NEW APPROACHES TO INTERNATIONAL MEDIATION

Recent Titles in Contributions in Political Science
Series Editor: Bernard K. Johnpoll

NEW APPROACHES TO INTERNATIONAL MEDIATION

Edited by

C. R. Mitchell and K. Webb

Contributions in Political Science, Number 223

Greenwood Press
New York · Westport, Connecticut · London

89-7455

Library of Congress Cataloging-in-Publication Data

New approaches to international mediation / edited by C. R. Mitchell and K. Webb.
  p. cm. — (Contributions in political science, ISSN 0147-1066; no. 223)
  Bibliography: p.
  Includes index.
  ISBN 0–313–25974–7 (lib. bdg. : alk. paper)
  1. Mediation, International. 2. World politics—1945–
I. Mitchell, C. R. (Christopher Roger), 1934–   . II. Webb, K.
III. Series.
JX4475.N45 1988
341.5' 2'19—dc 19   88–10252

British Library Cataloguing in Publication Data is available.

Library of Congress Catalog Card Number: 88–10252
ISBN: 0–313–25974–7
ISSN: 0147–1066

First published in 1988

Greenwood Press, Inc.
88 Post Road West, Westport, Connecticut 06881

Printed in the United States of America

The paper used in this book complies with the
Permanent Paper Standard issued by the National
Information Standards Organization (Z39.48—1984).

10 9 8 7 6 5 4 3 2 1

To Adam and Emily and Joanna and Laura

Contents

List of Abbreviations

AAA	American Arbitration Association
AACC	All Africa Conference of Churches
ABA	American Bar Association
ACAS	Arbitration and Conciliation Advisory Service
ACR	African Contemporary Record
ADR	Alternative Dispute Resolution
ANC	African National Congress
CAC	Central Arbitration Committee
CAC	Centre for the Analysis of Conflict
CASIN	Centre for the Applied Study of International Relations
CCIA	Commission of the Churches on International Affairs
CDR	Christian Democratic Union
CIA	Central Intelligence Agency
COPRED	Consortium on Peace Research, Education and Development
CRS	Community Relations Service
CRS	Conflict Research Society
CSU	Christian Social Union
DPE	Departement politique federale
DTA	pro-Democratic Turnhalle Alliance
EPG	Eminent Persons Group
EEC	European Economic Community
FEC	Federal Executive Council
FLN	Front pour la Liberation Nationale
FLS	Front Line States
FMCS	Federal Mediation and Conciliation Service
FMG	Federal Military Government
GATT	General Agreement on Tariffs and Trade

ICJ	International Court of Justice
ICRC	International Committee of the Red Cross
IG	Interessengemeinschaft Deutsch Sprachiger Sudwester
JCA	Joint Christian Aid
MCF	Movement for Colonial Freedom
MNR	Mozambique National Resistance
NATO	North Atlantic Treaty Organisation
NCPCR	National Conference on Peacemaking and Conflict Resolution
NIDR	National Institute for Dispute Resolution
OAS	Organisation of American States
OAU	Organisation for African Unity
OR	Operational Research
PCIJ	Permanent Court of International Justice
PDQ	Personal Damage Quotient
PLO	Palestine Liberation Organisation
PPS	Preliminary Problem Structuring
SADF	South African Defence Force
SAG	South African Government
SCR	Security Council Resolution
SIA	Special Interim Authority
SMC	Supreme Military Council
SPIDR	Society of Professionals in Dispute Resolution
SSLM	Southern Sudan Liberation Movement
SVP	South Tyrol People's Party
SWAPO	South-West Africa People's Organisation
SWAT	Special Weapons and Tactics
SWATF	South West Africa Territorial Force
TNC	Transnational Corporation
UDF	United Democratic Front
UNCTAD	United Nations Conference on Trade and Development
UNGA	United Nations General Assembly
UNITA	Union for the Total National Independence of Angola
WCC	World Council of Churches
WCG	Western Contact Group

Preface

This collection of papers had its origins in a workshop held at the University of Salzburg under the auspices of the European Consortium for Political Research. The convening of the workshop was partly intended to discover who, in Europe, was carrying on research into mediation and conciliation, in both civil and international society. We had hoped to find a new surge of interest in Europe to match that taking place in North America but in the event found that only a few institutes and scholars were working in the area. This was somewhat disappointing but it turned out that, with a small circle of interested scholars, ideas could be exchanged and developed easily and regularly, contacts kept up and informal meetings occasionally arranged. We thus owe the European Consortium a considerable debt of gratitude both for its help and encouragement, particularly from Professor Ken Newton and Ms. Valerie Stewart, and for supporting the initiative that led to this book.

The initial set of papers presented at the seminar in Salzburg were mainly concerned with relatively conventional aspects of international mediation, although some reflected the innovations in thinking that were already starting to affect traditional ideas about the nature of the inter-mediary process—ideas about "biassed" intermediaries, the conception that mediation was a regular (if usually informal) process in many international organisations, and the questioning of the nature of "neutrality" as displayed by a mediator. Further consultation led us to consider the idea of adopting a broader framework for the proposed book, and we became convinced that attention should be directed towards the use of mediation in intra-national as well as international disputes so that parallels and similarities could be emphasised and the whole approach viewed as a universal means of "managing" human conflicts, applicable and, indeed, utilised in a wide variety of settings.

Fortunately, we were able to add a number of papers that fitted in with this theme and which—in our eyes—pointed up both the commonalities of informal mediation in various social "arenas", and the new processes being tried out. Joseph Pickvance agreed to write about his experiences in the South Tyrol, and Hendrik van der Merwe about the problems of acting as an intermediary in South Africa. Hezekiah Assefa produced a fine analysis of the World Council of Churches' activities in trying to terminate the civil war in the Sudan. Our initial draft for this book, therefore, had moved from the somewhat disparate collection of preliminary papers presented at Salzburg to a far more coherent set that dealt with new intermediary approaches in terms of new analytical questions, new techniques and new areas of application.

For this reason, students of international relations may be struck by the fact that many of the new approaches mentioned in the chapters here are not necessarily applied to strictly international conflicts, and some may question the use of the term "international" in our title. However, as we argue in Chapter 1, our feeling is that ways of dealing with conflicts should be regarded as forming part of a range of practices and techniques that might be used either domestically or internationally, and that a division between those which are used (and perhaps "work") at one level and those used at another is probably a false and certainly an obfuscating one. Hence our decision to be eclectic as regards the range of topics covered in this collection, and our decision to include studies of the Tyrol question and the Sudanese Civil War, as well as of the Falklands/Malvinas dispute and the Namibian conflict.

Many people contribute to symposia, quite apart from editors and authors, and we would be less than grateful if we did not take this chance of publicly thanking those who helped us produce *New Approaches*. Not least of these was Mildred Vasan, our editor at Greenwood Press, who put up with delays and agitations with calm and understanding, as well as offering good advice on the manuscript when it was in gestation. We are grateful to Jennifer Mathers, who did sterling work on the bibliography, and to Dr. Christopher Pope, Lt. Commander Peter Hamilton, and Mr. Richard Jeffreys at City University, who helped with our computing and word-processing problems, which were many. We owe much thanks to a large number of secretaries who worked on various drafts and re-drafts of the work. At City University these included Joyce Bernard, Maria Correa, Helen Darmody, Ann Harris, Doreen Schlesinger, Melanie Skinner and Pauline Swierkot. At the University of Kent we should thank Mollie Roots for her help in this and many other projects.

Finally, we should pay tribute to our authors, who supplied re-drafts, references, bibliographies and further re-drafts in a helpful and uncomplaining manner over a long period of time, thus helping to make our task easier and the book a better joint project. Without them, none of this could have happened.

C. R. Mitchell
K. Webb

NEW APPROACHES TO
INTERNATIONAL MEDIATION

1

Mediation in International Relations: An Evolving Tradition

C. R. Mitchell & K. Webb

The use of intermediaries in settling disputes between states and their governments has a long and honourable tradition in international relations, although the precise form such mediation takes has varied from era to era. Intermediaries and third parties frequently became involved in efforts to end disputes between Greek city states,[1] although the main records left of such activities concern arbitrations rather than mediations (Adcock & Mosley, 1975). Between 211 and 206 B.C. a group of intermediaries from Athens, Rhodes, Egypt, Chios, Byzantium and Mytilene made strenuous efforts to bring an end to the conflict between Macedonia and the Aetolian League which was ruining trade in the area (Walbank, 1940). The Romans often utilised intermediaries as go-between or sponsors of settlements in the inevitable conflicts that attended the establishment of their hegemony in the Mediterranean region (Epirus played such a role in the first war between Rome and Phillip V of Macedon, helping to bring about the Peace of Phoenice) and not infrequently enacted that role themselves. One of the functions that a member of the newly developing profession of diplomat might be called upon to fulfil in the Renaissance world was that of intermediary between conflicting Italian city states. (As Mattingley notes [1955, p. 74], many of the resident ambassadors in the Vatican assisted Nicholas V in his mediating efforts to bring peace between Venice and Milan in 1454—efforts that eventually led to the Peace of Lodi.)

With the establishment of the modern inter-state system in the period following the Peace of Westphalia, the need for impartial intermediaries—"honest brokers" in Bismarck's famous phrase—did not diminish. Indeed, it could be argued that, with the growth of purely inter-state conflicts taking place in an international system characterised by doctrines of sovereign equality, an absence of any recognised, overarching authority, and each element in that system acting freely in pursuit of its own best interests (however egotistically defined), it was inevitable that the need for disinterested brokers and intermediaries should, if anything, increase.

THE ROLE OF MEDIATION IN INTERNATIONAL CONFLICTS

In both European and North American writings on international relations, the explanation for the use of intermediaries and the reliance of third-party action (whether defined as mediation, conciliation, good offices or simply fact finding) has usually started from an assumed distinction between the natures of domestic and international society. In both it is generally accepted that conflicts of interest will inevitably arise between individuals, organised groups and (eventually) governments. However, it is then conventional to contrast the markedly different means of managing or settling such disputes within the two forms of society.

On the one hand, it is argued, conflicts within domestic societies take place in an environment characterised by a legitimate, and usually widely accepted, central authority with a monopoly of power (the state) and a set of rules and structured institutions for determining the outcome of any conflicts that arise within its boundaries. Thus, civil courts apply rules to settle disputes between individuals or corporations. Formal industrial relations courts or arbitration tribunals determine solutions to industrial disputes or monitor the workings of agreed collective bargaining procedures. Electoral systems are developed to settle conflicts over who will occupy political authority roles within the country and how the occupancy will be reviewed (and perhaps changed) periodically. A reversion to violence to settle some salient dispute—a riot, a secessonist movement, a civil war—is taken to be a sign that the society so afflicted has, in some sense, "broken down" or that its methods for managing conflict have, perhaps temporarily, proved inadequate.

The image projected by conflict management systems in this ideal domestic society is thus typified by formal rules and structure. Adapting a phrase used by Lucy Mair to describe political systems in African tribal societies, conflict management is a matter of courts, codes, constables and consensus (Mair, 1964). Within this battery of formal and semi-formal means for dealing with intra-societal conflict one finds the occasional use of informal, relatively unstructured mediation or conciliation, such as the Federal Conciliation and Mediation Service in the United States, or ACAS in the United Kingdom, but, until comparatively recently, the use of such techniques for managing domestic conflicts was the exception rather than the rule.

While such an image of the management of conflicts *within* society may be something of a caricature, conventional writings about international relations tend to contrast it strongly with the management of conflict in what Hedley Bull, among others, characterises as "the anarchical society" of world politics (Bull, 1979). We do not wish to go deeply into the debate about the starkness of this contract, although we feel that much of world society is as ordered and consensual as many domestic societies and frequently not as violent or anarchic as others (Cyprus, the Lebanon, Ethiopia, the southern Sudan come immediately to mind). However, it is undoubtedly the case that, at this level of world society: (1) the probablility of major conflicts of interest developing are at least as great as within domestic society; (2) there is no centralised, legitimised authority to establish and operate any formal system for conflict management; and, hence (3) the processes by which international disputes are managed and (perhaps) settled have to be largely informal and largely dependent upon their acceptability to those independent and "sovereign" entities engaged in the conflict. If they are not acceptable, they are not used.

Again, it is possible to over-draw this distinction. It is certainly the case that the period since the ending of the Thirty Years War has seen numerous efforts to establish institutions and processes for managing international conflicts successfully. These have been both *intellectual* efforts—and Hinsley (1963) has written a full account of the various ideas put forward since 1648 for avoiding, ending or ameliorating the wars that arise from international conflicts of interest—and *practical* efforts, which have resulted in the establishment of both international and regional institutions at least part of whose function has been the management of international disputes. In this century alone there have been two major attempts to institutionalise on a global basis the conflict-managing and peace-maintaining functions carried out in the nineteenth century on an ad hoc basis by the then Great Powers (the "Concert of Europe"), by concerned neighbouring governments, or by other "honest brokers". Both the Council of the League of Nations and the Security Council and secretary general of the UN have, predominantly, a conflict-management function to fulfil within their respective organisations, and a similar function is present in regional organisations such as the OAS, through its secretary general (whose role was recently strengthened at the meeting in Cartagena in December 1985), or the OAU formally through its Committee on Mediation and Conciliation but more practically through a series of ad hoc missions to various African parties in conflict.

It is also the case that similar effort has been devoted to establishing legal processes for managing conflicts (the "courts and codes" of Lucy Mair's formulation) within the world society. Courts and legal processes featured largely in many of the schemes reviewed by Hinsley to abolish wars or settle international disputes without recourse to arms and violence.

More practically, marked interest in arbitration processes at the ending of the nineteenth century gave rise to the Permanent Court of Arbitration at the Hague, while the establishment of the PCIJ as an integral part of the League of Nations system in 1919 (and its continuation as the ICJ in the post–Second World War world) demonstrated the hope that major inter-state conflicts could be institutionalised within a legal structure and process (as well as the dominance of the *domestic image* of managing conflict when decision makers came to consider appropriate structures and procedures for conflict management at an international level).[2] However, in spite of both intellectual and practical efforts to transform the practices of international conflict management more firmly into the image of (apparently) successful domestic conflict management, any institutions successfully established have had to confront basic problems of legitimacy and acceptability, different—at least, in degree—from those in most domestic societies. Although it is true to say that much of international law works in much the same way as domestic law, particularly in the functional and commercial fields, it more obviously relies on concensus when major international conflicts of interest arise. Frequently, a consensus even to *use* the available system of courts and codes (or arbitration processes) is absent. Doctrines of "auto-interpretation" and even outright defiance limit the jurisdiction and effects of international courts in handling vital conflicts of interest. Principles of non-interference and domestic jurisdiction similarly limit the use of legal procedures in many disputes which may begin domestically but have a major impact on international relations by spilling over the territorial (and other) boundaries of states and involving other parties. (We think here of the conflicts "within" El Salvador and Nicaragua, or that "within" the United Kingdom in its province of Northern Ireland.) Governments do take conflicts of interest to arbitration—Egypt and Israel in the Taba Dispute is a recent example—but such instances are rare, infrequently involve salient issues and sometimes result in an award which is steadfastly ignored by one of the parties to the dispute. (We recall the abortive British arbitration award in the dispute over the Beagle Channel.)

To some degree, the brief outline above may paint too gloomy a picture, and we will have reason and opportunity to modify it later. However, it undoubtedly provides some explanation of why many international conflicts of interest rely for their solution either upon bargaining and compromise between the parties involved—which inevitably involves the use of some coercion and, at times, outright physical force on the part of the adversaries—or upon the activities of some third party acting as a channel of communication to overcome a deadlock, to suggest alternative formulae, to get the parties to re-examine their options and positions, to supply rewards and inducements for concessions or to perform all the other functions that have become characteristic of international intermediaries in the late twentieth century.

The above discussion has been a somewhat round-about way of explaining both the prevelance and the importance of mediation and the intermediary in international conflict management. Its main focus has been on the role of intermediary processes, given the relative weakness of other modes for handling conflicts of interest at the international level, and the continuing need for skillful mediators and conciliators in world society. However, we do not wish to give the impression either that (1) the nature and functions of international mediators have not changed markedly as a result of new problems but also new ideas arising, or that (2) the role of mediation and conciliation have remained relevant only in international rather than domestic society. Quite the opposite seems to us to be the case. Confining ourselves, for the moment, to the first point, it is clear that the nature and form of mediation in international relations changes over time as new forms and innovations are developed and become accepted by members of international society. That forms of mediation change considerably as the structure of international society changes was clearly revealed in an early study by LeVine (1972), who analysed the set of major mediation initiatives undertaken to deal with inter-state disputes during the period 1815 to 1960. Among LeVine's findings was the intuitively plausible one that the balance of activity in mediation in terms of *who* undertakes intermediary initiatives had swung decisively from the middle of the nineteenth century to the middle of the twentieth century. Whereas the typical mediator in the mid-nineteenth century was a major European power or a coalition of neighbouring governments, since the Second World War the pre-eminent type of mediator (or provider of good offices) was the representative of an international organisation, either an executive official (the UN secretary general) or a specially appointed committee (the OAU mission to Nigeria during that country's civil war).

However, LeVine also noted that in the period 1945–65 both major and lesser powers continued to play roles as mediators. This fits in with our own observation of recent trends away from using major international organisations such as the UN as intermediaries (or even for peacekeeping purposes) and towards the use of powerful governments in an intermediary role, such as the United States in the Middle East. It also reinforces our contention about mediation changing as regards both to practitioners and processes as the nature and structure of world society alters.

We therefore would begin by arguing strongly that mediation seems to us to have changed considerably since 1945, and it is this theme that underlies this present volume. What, then, in the light of this argument, are the interesting and useful innovations in the field of mediation that might add to the (scarcely adequate) battery of processes for managing international conflicts? Some answers to this question are given in the chapters that follow.

RENEWED SCHOLARLY INTEREST IN MEDIATION

Certainly one recent development concerning mediation in international disputes has been the growth of scholarly interest in the field over the last decade. The need for this growth is, in itself, somewhat surprising. Given the rather limited range of conflict management techniques available within world society, it would have been reasonable to suppose that a major effort would long ago have been devoted to understanding the process of mediation, the role and function of intermediaries, the qualities necessary for a good mediator and a successful mediation initiative, the appropriate stage of an international dispute at which intermediary action might have the best chance of success and the most appropriate source of an intermediary initiative, bearing in mind the nature and complexities of particular types of conflict. In other words, there would exist at least the beginnings of a useful, explanatory and (perhaps) predictive *theory of mediation*, culled from a comparison of the many examples of that process in managing international disputes.

Nothing could be further from the truth. Comparative academic study (and hence understanding) of international mediation was, until very recently, characterised by almost complete neglect. Until the late 1960s, the academic scene showed an almost total lack of up-to-date, comparative work on the nature of informal third-party efforts at peacemaking via mediation or conciliation. The only exceptions to this generalisation were a number of case studies of recent (and not so recent) examples of intermediary initiatives (for example, Barros' [1968] study of the Aland Islands) and an excellent if anecdotal distillation of the experiences of a private Quaker intermediary, Elmore Jackson (1952).

In the late 1960s, three books appeared that indicated that the long scholarly neglect of intermediary processes was about to end. Of the three, only Oran Young's *The Intermediaries* (1967) was centrally concerned with the activities of traditionally conceived third-party mediators and conciliators dealing with international conflicts. However, as we argue below, both John Burton's *Conflict and Communication* (1969) and Richard Walton's *Interpersonal Peacemaking* (1969) were to prove part of an academic movement that not only rapidly expanded the study of processes and techniques relevant (and useful) to international intermediaries, but also tied the analysing of international mediation into a much broader field which included mediation, conciliation and other newer processes at all social levels, whether domestic or inter-state.

Not that there was an immediate flood of conceptual, analytical or comparative studies at the start of the 1970s. However, by the end of that decade, the comparative analysis of mediation and scholarly attempts to develop general principles and theories of mediation and even the broader field of "conflict management" were well under way. Looking back, it seems reasonable to argue that there were a number of major changes, partly scholarly, partly historical, that underlay the growth of interest of which this present volume forms part.

The first of these changes was that the study of third-party activity in helping to end international disputes was a natural continuation of the interest in negotiation and bilateral bargaining that arose in the late 1960s and early 1970s. To some degree, this intellectual fashion had its beginnings in the work on formal models of bargaining behaviour and "rational" choice that began with Von Neumann and Morgenstern in the 1940s. What was different about the interest in negotiating processes in the 1970s, however, was that it took the form of enquiring empirically about how negotiators actually behaved in historical situations, rather than how they ought to behave (theoretically) to achieve some "optimal" solution. One major aspect of this interest was an effort to tap and systematise the existing wisdom of practising negotiators (and even to borrow ideas from others who fulfilled the bargaining role more regularly than practising diplomats, such as union or management negotiators), an effort that produced the "formula-detail" model of negotiating processes as an alternative to the conventional "concession-convergence" model (for details, see Winham, 1977; Zartman, 1977).

Thus, retrospective studies of particular negotiating cases were undertaken, such as Campbell's study of the bargaining over Trieste in 1954 (Campbell, 1976); major efforts made to compare and categorise the experience of retired diplomats and decision makers who had been involved in negotiation (Zartman & Berman, 1982); comparative and experimental studies undertaken about the psychological aspects and stresses of negotiation (Druckman, 1977); and efforts made to discover and describe what forms of private and unofficial bargaining had assisted political leaders in ending, or at least modifying, the endless series of disputes that had characterised world society since 1945. It is not too much of an exaggeration to claim that, during the 1970s, negotiation was one of the (if not the) predominant growth areas in international relations scholarship.

Eventually, as an inevitable end product of this scholarly activity, a series of works consolidating conceptual, historical and even experimental work on the process of negotiation and dispute settlement appeared, some from the pens (or word processors) of political scientists (Raiffa, 1982), some from social psychologists (Pruitt, 1981) and others from a variety of interesting backgrounds, such as anthropology (Gulliver, 1979). What was significant about all of these works was that they contained at least one chapter on the role of third parties (either as mediators, conciliators or facilitators) in helping bilateral bargaining processes. From that point on, the next logical step was to extend comparative and systematic scholarly analysis to the role of third parties and to the nature of the mediation process itself.

This logical extension of analytical and comparative work is now taking place. Previous work, both experimental and historical, is being consolidated and new work undertaken. Academic fashion in international relations studies is now swinging away from the analysis of negotiation and more towards mediation. Already comparative studies of mediation initiatives are being published (Touval & Zartman, 1985), retrospective analyses of third-party roles in terminating disputes being undertaken (Bendahmane & McDonald, 1986) and efforts being made to trace through the fortunes of intermediaries in specific protracted conflicts, such as that over Palestine (Touval, 1982). As with the analysis of negotiation, this work is highly eclectic. Concepts, models and insights are borrowed from the study of mediation at social levels other than the international. (For example, ideas from Wall [1981] have particularly influenced some of the contributors to this volume.) Similarly, the activities of private and unofficial intermediaries are also being explored to see what general insights might be gained from their wealth of practical experience in mediation (see Curle, 1986), while there are even efforts being made to move towards a general theory of international mediation.

A second major reason for the development of interest in the subject of international mediation during the 1970s has been the high-profile use of this technique by political leaders and decision makers in dealing with some of the protracted and intractable conflicts that erupted or repeated during the decade, particularly those in the Middle East. In many ways, this could be regarded merely as a more widely publicised return to the use of mediation as a tool by great-power "honest" (or less than honest) brokers and as nothing very new. However, it seems to have been that case that the activities of Secretary of State Haig in the Falklands/Malvinas dispute, of Lord Carrington over the struggle in Zimbabwe, of President Carter at Camp David, of Philip Habib in the Lebanon and particularly of Dr. Kissinger in a series of initiatives, shuttles and dramatic wheelings and dealings in the Middle East, all contributed to making the study of intermediaries and mediation both publicly fashionable and of scholarly importance.

The results of this focussing of attention on shuttle diplomacy and dramatic mediations have been varied and complex. One has, inevitably, taken the form of a new set of studies of particular cases of mediation (Quandt's excellent book on Camp David [1986], for example) or on particular mediators (Rubin's [1981] collection of papers on Dr. Kissinger). Another has been a temporary, and rather unfair, neglect of the less spectacular efforts of the representatives of international organisations who continue to play a quiet role as important intermediaries and conciliators. (We should, however, mention Sydney Bailey's distinguished two-volume study [1982] of the UN's contribution to the ending of wars and the achievement of some form of peaceful settlement.) A third has been a revival of analytical interest in the role of interested and resource-rich governments, acting to end a dispute on terms satisfactory not merely to the adversaries but also to the intermediary. The most glaring contrast exists between this type of interested intermediary, with a major stake in outcomes, and the ideal disinterested and impartial third party found in textbooks. This has led to interesting scholarly work on the concept of the *biassed* intermediary which has influenced several contributions to this present volume.

ADR: MEDIATION AND CONCILIATION IN DOMESTIC SOCIETY

We have mentioned the eclectic nature of the revived study of international mediation, and this seems to us to provide the third most exciting source of new ideas and energy in the study of international mediation.

That this third influence should emerge at all is something of a paradox. Earlier, we argued that there existed a widely held perception of marked contrast between conflict management within domestic society (relatively orderly, institutionalised and rule bound) and that within world society (relatively ad hoc, decentralised, norm bound at best and coercive at worst). We also implied that this "domestic image" of conflict management, with its structure and its regularities and its codes, had tended to be the ideal to which reformers of world society aspired, so that conflict-management processes such as conciliation, mediation and negotiation were regarded as the best one could achieve within the prevailing (tempered) international anarchy—and a very second best at that.

In retrospect, it is possible to see a number of intellectual influences at work in breaking down this stark intellectual contrast between managing conflict within and between states, and thus contributing to our paradox of renewed interest in the general phenomenon of third-party mediation. A general background phenomenon has been the intense debate among scholars about the nature of "international relations" and of international society and of whether and how this society differs from domestic society. New perspectives, identified variously as the "interdependence" or the "world society" approaches to analysing global problems (such as conflict and its amelioration), have emphasised the frequent need for parties in conflict to seek solutions for conflicts outside the conventional state-centric and power-broking structures familiar to nineteenth- and early twentieth-century diplomacy and coercive negotiation. In an interdependent world, the opportunities for new actors to play the role of honest broker have increased geometrically, with the result that such bodies as the Lome' Secretariat, GATT, the Club de Paris and even NATO have become intermediaries on a segmented, specialised basis.

Another factor reinforcing this erosion of the intellectual international/ domestic dividing line has been the increasing interpenetration of states since 1945. More and more "domestic" issues have tended to become internationalised in a variety of ways and this is particularly so over major domestic conflicts, many of which become transnational or international very rapidly. Lebanon, Cyprus and Northern Ireland are cases in point, as we mentioned above, while the same is true of conflicts in South Africa, Namibia and even the South Tyrol. With such conflicts, the issue is whether they should be managed as though they were domestic conflicts, through the application of rules and codes, or treated as though they were—at least in some senses—quasi-international and thus to be dealt with through negotiation or mediation.

However, our mediation paradox mainly arose because it was the very "second-best" processes for ending disputes that began, in the 1970s, to be re-adapted for much wider use in many domestic societies (ostensibly relatively stable and successful in managing most forms of conflict within their own boundaries). Moreover, a wide range of practitioners and observers of domestic conflict management also began to argue that these informal and unstructured means of searching for a settlement to a conflict had great advantages lacking in the more formal, legal approaches. For one thing, they enabled those directly involved in the dispute to retain control over the process of negotiation and settlement so that, in the words of one practitioner, they "owned"—and felt they owned—their solution, which, it was claimed, made that solution more stable and acceptable. For another, informal processes of resolving disputes enabled the parties to explore the nature of the (often underlying) issues—the so-called "hidden agenda"—and deal with each other's *interests* rather than public bargaining *positions* (Fisher & Ury, 1981). Again, it was argued that new approaches[3] to managing inter-personal, intra-organisational, intra-communal and communal conflicts were, in fact, less expensive, time consuming and coercive than conventional ways of managing conflicts. Moreover, they were more satisfactory to the adversaries involved and more likely to produce long-lasting (because self-supporting) solutions to disputes.

The adoption of both traditional and innovative ways for handling conflicts within domestic societies began in North America in the 1970s and by the middle of that decade had started a genuine revolution in the thinking about and practice of handling disputes. New ideas had also been evolving in Europe, Scandanavia and as far afield as Australia and New Zealand. Under the general label of *Alternative Dispute Resolution* (ADR) the change had begun to affect conflict management within and between large organisations, as well as conflicts of interest over the environment, within divided communities and in local neighborhoods and families. Dennis Sandole's chapter in this book provides a broad overview of the ADR phenomenon, and we do not feel it necessary to go deeply into its nature or effects in this introduction. However, it is necessary to make three general points which link the ADR movement in domestic societies to our work on the practice and study of mediation at the international level.

Firstly, the ADR movement went far beyond the simple revival of informal mediation and conciliation processes to "get parties together" so that they could jointly search for solutions. The movement was genuinely innovative in that major efforts were made to devise and use new forms of conflict management involving new institutional settings for conflict management (community mediation centres, consultant facilitators, environmental dispute resolution workshops) as well as new types of third parties in a variety of roles and functions. It is true that part of "innovation" involved the application of tried and tested processes such as mediation, arbitration or even "shuttle diplomacy" to different classes of conflict (disputes between neighbours, conflicts over children during divorce, accident claims, even criminal misdemeanours involving offenders and victims). However, another aspect was genuinely innovative in terms of new and experimental processes (problem-solving workshops, mini-trials, simple facilitation of communication) which were developed to help parties in ther own search for an uncoerced solution to their own dispute.

The second point is also somewhat paradoxical in that many of the assumptions, much of the theory and some of the actual techniques that formed part of the domestic ADR movement of the 1970s and 1980s had themselves been developed in the 1960s to try to deal with disputes (and to improve on the existing techniques of traditional mediation and conciliation) at the international level. We have already referred to the work of John Burton and his development during the 1960s of non-directive, facilitative approaches and problem-solving workshops in efforts to manage international conflict (Burton, 1969). Many of the ideas underlying Burton's pioneering work were carried over into the thinking underlying domestic ADR in the 1970s, together with ideas from organisational and industrial problem-solving (Walton, 1969; Blake et al., 1964). Moreover, the use of problem-solving workshops, facilitation and non-directive intervention in helping to manage interstate and major inter-communal conflicts had also been carried on by scholars such as Kelman and Cohen (1976), Doob (1970), Levi and Benjamin (1977) and Azar and Burton himself (Azar and Burton, 1986). Hence, at the level of international dispute settlement, there was already a small but growing tradition of innovation in the form of intermediary activity available.

Finally, we would like to stress the way in which new ideas and approaches from domestic ADR contributed to what we regard as a major ferment in both the practice and study of mediation, conciliation and other informal approaches to international conflict management. It seems to us that there are several "new" features of current approaches to analysing and practising international mediation. One is the simple development of new interest in the systematic study of the phenomenon of mediation, conciliation and the work of intermediaries within the world society. Another is the changing pattern of activity (new types of party involved, new techniques applied, new roles for third parties, old approaches revived with new twists) that characterises the use of mediation and conciliation in the 1970s and 1980s. Lastly, there is the ADR revolution within domestic society, which has had the effect of both introducing a fruitful interaction of ideas and techniques from the two sides of the perceived domestic/ international divide, and breaking down the assumption that there are two quite distinct arenas for the practice of conflict management such that techniques appropriate to one arena have little application in the other.

There has also occurred a modification of an inherent conservatism that affected thinking about methods of conflict management. The willingness of practitioners in domestic societies to experiment with new approaches to domestic disputes now appears to be "rubbing off" at the international level. This willingness to think about innovatory approaches—the use of new types of intermediary, the employment of new means of dialogue in unusual settings and forums—is reflected in many of the chapters that follow. This is one sense in which we talk about "new" approaches to international mediation.

CURRENT THEMES AND ISSUES IN INTERNATIONAL MEDIATION

From our brief account of the development of scholarly and practical interest in the process of international mediation and conciliation, it will be apparent that both the practice and study of the subject are in a rather confusing—if exciting—condition. Intellectual debates continue about such topics as the nature of the mediation process (many people, apparently including Dr. Kissinger himself, argue that the processes adopted during his efforts to find a settlement in the Middle East are a form of triangular negotiation rather than mediation); about the type of conflict best suited to informal mediation and conciliation processes; and about the type of institution best suited to carry through such a process. There is considerable doubt about whether mediation processes can work effectively in conflicts of value or in domestic disputes (such as within South Africa) where fundamental change rather than minimal adjustment through concession is at issue. Different positions are taken on whether mediation can occur in situations of profound power or resource imbalance, where successful mediation may merely involve the perpetuation of what seems, to many, a relationship of inequality and injustice.

Equally, there is considerable confusion about what noticeably "new" aspects of mediation and conciliation should first engage scholarly attention. There are many new types of actor currently engaged in both traditional and innovative forms of mediation in both domestic and international arenas. (For example, the Contadora Group and the Western Contact Group may have forerunners in the group of interested Greek states that tried to make peace between the Simarchy and the Aetolian League over 2,000 years ago, but they are new in that they operate from or in co-ordination with delegations to a global inter-governmental organisation.) Should attention be focussed on the new types of actor, the new processes or both? Similarly, the old pattern of great-power involvement in an intermediary role seems to be re-asserting itself, but to what extent are contemporary "biassed" mediators merely utilising the traditional tools of interested great powers to ensure an outcome to their liking? What new roles might there be for unofficial diplomats or private intermediaries, particularly in using new techniques such as problem-solving workshops or facilitated private meetings between the representatives of conflicting governments or communities?

These are some of the issues that concern the scholars and practitioners that have contributed to this present volume. They are issues that arise from the arrival of new actors, new processes and new arenas for mediation in contemporary world society. Naturally, not all of the possible range of questions thrown up by the new features of contemporary international mediation can be covered in the chapters that follow. However, many of the major points of debate find some treatment or mention in the collection presented here. For example, the theme of new actors involving themselves in the intermediary role underlies both Vivienne Jabri's review in Chapter 6 of the problems afflicting the Western Contact Group as an interested coalition trying to mediate and Andrew Williams' account in Chapter 9 of the work of CASIN in Geneva. Peter Bennett's chapter (Chapter 11), in contrast to the one on the Western Contact Group, concerns itself more with the potential of new tools and techniques for an intermediary and explores whether some of the methods of "decision aiding" (normally employed to help parties in cooperation think through an optimum course of action) might help an intermediary striving to build bridges between adversaries in conflict. Both Joseph Pickvance (Chapter 7) and Hendrik van der Merwe (Chapter 10) take up the theme of private, informal and low-profile intermediary activity. From their own experiences in the Tyrol and South Africa they comment on the lessons they have learned from their own roles as intermediaries, while Hezekiah Assefa outlines in Chapter 8 the work of another private intermediary—the World Council of Churches in its Sudanese mediation initiative.

There are more familiar, recurrent issues as well. Douglas Kinney (Chapter 5) draws upon his own major study of the Haig initiative during the Falklands/Malvinas crisis to illustrate lessons about aspects of traditional, great-power mediation. Christopher Mitchell examines in Chapter 3 some of the reasons, rewards and risks of playing the part of an international mediator, by implication broadening the concept of the "biassed" mediator and suggesting that the conventional dichotomy between an impartial and an interested intermediary may be misleading. John Stephens (Chapter 4) takes up a crucial practical problem for potential intermediaries and asks what is likely to affect a mediator's success in having his offer of help accepted by parties in conflict, while Keith Webb (Chapter 2) considers the dilemma of any third party contemplating intervention into an imbalanced conflict, where considerations of the justice or injustice of the adversaries' positions have to be weighed against the desirability of attempting to bring to an end overt violence, death and destruction. Finally, Dennis Sandole, in Chapter 12, reviews and comments upon the new ADR "revolution" and offers a guide to that "paradigm shift" in thinking about the management of conflict.

This brusque check list tends to conceal much more than it reveals and too neatly categorises chapters that interlock and take up themes and issues from one to another. (For example, the dilemma centrally discussed in Webb's chapter runs as a continuous thread through van der Merwe's reflection on intermediary action in South Africa.) While the chapters are individual in themselves, they do reflect both the diversity of ideas about international mediation (and its growing connection with domestic dispute resolution) and the emergence of a number of central themes in the current literature. We feel that such connections promise well for our future understanding of both traditional means of managing conflicts and for their improvement and increased variety as new innovations are developed and "field tested" in domestic and international arenas. If this present volume makes any contribution to this scholarly understanding or to practical innovation, we will be more than satisfied.

NOTES

1. Adcock and Mosley (1975, p. 212) report one offer from Megara to mediate between Athens and Sparta during the time of King Aegesopolos. The offer was rebuffed, with the Spartan comment that the Megarans were hardly likely to know more about justice than did Athens or Sparta!

2. Many writers have commented on the dominance of this "domestic image" of conflict management in thinking about optimal arrangements for dealing with international disputes; on how institutions at the international level are often unfavourably compared with those characteristic of civil society; and on how any progress in improving international conflict management is usually assumed to be in the direction of global governments, international courts and police forces and enforced international laws. Less frequently, some have raised the issue of the appropriateness of this image.

3. It would perhaps be more appropriate to regard these as traditional but neglected forms of community conflict management—at least in industrialised and urbanised societies. One of the earliest of the community dispute resolution services in the United States was established at least partly as a result of an American anthropologist returning from West Africa, having observed and been impressed by dispute resolution processes there.

2

The Morality of Mediation

K. Webb

The act of mediation is not a neutral act; it is a moral and political act undertaken by the mediator to achieve desired ends. The mediator may claim to be neutral with respect to the values and claims of the combatants, but the activity of mediating is still a declaration of values held by the mediator. This is, perhaps, most clearly evident where the third party is powerful with respect to the combatants and is neutral between them, but has an interest in peace. It is still true, however, where the mediator has no obvious material or political interests in the outcome but undertakes the activity of peacemaking nonetheless. Examples here are numerous: the activities of Quakers in the Nigerian Civil War, or in the South Tyrol Settlement (see Chapter 7); the role of the Council of African Churches in the Sudanese settlement; the activities of the Centre for Intergroup Studies or the Foundation for International Conciliation in South Africa (see Chapter 10); or the numerous workshops organised by the Centre for the Analysis of Conflict (Banks, 1984a). In a sense the activities of such groups are analogous to the more familiar role of the family mediator: if the family mediator placed no value on the institution of marriage itself, and upon the desirability of amicable and productive relationships within that institution, then the activity would be largely pointless. All family counsellors or mediators believe in the value of marriage itself, while mediators in general tend to believe that the ending of behavioural violence and its consequences for quality of human life is preferable to its continuance. It follows, from the fact that mediation is undertaken to attain certain values, that mediators see this activity as giving the highest probability of achieving those ends, and it also follows that there may be cases where those ends are more likely to be achieved through not mediating. The values of the mediator may be best achieved by allowing a conflict to run its course rather than intervening to prolong a damaging and inequitable relationship. Mediation is thus a means to particular ends rather than an end in itself, and the more effective the techniques of mediation become through research and practice, the more important it becomes to recognise this point. Picking up again the analogy of the family mediator and leaving aside the case where marriage is seen as sacrosanct and to be saved or endured at any physical or psychological cost, there may be cases where the valued ends of the mediator are best achieved through separation or divorce; such may be the case where wife-battering, adultery, incest or cruelty are seen as being unlikely to cease and the physical or psychological health of one or both partners, and possibly also children, are constantly endangered. In such a case while the institution of marriage remains valued, the family mediator may believe that morally it is not a case for the exercise of his skills.

The central point being laboured is that undertaking mediation to end or resolve a conflict is not an automatic response to the perception of a conflict, that it is something undertaken to attain given ends that in some cases may be better achieved by other means. For example, to attempt to mediate between the Greek and Turkish Cypriots over the re-unification of Cyprus pre-supposes the normative value that unity is desirable, while it is at least conceivable that in the long run division and separation may lead to greater peace than unsuccessful attempts at integration.

This utilitarian point is obvious and important and has certain implications for the ongoing and divisive debate within the peace and conflict literature with respect to the "objectivist" and "subjectivist" schools of thought (Mitchell, 1981a, pp. 12–42). The objectivist perceives the "real" nature of conflict to be embedded in the social structure and independent of the perceptions of the actors in the situation. The actors might see the shadows on the wall; the analyst with his social-science searchlight illuminates the real structure of the situation. The subjectivist, however, recognises conflict only insofar as it manifests itself in the perceptions of the actors; conflict exists only insofar as there is a perceived incompatibility of goals. The former case, while stressing important aspects of reality, can become blatantly imputational and value-based as well as using language in unacceptable ways; is inequality what we mean by conflict? The latter case, linguistically precise and readily operational, pushes aside such problems as belonging to a different universe of discourse.

In many cases in social science, differences in epistemology are not reflected in practical research activity, since there is little difference in what is actually done. This is not one of those cases. Whether one is an objectivist or a subjectivist leads to very different action prescriptions. The objectivist often perceives mediation as being a mere manipulatory device designed to pacify the weaker party to the extent that it does not radically restructure and reorder social relations. The emphasis would be, therefore, on changing the social structure that gives rise to conflict, which in practice means an adherence to revolutionary doctrine and usually to violence. The aim would be to cause and sharpen social antagonisms, perhaps through empowerment, as a prelude to their ultimate resolution in a just and equal society (Groom & Webb, 1987). To achieve peace, conflict and violence are adopted as means. The subjectivist takes a very different view. His focus is not the social structure but the conflict as defined by the goals and perceptions of the actors. Since conflict is dependent on the perceptions of the actors, change in those perceptions can lead to an end to the conflict. Here manipulability is seen as a positive rather than a negative factor, and since the task undertaken is not so Herculean, it can be attempted more frequently and with a higher probability of success.

To the extent that conflict is so differently viewed, it can probably be classified as an "essentially contested concept". As such the possibility of agreement over the meaning of conflict is slight. Nor, necessarily, should agreement be sought or forced, for each side of the argument brings valuable goods that serve as a corrective to the emphasis of the other. The problem comes at the level of practice; how can two such disparate versions of the world operate in such a way as to maximise the values of each and yet not tear the discipline apart in internecinery academic warfare? The answer advanced in this chapter is that so long as the focus remains unshifted the argument will continue unabated, but if the focus is shifted to the level of practice (bearing in mind the values of each school), considerations can be brought to bear with the consequence that the distance separating each from the other declines markedly. Underlying this approach, however, is an assumption akin to the proviso on the sanctity of marriage in the previous example, and that is that physical violence is not in itself morally wrong in all circumstances. Hence, where a pacifist position is held this chapter can have no relevance.

PERCEPTIONS OF CONFLICT

The strong version of the objective perception of conflict is that it may exist independently of the perceptions or beliefs of the actors in a particular situation.

. . . conflict is conflict of interest. Interest is not seen as a matter of subjective definition but as determined by the social structure. In other words, conflict is given an objectivistic definition. Conflict is incompatible interests built into the structure of the system where conflict is located. A class conflict, for example, is not a conflict because the classes have incompatible goals, fight each other, and hate each other. It is a conflict because the social structure is such that one class loses what the other class wins. [Schmid, 1968, p. 226]

Here, of course, we have a re-statement of a very old social-science doctrine, that people may have real interests that they themselves do not recognise. Such an argument is the mainstay of much radical thought and brings to the fore three central points. First, the observer is interpreting the subjective experience of the actors in a way that may be very different from the way in which the actors perceive the situation. There is nothing inherently wrong with this practice, and it is common in social science. The analyst may define a situation as marked by a "balance of power" where the actors merely feel frustration and impotence. A group may be said to possess "ideology" as a hypothetical construct, even if the ideational structure does not conform to the belief system of any one member of the group. The point with both cases is that the general term re-labelling and reinterpretation is operationally related to the subjective experience of the actor; the empirical procedure whereby a subjective experience is to be included under that label is capable of public specification. According to this criterion the objective definition of conflict is perfectly acceptable: a conflict exists where there is structural violence. Secondly, there is the inevitable question of imputation. The observer is charged not merely with reinterpreting the subjective experience of the actors, but with imposing his values in the process of so doing. Hence, to ascribe conflictual relations to a situation where the participants deny that there is conflict can only be done by emphasising a feature of the situation that has little significance for the actors, this feature being given importance due to what is valued by the observer. However, while there may be cases where we can justify imputation, Mitchell (1981a, p. 22) stresses a further problem:

A further difficulty with this objectivist approach can be seen by pushing its major argument to its logical conclusion and by recognising that two observers holding different sets of values will interpret the situation in radically different ways.

Schmid admits this point, considering it an "obvious weakness" but rather than rejecting the imputation considers that its validation presents a "challenge" (Schmid, 1968, p. 227), while Curle (1971, p. 5) happily and openly admits a value bias. The subjectivist charge of imputation is clearly well made, but what is less clear is whether the subjectivist is himself altogether untainted. In undertaking mediation, and in attempting to persuade parties to a conflict that there is a better mode of interaction, the subjectivist clearly believes that he is aware of the interests of the parties better than they themselves may be, even though, as is often the case, the parties initially reject the intrusion of a mediator.

The objectivist, however, is not entirely defenceless in the face of the value-bias allegations made against him. We could suggest, for example, that the selection of any data presupposes some perspective upon which the criteria of selection is based. Thus the charge of bias in the objectivist assessment holds true, but it does not differentiate the objectivist position from other positions with respect to values and selectivity. Ultimately, if pursuing this line of argument, we would finish up discussing paradigms, and there is little doubt that the Marxist paradigm, upon which the objectivist position draws, comes close to the classical scientific notion of a paradigm and shows little sign of degeneration in the sense pointed out by Lakatos (1970, pp. 173–74). It is the case that while potentially there is a plethora of alternative "objective" articulations, the fact is that these are limited to particular articulations with widespread support among scholars. What we should be concerned with, then, is not the value base of the objectivist approach—since all approaches are value based—but whether it is a fruitful approach.

The objectivist could also defend himself on perfectly reasonable social scientific grounds by making reference to the role of power in conflict. The development of alternative aspirations—a necessary condition for the emergence of incompatibility of goals—is itself a function of opportunity and the distribution of power. Just this point is made by what Eckstein calls "inherency theory" (Eckstein, 1980) and hence the emphasis in the literature on social control (Webb, 1986). Approached from a radical perspective, terms like "false consciousness" or "repressive tolerance" might be used. Approached from a different perspective and using an alternative vocabulary, the non-emergence of incompatible goals might be described in terms of the reduction of dissonance on the part of either individuals or groups. In either case the structure of the argument is essentially the same, that the non-emergence of such goals is a function of the distribution of power which includes control of ideological propagation and hence the encouragement of conformity. In general we might suggest that where power differentials are great, and the possibility of dissent limited, and where the cost of dissent is high, the tendency will be for subordinate groups and individuals to reduce dissonance by conforming, by accepting the legitimising myths of society, by restricting the scope of comparative social references or by withdrawing psychologically. Thus Oberschall (1969), in the context of developing countries, notes that there is a reality principle involved in the emergence of alternative aspirations; people will develop serious aspirations about objects that they feel are attainable. Similarly, Korpi (1974), writing in the context of bicommunal conflict, notes that aspirations will change in part as a result of changes in relative power balances. Thus, in at least some cases it would seem to make sense to suggest that an incompatibility of goals is inherent in the structure of society and would emerge if the balance of power in society were to change. To argue otherwise is to believe that there are groups in contemporary society who, if they had the power to bring about change, and were aware of the situation, would still willingly opt for high rates of infant mortality, lower longevity and greater probabilities of disease, poverty, undereducation and life chances in general.

It is impossible to separate the idea of structural violence from that of the objectivist definition of conflict; it is implied in the zero-sum conception contained in the previous Schmid quotation. Structural violence may be defined as damage that accrues to individuals or groups due to differential access to social goods and due to the normal operation of the social system. Structural violence thus conceived is not an unusual phenomenon but a feature of most contemporary social systems. It can occur in relation to class, ethnicity, language, religion or family role, and is, it is claimed, prevalent in the international system of stratification (Hoivik, 1971; Kohler & Alcock, 1976). It is important to recognise that it is not inequality per se and the subsequent life chances that flow from this that are indicative of structural violence, but only where this is a consequence of an enduring relationship between parties and hence in principle amenable to rectification.

An important aspect of this perspective is the blurring of the distinction between behavioural and passive violence. The sin of omission is as wrong as the sin of commission. The absence of much-needed medicine, food or fertiliser has very similar effects to the presence of a bullet, bludgeon or blade; the victim is maimed or dies. The similarity of effect is matched by the similarity of cause; one group is doing something to another group. The only significant difference is in the level of awareness; where the violence perpetrated is structural it may be legitimised, accepted fatalistically or compensation sought in other ways. However, the distinction between behavioural and structural violence is not one of fundamental difference between cause and effect, but merely a difference of means. According to the comparative study of Kohler and Alcock (1976), structural violence is far more prevalent than behavioural violence and causes far more human damage, and they conclude with the statement that "wealth cannot only buy a higher standard of living, it also buys life itself".

Hence, the general line taken here is that the objective definition of conflict, far from being either metaphysical or unduly value-based, has much to be said in its favour. It raises important questions about aspects of social existence that can only be ignored at the risk of trivialising the notion of conflict. Consider, for example, the notion of conflict resolution. The subjectivist will often make a distinction between the mere termination or ending of a particular conflict, and the resolution of a conflict. A termination or settlement of a conflict such that the actors no longer perceive themselves to have incompatible goals may be achieved to the satisfaction of the actors, but the subjectivist may deny that a resolution has been achieved if the underlying structural relationships remain unchanged. Thus, at some stage the conflict can be expected to revive. On some occasions at least, then, the subjectivist is driven to the idea that conflict is embedded at least potentially in the structure of situations and that resolution may only be achieved through structural change.

An example may clarify this point. If, as Hadley Cantril (1965) asserts, most of human conflict is over welfare values, and these welfare values are disproportionately distributed according to some social cleavage which has already been the basis of social mobilisation, even while settlement may be achieved on particular issues, the probability of future mobilisation along that cleavage line remains high if the structural relationship between the groups is not significantly changed. Glass will break more easily along a previously scored line. A settlement that "pacifies" with respect to particular issues and which brings an end to overt conflict behaviour, and yet which does not adjust the fundamental disproportionality of distribution or the underlying causes of the conflict, would be termed by the objectivist "negative" peace in that the relationship between the parties would still be associated with arrested development, the full flowering of human potential being limited by the structural relationship. Hence, while the structural relationship between France and Germany remained unchanged, with Germany dynamically seeking a place and role in the international system which was resisted by other powers (Howard, 1983, pp. 7–22) there was a hundred years of "unpeaceful" peace (Curle, 1971, pp. 9–17) interspersed with war, while a change in the structural relationship between these parties within the European Community has made war between these actors unthinkable. A resolution of the conflict required not merely a cessation of hostilities, or even a change of perception on the part of the actors, but a significant change in the structure of the relationship between the parties.

The rejection of negative peace or "pacification" by the objectivist is allied to the charge made against the subjectivist that the mere termination of behavioural violence is essentially and inherently conservative:

Power and influence are needed to carry out the policy implications and recommendations of peace research. The peace researcher will have to ally himself with those who have power in the international structure. . . . The rich and powerful nations of the world are also the most anxious to maintain the international system. [Schmid, 1968, p. 221.]

This point is clearly demonstrated in an industrial setting. Suppose a putative mediator were to attempt to intercede in a dispute such as the 1984 coal strike in Britain; his credibility as a "responsible" actor to the dominant party would depend upon his acceptance of the prevailing hierarchical structure of British industry and society. Hence the range of possible terminations of the conflict, some of which would be structural resolutions, would be severely limited and include only those defined by the objectivist as negative peace. The mediator becomes, in this light, an ally of the dominant party, manipulating the weaker party to accept a settlement that does not change the structure of the relationship (see, for example, this argument applied to the doctrine of empowerment in South Africa in Groom and Webb [1987]). The subjectivist response to this charge is relatively simple and understandable; the mediator as a social actor can do little to change the structure of the world but can at times do something to ameliorate the more obvious and damaging aspects of social discord. To him, the greatest crime is to do nothing because he can only do a little.

At the end of this long, complex and at times acrimonious disciplinary debate, the question of practice still remains. When should the mediator bring his peculiar skills into play, and when should he let events take their course in the hope of a more thorough-going structural resolution. It could even be the case, if it can be demonstrated that at the level of practice the gap between the objective and subjective approaches is not that wide, that the subjectivist mediator may feel inclined to follow Schmid's prescription and learn "how to sharpen conflict relations", a view that is implied in certain interpretations of the problem-solving workshop approach (de Reuck, 1974, 1983; Light, 1984).

TO MEDIATE OR NOT TO MEDIATE?

The argument that will be put forward here is that, in spite of the history of the debate, there is no necessary contradiction between these two schools and that they can be reconciled within the field of peace research and mediation in such a way as to make the disciplinary division redundant at the level of practice. Both approaches are equally good and neither implies the total negation of the other. For, unlike the Freudian–Behaviourism or the Darwinian–Lamarkian debates, we are not looking at stark alternative theoretical perspectives but rather at different ways of construing and developing a single basic value. Since neither approach is wrong, it follows that there is no good reason to reject the prescriptions that flow from either since both will be applicable where the situation is congruent with the particular approach adopted. Seeing the problem in this pragmatic light means that a decisional procedure is necessary in order to evaluate the morality of different course of action. Hence, we wish to know when it is the right and proper thing to attempt mediation, when intervention should be avoided and when we should attempt to forment and develop a conflict. Just as the marriage guidance counsellor has implicit criteria to guide his action, so also should the mediator in the larger sphere.

It should be clear from what has been said that in this writer's opinion values underlie all social-science perspectives. Social-science approaches do not differ between those that are value free and those that are normative, but only in the different normative underpinnings of different perspectives.[1] In the two approaches we have been looking at there is, however, a single basic value that underpins them both, and that is the humanitarian value that damage to individuals is wrong, and any steps that can be taken to reduce or eradicate that damage should be taken. To aid in showing this, the concept of a "Personal Damage Quotient" (PDQ) will be utilised. This in essence does not differ too much from the concept of structural violence except insofar as the cause of the damage is left open, and rather than being aggregatively constructed damage is conceived of at the level of the individual. Were we to pursue its operationalisation we would set up socially constructed standards for comparison along the dimensions suggested in the structural violence literature. However, for the argument of this chapter it is the concept of PDQ that is more important than its operationalisation or empirical demonstration.

To argue that the idea of PDQ underlies both objective and subjective approaches is not difficult. To the subjectivist, whose major but not only concern is with the more extreme forms of conflict, we merely ask why the attempt to resolve, reduce or mediate conflicts? The first response might be that certain forms of conflict are wasteful, expensive, inefficient and non-productive. But when pushed further about the meaning of these words in human terms, the idea of personal damage would soon come to the fore; violent conflict leads to death and maiming, the preparations for conflict are detrimental to health and education due to the mis-allocation of resources, starvation and disease are often preceded by violent conflict and the militarisation of society cuts into valued developmental freedoms.[2] These are all terms which suggest that the activity of attempting to resolve or mediate conflict perceived as socially and individually deleterious is motivated by the damage perceived to be inflicted upon both combatants and non-combatants alike in violent conflict and contemporary warfare.

For the objectivist the acceptance of PDQ as a basic value is clearer and more direct; after all, conflict is defined in part by something close to the structured aggregate of PDQ. To accept PDQ as an underlying concept in both approaches is, however, to come close to accepting one of the major thrusts of the objectivist argument, that there is an equivalence in the effects of both structural and behavioural violence, the only difference being in the means by which the damage is caused.

Having suggested a basic value it now becomes possible to answer the question, "When should mediation be attempted, and when should other courses of action be selected?" The evaluation will rest upon the assessment of comparative outcomes following the supposed adoption of different course of action. Hence, evaluation will rest upon a number of hypothetical statements of the sort "If X then. . . ." This procedure, of course, presupposes some general and public knowledge about probable outcomes that can be utilised decisionally. Hence, when faced with a practical situation a number of questions suggest themselves, and it is in relation to the answers that a course of action is decided upon.

Initially we may conceive of two interacting dimensions, the behavioural/structural origins of PDQ and the level of PDQ that exists in a particular conflict situation, or which may come to exist in a particular conflict. This schema is not fully adequate in that most situations will be marked by both behavioural and structural origins of PDQ. This makes sense in that physical violence is frequently used to maintain a state of structural imbalance. This minor problem can be reconciled by allowing the appearance of a particular case twice, with the origins of PDQ parcelled out between structural and behavioural (Figure 2.1).

The first point to note is that not all conflicts are structural in the sense that damage to persons emanates from the normal operation of the system and particularly the system of distribution. The war between Iran and Iraq is a case in point; the level of PDQ within each country did not derive from the relationship between them, for both occupy broadly similar positions within the international stratification system. While there is a level of PDQ within each country that has a structural basis, with respect to the conflict between the countries the origin of PDQ is almost wholly behavioural. Within Britain, to take another case, there is structural violence, but compared with many other nations and cases it is relatively slight, and such is the level of legitimacy in British society that the degree of coercion needed to maintain the existing mode of distribution is low. In South

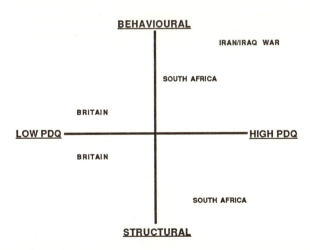

Figure 2.1.

Africa the case is very different; the level of structurally derived PDQ is very high, and it is maintained by high levels of physical coercion that would seem to be on the increase.

As a general rule, we might suggest that moral problems of mediation do not emerge where the amount of PDQ is non-structural in origin and stems from the conduct of the conflict itself. The action of the active mediator is ultimately justified by reductions in the level of PDQ, and where a settlement is achieved in a conflict which does not perpetuate or institute a structural basis to PDQ then the action of mediation may be considered as legitimate.

This consideration is relatively simple and straightforward and largely uncontentious. It could be agreed by both schools with little problem, for the objectivist approach does not reject the idea of negative peace, but suggests that there are situations where it does not go far enough (Schmid, 1968, p. 223). The real problems begin to emerge where we have to trade values in the context of uncertain expectations. Here, however, we can utilise our basic value to aid us in our decision.

For the sake of exposition let us imagine a hypothetical country—North Gondoland—which is marked by bicommunalism. The dominant tribe, the Mingoes, have control of a disproportionate share of the available resources, positional, honorific and material, and have a life-expectancy of several years more than the subordinate tribe, the Mungels. There is no overt behavioural violence and conflict in North Gondoland, the reason being that the Mingoes have such an overwhelming preponderance of coercive capacity that any attempt by the Mungels to rectify the situation would lead to bloodshed and massacres. For the potential mediator to foment conflict by arousing consciousness or empowering the Mungels may, given the balance of power, have the effect of increasing the levels of PDQ without any real immediate hope of decreasing the degree of structurally derived PDQ. If, however, consciousness was otherwise aroused, with perhaps training camps for dissidents in neighbouring countries, etc., our action as a mediator would be related to the trade-off in life-years (as a simple measure of PDQ) between encouraging and aiding the revolt on the basis that in the long term the level of structural violence would be decreased, as against the number of life-years that would be lost in the actual prosecution of a violent conflict. If, for a population of 100,000 Mungels, the average loss of man-years structurally derived is five per person, the potential cost of not revolting is 500,000 man-years, while the actual cost of revolting is the physical damage incurred through violence.

In the advocacy of violence to achieve peace, or in the selection of mediation to achieve peace, there are two qualifications on any straight man-year calculation, both of which are implied by the primary value. The first is that violence can only be advocated and supported where the probability of success is reasonably high. Here, of course, this analysis veers from that of Schmid, who sees this as a general strategy to be adopted in the presence of structural violence. For, where the probability of success is low, and violence is engaged in, then the level of PDQ will rise quickly with little prospect of long-term compensations.

The second point is perhaps more fundamental, and it is that all means must be attempted to reduce the disproportionality that gives rise to structural PDQ prior to the adoption of violence. Violence can only be advocated where the long-term benefits can reasonably be seen to outweigh the contemporary costs. There are, however, many ways of attempting to reduce structural PDQ other than using violence. There are, for example, wholly non-coercive interventions. The mediator may seek to make the dominant party aware of the potential long-term costs to that party of a situation of structural violence. Or there are economic and political non-violent coercive strategies that can be utilised. The advocacy of revolt must be in inverse relation to the possibility of reform. Hence, in South Africa the intransigence of the regime over many years in a situation of high structural violence would seem to indicate that reform is unlikely in the forseeable future, and hence the argument for violence is that much stronger. In Britain, where the disproportion and its effects is not so great, but where, for example, infant mortality still varies greatly between classes, reform seems far more attainable and hence the resort to violence less acceptable.

CONCLUSION

The morality of mediation is, like all morality, complex and marked by the absence of absolute rules which are universally accepted. The primary value advanced here—the level and distribution of PDQ—is a value, but one with a wide consensual base and which can be accepted by both the objectivist and the subjectivist and utilised by both decisionally. As a prescriptive rule the primary value widens the legitimate scope of activity for both the objectivist and the subjectivist. The objectivist need not be so dismissive of negative peace and the attempts to promote it. A more realistic perception is encouraged that does not deal in blanket generalisations, and with this increased realism comes an acceptance of mediation as a valuable and moral act even though the structure of the world is not changed. A similar widening occurs for the subjectivist with the realisation that there may well be occasions when to attempt to end a violent conflict through mediation, but without changing the structural basis of the conflict, may not be the best course of action. In general, then, mediation is not something that should be done automatically but is a course of action designed to achieve certain humanitarian ends, and there may well be cases where those ends are best served by not mediating.

NOTES

1. Far from being a weakness, the fact of value intrusion in social science maintains the relevance and significance of social-science work. Without values, social science would be arid, sterile and probably wholly inapplicable to society.

2. The fact that this is a value construction rather than a description of the consequences of violent action can be demonstrated by construing many of the same factors in an entirely different manner. Thus, engagement in violent conflict may lead to martyrdom, paradise or glory, and militarisation to discipline and a sense of unity.

3

The Motives for Mediation

C. R. Mitchell

In the spring of 1983 the diplomatic world was startled by the sudden
announcement (from Los Angeles Airport) that Miss Elizabeth Taylor was
intending to undertake an initiative to bring about peace in the Middle
East. The film star stated that she intended to embark on a ten-day trip to
the region, during which she would meet with Prime Minister Begin and
President Gemayel of the Lebanon. The object of the trip would be to try
to create peace between Israel and Lebanon. Later scrutiny of the
international press failed to reveal whether Miss Taylor had, in fact,
embarked upon her mission, although subsequent events involving
Lebanon and Israel would indicate that, if indeed she had, her initiative
had achieved less than optimum results. The whole episode might well be
dismissed as having more to do with the film star's wish to keep herself and
her image before the eyes of a somewhat diminishing public, together
(probably) with some residual and praiseworthy desire to "do something"
about the costly and dangerous cluster of disputes revolving around the
Lebanon.

Miss Taylor's initiative does, however, highlight one aspect of other,
more seriously intended and "professional" mediation initiatives. This is
the undoubted fact that the intermediaries themselves possess diverse
motives for choosing that particular form of behaviour (or the "role" of
intermediary) towards the conflict situations they are attempting to effect.
Paradoxically, the fact that intermediaries possess goals and objectives that
they attempt to further through mediation, quite apart from other forms of
third-party involvement, has been a neglected aspect of the neglected study
of third-party activities. It tends to be assumed that, while the adversaries

in the conflict possess goals and objectives that underlie the behaviour they undertake—the incompatibility of which, indeed, forms the basis of the dispute—any intermediary is wholly or, at worst, largely motivated by a desire to bring about a settlement restoring peace and stability to the adversaries' relationship and terminating the conflict in some satisfactory manner. "Peace", as Dr. Kissinger once remarked, "is also a value".

The starting point for this present chapter, however, is that the goals and objectives of any mediator, from individual film stars to special representatives of the UN secretary general, should not be taken for granted and are a proper subject for academic analysis. Furthermore, the underlying motives from which an intermediary initiative arises and which sustain it[1] are likely to have a marked influence on the way that an intermediary conducts the process, on the manner in which the parties in conflict react to the intermediary's activities and on the eventual outcome particularly in terms of the form any final settlement might take.

That mediators have clear motives of their own, and that these are not necessarily confined to the rapid establishment of an acceptable peace might occasion no surprise to a student of nineteenth-century international relations. As LeVine (1971) has pointed out, the overwhelming number of intermediary activities during the period 1815 to 1914 were carried out by national governments, usually those of the "Great Powers" of Europe, and in most of the cases it was seldom argued that these powerful and interested intermediaries acted as they did solely from an altruistic desire to end a conflict and restore a peace satisfactory to the adversaries. Frequently, the intermediary role was played by some highly interested government undertaking that role with the aim of helping to achieve a new situation more to its own liking. Bismarck may have ostensibly acted as an "honest broker" during the Balkan crisis of 1876 and at the Congress of Berlin, but the "broker" during that episode possessed an obvious interest in supporting the claims of Austria-Hungary and in ensuring that Russian gains in the region were kept to a minimum.[2]

It is only in recent years, partly as a result of the rise of international governmental or non-governmental organisations to prominence as "conflict managers", that it is frequently assumed that third parties' motives for acting as peacemaker are to bring about an acceptable termination and no more. Hence, academic writings (Young, 1967; Mitchell, 1981a) have tended to characterise the necessary qualities of a successful intermediary as "neutrality", "impartiality" and "disinterest in the final outcome". Recent works by Touval (1982) and Rubin (1981) have gone some way towards questioning that assumption. However, the former's implied classification of intermediaries into "biassed" and (by implication at least) "non-biassed" (Touval, 1975) leads to the conclusion that there are at least some practising intermediaries whose sole, or major, interest remains the achievement of a peaceful settlement, whether its nature and whatever its effect upon the intermediaries' other interests.

It would be easy enough to begin with the opposite assumption—that all intermediaries possess motives and reasons for undertaking that role quite apart from any desire to bring about a satisfactory peace settlement. This starting point does not seem unreasonable, and if this is the case, we need to think about what might usefully be said concerning the nature of intermediary motivations and the manner in which these can be helpfully classified. What are the reasons for parties becoming intermediaries in the first place, and how might these reasons affect intermediary behaviour and performance?

TWO LEVELS OF "MOTIVATION"

The process of mediation is customarily carried out by individuals, sometimes by single individuals, and this fact can, to some degree, be misleading in any consideration of the "motives" for that process. At the level of the individual (or the head of the team), the nature of motivations involved can run from a genuinely altruistic desire to bring an end to some conflict regarded as tragic or misguided, to a wish for an increase in personal status and reputation, or a desire for a "place in history". For a professional bureaucrat, an international civil servant or a diplomat, rewards may be the sense of gratification from a job well done or an attempt made in difficult circumstances. More mundanely, they may be an increase in personal standing or career prospects within an organisation or diplomatic service. For a private, unofficial intermediary, the motives may involve gaining access to important political figures, well-known statesmen or other famous names. They may involve a sense of, for once, being in a position to affect important events, of being in a position of influence, of having (and wishing to retain) a sense of being at the centre of crucial decision. Such motives can co-exist with the most worthy aims of ending fighting and bloodshed, promoting agreement or discovering ingenious solutions to intractable problems.[3]

At this individual level, underlying motivations can be conscious or unconscious. They can range from highly altruistic, other-directed motives to those involving personal advancement and material benefit and a wide variety of ego-enhancing (and ego-defensive) reasons. In certain circumstances, the motive for undertaking a particular mediation can simply be that of professionalism. The individual intermediary is part of an organisation that provides such a service on a regular basis, as is the case with the conciliators of ACAS, the Federal Mediation and Conciliation Service, the American Arbitration Association (AAA) or the Central Arbitration Committee (CAC), so that the particular individual involved is merely "doing his job", performing a skill learned over a number of years. In all these cases, the "motivations for the mediation" are those arising from the nature of the individuals directly enacting the role.

On the other hand, it is usually the case that the individuals actually carrying out the mediatory process belong to, or represent, some institution, organisation or government. To a large degree, they undertake the intermediary role for reasons which have to do with the "motivations" or, more realistically, the objectives of that organisation. This argument is easy to see with intermediaries such as Henry Kissinger, Alexander Haig or Philip Habib, all of whom have acted in the intermediary role for the U.S. government. It is also clear in the case of individuals (Sr. Gallo-Plaza) or groups of individuals (the Committee of African Elder Statesmen in the Middle East) formally representing an international organisation, such as the UN, the OAU or the European Community. It is less clear in the case of those individuals usually called "private" or "unofficial" mediators, but it seems reasonable to argue that individuals such as Canon Burgess Carr mediating in the Sudanese Civil War, Mr. Elmore Jackson acting as go-between for President Nasser and Mr. Eshkol, or Mr. Olof Palme mediating betwee Iran and Iraq could reasonably be regarded as part of the All-Africa Council of Churches, the Society of Friends and the UN Secretariat, respectively. I would argue that so rare is the case where an individual acting as an intermediary represents "only himself" that such instances prove the rule that all intermediaries can be regarded as part of some intermediary organisation, supporting and controlling the individual(s) acting on its behalf and in its name.[4]

This argument leads to the conclusion that there exists at least a second analytical level at which "motives for mediation" need to be analysed and explained. (It also suggests that, at this second level, the term "motives" might not be appropriate.) It seems unarguable that organisations, institutions and governments acting as intermediaries can so act in order to achieve internally set and agreed goals, to fulfil established objectives, or to bring about some future state of affairs which they desire. Thus, what might be termed "institutional motives" for mediation can be added to those more private ones of the individuals directly mediating. In many ways, it seems more appropriate to make a clear distinction between the two levels, and doing so might best be facilitated by using the term "motives" for the goals that are particular to individual mediators and by labelling the organisational equivalent of individual motivations the "objectives" of the mediating body. It also seems a sensible starting point to regard the latter as being the most important influences upon: (1) any decisions to launch an intermediary initiative; (2) the manner in which the mediating process is carried out; (3) the type of solution sought by the third party; and (4) the final outcome of the mediation process. In other words, while acknowledging the part played by the personal ambitions, fears, wishes and perceptions of (for example) Dr. Kissinger helping the disengagement of Israeli and Egyptian forces in Sinai, concentrating upon the objectives of the U.S. government policy at that time is likely to provide the key to understanding the U.S. role in the triangular mediation process that led to the Disengagement Agreements.

Concentrating upon the *institutional objectives* of the intermediary is one way of analysing an important part of the overall mediation process. Indeed, one sensible way of answering questions as to why the intermediary is undertaking such a role is to look for the advantages (both direct and indirect) to the intermediary in fulfilling that particular role, at that time and in that manner. In brief, the intermediary can be regarded as *choosing* the role because some form of benefit accrues from it. The next question to ask is how one might describe such benefits and then usefully classify them to begin the task of suggesting associations between certain types of intermediary and certain classes of benefit. The second section of this chapter begins this process of description and classification.

INTERMEDIARY REWARDS

Summarising the argument so far, it is—in plain language—that institutions undertaking an intermediary role in any conflict do so because they obtain some reward for so doing. These "rewards" can take a variety of forms. The type of resource, reputation or other non-material good regarded as a desirable reward accruing from being an intermediary obviously differs according to the institution undertaking the role. What is a major reward to the World Council of Churches would probably be an irrelevancy to the Soviet or U.S. government, while the reverse is equally the case. Like beauty, the nature and value of "rewards" lie in the eye of the beholder and are closely related to the value system espoused by the intermediary institution.

It must not be thought too cynical to argue that intermediaries perform their role because they gain something from the performance. Roles involve benefits. However, a necessary analytical distinction needs to be made between benefits that derive from: (1) engaging in the behaviour of an intermediary, irrespective of outcome (process rewards); (2) achieving some form of settlement of the dispute in question which is at least minimally satisfactory to the parties (achievement rewards); and (3) achieving a particular, sought-after settlement which, apart from at least minimally satisfying the parties, also advances the interests of the intermediary (settlement rewards).

The latter two sources of benefit are familiar and understandable, but the idea that it is possible to derive benefits from performing the role of intermediary may initially seem a little bizarre. However, there are many situations in which the very act of mediation itself produces benefits for the intermediary. It can help to hold together a coalition or a membership of an international organisation that is divided in its views of a conflict between outsiders or even some of its own members. In such circumstances, mediation can be a kind of "lowest-common-denominator" strategy: the only policy upon which all members of the coalition can agree. Alternatively, mediation may be a strategy by which a third party avoids having to choose sides in a dispute from which it cannot remain wholly aloof.

Both these elements appear to have been involved in African governments' decision to launch an OAU peace mission to the Middle East in 1971. The establishment of the OAU Committee of Presidents can be seen partly as an effort to find a policy that maintained (if only temporarily) African solidarity on the Middle East dispute, while at the same time avoiding the unwanted choice of offending Arab members of the OAU (especially Egypt) or lining up clearly against Israel.[5]

Noting the distinction between process, achievement and settlement rewards leads to a further point about the nature of benefits to be derived from the role of intermediary. This is the rather obvious one that the nature and number of rewards derived from the role can alter over time, so that what are benefits at one stage can cease to be so (or become less salient) later in the conflict. This argument is easy to grasp in the case of rewards derived from the process of mediating. (The relative failure of the OAU presidents' efforts to extract concessions from Israeli and Egyptian governments gradually discredited their mission, exacerbated divisions among OAU members and led, eventually, to almost total African disarray in the United Nations when the issue of the Arab–Israeli conflict was discussed in December 1971.) However, it is equally applicable to the benefits derived from helping to bring about, and being associated with, a "successful" settlement. Any credit derived from being associated with the 1973 peace settlement in Vietnam rapidly backfired once that settlement collapsed with the rapid and complete North Vietnamese conquest of the entire country two years later. Benefits deriving from having helped construct a temporarily successful peace settlement can rapidly turn into discredit if that settlement collapses or rapidly "goes bad".

Even if we concentrate on the rewards which might accrue to intermediaries enacting such a role, our most basic question remains how to begin analysing the various types of reward that might provide pay-offs to a government or other institution contemplating mediation. An initial analytical step might be to ask (1) where such rewards might arise, and (2) what type of benefit they might confer.

SOURCES OF REWARD: THE FOUR "ARENAS"

Any question of *source* of rewards from intermediary activity directs attention to the various sectors of a third party's overall environment which can be affected by the latter's taking up such a role. We term these "arenas". In this regard, Wall's model of the structure of mediation can be helpful (Wall, 1981). Wall suggests that the structure of any mediation "system" is more complex than the triad customarily envisaged. In the latter, two parties interact, using coercive and other strategies to obtain their goals, but have their behaviour modified by an intermediary attempting to influence both adversaries and their behaviour. Instead, Wall proposes a structure which has at its centre a triangular bargaining process involving the adversaries and the intermediary, but which also involves interaction (1) between the intermediary and the internal supporters (the *constituency*) of each of the adversary parties; (2) between the intermediary and his own constituency; and, by implication, (3) between one or both of the parties in conflict and the intermediary's own constituency.[6] Wall's model also includes other third parties as part of the environment of both intermediary and adversaries, implying other possible third-party roles than that of intermediary. The original model is set out in Figure 3.1.

Although Wall's work serves as an excellent basis for analysing whence intermediaries might derive rewards, it seems useful to make it slightly more complex, at least to assist analysing international mediation where the overall environment for any intermediary is likely to be yet more

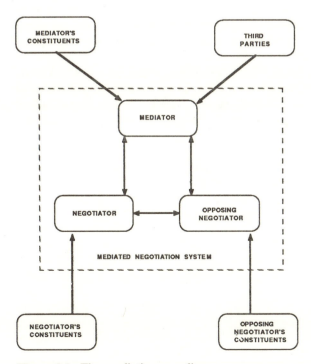

Figure 3.1. The mediation paradigm.

complex. This is especially the case if we consider Wall's category of "Other Third Parties", for these might take a wide variety of different roles in regard to the conflict being mediated. One major category of actors in any international conflict might well be other governments or organisations acting in support of one or other of the adversaries, fulfilling the role of "ally" (or patron) to turn the conflict and its outcome to their own advantage. The role of the Front Line States in the Rhodesian/ Zimbabwean struggle might well illustrate this type of role—not directly engaged as a *party* to the central dispute, but closely interested in both course and outcome and acting to provide advantages to one side against the other.

Another role for third parties might well be that of someone with a direct interest in the conflict but with little preference for one or other party to the dispute. Thus, for many conflicts there exists an interested international or regional group of *affected others* with a direct interest in some specific—and frequently threatened—value deriving directly from the adversaries or in some more general good which they wish to see preserved. Japanese interest in preserving oil supplies from a Gulf region threatened by the Iran/Iraq War might be a good illustration of the former case, while the interests of neighbouring governments in dampening down regional conflict and instability lest it affects them (either externally or domestically) illustrates the latter. In contrast, it might be helpful to distinguish a third category of "third parties"; those with no immediate or direct interest either in the dispute itself or the regional system affected, but with a general interest in the preservation of international stability and the upholding of shared values—for example, in not using military force to bring about change, in respect for international or regional institutions or "the rule of law", or in the containment of forces making for violence and instability in a fragile world. Such third parties form an *audience* before which the conflict itself, as well as any mediation process, is enacted.

The modified version of Wall's model (illustrated in Figure 3.2) enables us to delineate the different arenas from which intermediaries might derive benefits and rewards, making the adoption or maintenance of such a role worthwhile. The model suggests that it might be fruitful to look for potential rewards for mediating governments and other institutions from the following sources:[7]

1. Benefits derived from having some effects on the conflict itself (via the settlement thereof) which includes those from the changed interaction between erstwhile adversaries, but also benefits derived directly from the parties themselves.
2. Benefits from affecting the regional environment within which the conflict is taking place.
3. Benefits from affecting other third parties involved in the overall structure of the conflict, such as allies and patrons of one of the adversaries, affected others or part of an international audience.

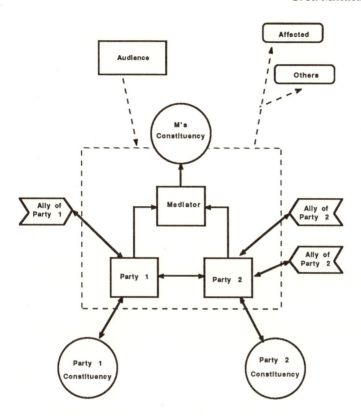

Figure 3.2. Third parties and the conflict system.

4. Benefits from affecting one's constituency, whether this is the salient interests in the political community (in Easton's sense) of a governmental intermediary, or salient blocs and factions within the overall membership of an international or regional organisation.[8]

REWARDS FROM THE CONFLICT AND FROM ADVERSARIES

The first of these sources of benefit for an intermediary is the most familiar, for conventional views of mediation are founded on the assumption that intermediaries derive their main rewards from ending the conflict in a satisfactory settlement. For a "biassed" or interested intermediary, benefits may derive from a settlement that increased either the safety of some good threatened by the conflict, or the intermediary's influence over one or both of the adversaries. For an "impartial" intermediary, rewards may derive from the establishment of peace and stability in part of the global system previously characterised by instability and lethal-conflict behaviour.

Although this arena for deriving mediator rewards is a familiar one, it can nonetheless provide a wide variety of types of benefit to a successful intermediary. An initial distinction can be made between those pay-offs that derive from changing the patterns of interaction between the adversaries and those which derive from establishing a new relationship between the intermediary and each individual party to the conflict. This first type of reward might well be exemplified by a hypothetically successful outcome to the Haig mission between Britain and Argentina at the time of the Falklands War, which would have had the considerable benefits to the intermediary government of reconciling two important allies, one European and one Latin American; removing the necessity for Britain sending large naval and land forces from the North Atlantic and Western Europe; throwing fewer strains on U.S. relations with other European allies; and avoiding the undermining (and ultimate downfall) of Argentine leaders—on whom the Reagan administration had spent much time and effort as part of its anti-Communist campaign throughout Latin America. Less hypothetically, we might quote the actual benefits to the United States following Camp David of ending the dispute between an actual ally (Israel) and a potential ally (Egypt) over withdrawal from Sinai.

Paradoxically, another way in which an intermediary can use that role to obtain benefits from the conflict being mediated is by trying to affect the actual course of that conflict through a judiciously timed mediation offer. Mediation can be used to delay or alter a trend within the conflict, to provide a breathing space for a favoured party against whom the tide is beginning to turn, to buy time for a client to regroup, reorganise, re-arm. Such a motivation for attempting to launch a mediation process may seem the ultimately cynical, but there can be little doubt that such ideas underlay the U.S. attempt to encourage an OAS peacekeeping and peacemaking mission into Nicaragua in June 1979. Had the effort succeeded, the main benefits to the United States would have been through obtaining a breathing space for their client, President Samoza, or allowing a change to a client in Nicaragua better able to prevent—or, at least, delay—the take-over of the country by the Sandanistas. On this occasion, however, the attempt to use the intermediary role for this purpose was too transparent. Neither the OAS nor the Sandanistas were willing to take part.

The second major class of benefits directly derivable from this arena are those which may accrue to an intermediary in terms of its relationship with one or other of the parties to the conflict. During the actual process of mediation, the third party can use its role to increase its own influence with one of the parties. It may be able to buy promises of future compliance or increased sensitivity to its wishes with rewards offered itself or with promises of concessions to be extracted from the other party to the conflict, over which a biassed intermediary may have some considerable influence.[9] One benefit to be derived by the United States from a successful Egyptian/Israeli mediation following the 1973 Middle East War was increased influence over Egyptian policy and future positions, and this seems to have been one of the objectives consciously pursued by Dr. Kissinger during his "honest brokership".

Moreover, once a satisfactory settlement has been agreed, the intermediary's hold on the adversaries can be sustained, and even increased, particularly if the carrying out of the terms of the settlement depends upon actions or guarantees by the third party. In a settlement such as the second Egyptian/Israeli Disengagement Agreement, commitments cut three ways, but the particular reward for the U.S. government was its increased influence on Egypt through its material help to President Sadat and its ultimate guarantee of the agreement.

Finally, some instances of mediation can be motivated by a wish to affect the internal structure or processes of one of the adversaries (usually an ally or client) in some "beneficial" way from which rewards will be derived. During U.S. and British efforts to bring about a settlement of the Trieste dispute between Italy and Yugoslavia, it was widely suspected (not least by the Yugoslavs) that the two Western governments were attempting to use a successful settlement as a way of shoring up Italy's threatened Christian Democrat government and also of obtaining its support for the planned European Defence Community. In the event, the first benefit was achieved, if not the second (Touval, 1975).

REWARDS FROM AFFECTING A REGIONAL ENVIRONMENT

Frequently, rewards from mediation derived from the conflict arena itself overlap (or are intimately connected with) those derived from that affecting the regional environment in which the conflict is embedded. In many respects, this category of benefits arises from a familiar phenomenon, the *neighbour mediator*, an intermediary initiative undertaken by a geographically proximate government or regional organisation. Frequently, the objective of such a strategy is to preserve regional stability by preventing the effects of the conflict spreading to neighbouring countries. A third party might take up the role of intermediary in the hope of bringing about a quick solution so that the conflict poses no danger to a client bordering directly onto the conflict. On other occasions, the motive might be to settle the conflict before it has any major "demonstration effect" on countries in the region with similar latent disputes, currently quiescent.

Much OAU intermediary activity in African disputes seems to arise from the fears of OAU members that they themselves might face similar conflicts in future if those that have reached an overt stage are not dampened down swiftly. OAU action with respect to border disputes can be explained with this in mind. Similarly, efforts to find a settlement to the Nigerian Civil War were given added urgency because many of Nigeria's neighbours, near and more distant, suffered from similar internal cleavages to those underlying the attempted session of Biafra. Other examples are even more specifically tied to fears of a "fall-out" effect. It is clear that a major motivation for Haile Selassi's associating himself with the WCC's Sudanese mediation mission was the fear that, if the internal conflict in the southern Sudan was not ended rapidly and satisfactorily, that dispute would again become further embroiled in his own secessionist movement in Eritrea to the detriment of Ethiopian success in the latter conflict (Howell, 1978).

Often, neighbouring countries exhibit clear and realistic understanding of the tendency of major and long-lasting conflicts to draw in other governments, so that rapid settlement of the dispute is seen as a way of preventing the "internationalisation" of regional disputes (see Rosenau, 1964). The desire to minimise Chinese opportunities for interference in Southeast Asia and beyond evidently plays a part in the efforts of ASEAN to bring about a stable relationship between Vietnamese and Cambodians—a motive especially relevant to the Thais.

Finally, as we have already mentioned, adopting the role of intermediary is one way in which a neighbouring government or organisation can avoid the awkward and frequently costly matter of taking sides in a regional conflict, offending an actual or potential ally.[10] Mediation is a means of *not* taking sides, of remaining neutral and of not suffering sanctions from the parties in conflict. We have already noted that this course of action was adopted by the OAU, particularly by pro-Israeli African countries, in 1971. A similar motivation clearly influenced the U.S. decision to play the role of "honest broker" in the initial stages of the Falklands War. This choice brought some criticism of "fence-sitting" from both of President Reagan's allies. However, acting as intermediary for as long as the Haig mission lasted delayed having to choose between an important European or Latin American ally, the costs of which were plain to Washington and duly paid in terms of loss of Argentine trust and support when the U.S. government finally supported Britain.

REWARDS FROM ALLIES, RIVALS AND AUDIENCES

It can, of course, be argued that the benefits of mediation for the intermediary arising from the *regional arena* are merely a sub-set of a broader category of benefits arising from the effects of the intermediary role on other parties, irrespective of where these are situated. This may be true, although a regional/global distinction seems useful. Whether such an analytical division is made, however, there is no doubt that the adoption of an intermediary role can bring benefits from a wide variety of parties in a wide variety of ways.

For example, on some occasions, an intermediary may be acting to win some material benefits from other governments or institutions, either for carrying out the role or for its successful conclusion (at least, as judged by the third parties that are targets for the effort). Both these objectives undoubtedly played a part in Dr. Kissinger's willing espousal of the intermediary role in 1973/74, when a major aim of U.S. policy was to use the role of "even-handed" intermediary to remove the Arab oil embargo—an outcome which only finally occurred after the successful agreement between Syria and Israel in the summer of 1974. (The Saudi government had insisted that "something be done for Syria" before the embargo could be formally resolved, although it was unofficially lifted after the earlier Israeli–Egyptian Agreement.) In another case entirely, the Western Contact Group's role in Namibia is not entirely unconnected with group members' wishes to preserve vital investments and mineral supplies, especially of urganium (see Jabri, Chapter 6 this volume).

At other times, the role of an intermediary can be adopted with a view to increasing one's own influence over patrons of the adversaries or over third parties in the region generally. (That is, adopting a more "even-handed" approach, so that its maintenance becomes a goal of such regional targets for which they are willing to pay a price.) Conversely, acting as an intermediary can be used as a deliberate strategy to exclude others' influence from the region—usually the influence of a global or regional rival. Touval (1982) argues that, in the mid 1950s, the U.S. aim of excluding Soviet influence from the Middle East (and, especially from Nasser's Egypt) was a major factor in the U.S. decision to launch a peace initiative as a parallel strategy to building up pro-Western alliances in the area. (The policy resulted in the Anderson mission to Israel and Egypt in 1955.) It seems clear that one major objective of Kissinger's shuttle diplomacy in the period 1973/74, and his adoption of a more "even-handed" approach to Arab–Israeli relations, was connected with his wish to keep the Soviets at bay in the Middle East and, particularly, to continue their exclusion from Sadat's Egypt. Similar objectives were said to underlie British and U.S. initiatives as intermediaries between Italy and Yugoslavia over the Trieste question in 1954. At least part of the mediator's shared motivation was preventing the development of closer relations between the Yugoslavs and the Soviet Union after the end of the Stalin era and strengthening Yugoslav political ties with the West (Campbell, 1976). In other circumstances, the intermediary role may be adopted less to affect the adversaries' allies or intermediaries' rivals as to influence an international audience. Becoming an intermediary can be partly a symbolic act, for example, dissociating oneself from the actions of one or other of the parties in conflict or one of their patrons. Secretary Dulles' actions at the time of Suez, helping to arrange a withdrawal, was partly intended to help America's allies (Britain and France) "off the hook". However, it was also intended to distance the United States from its allies' attack on Egypt.

A similar consideration seems to have played a part in Prime Minister Wilson's efforts with Premier Kosygin to act as "honest broker" between Washington and Hanoi in 1967, when the position of unquestioning supporter of the United States' action in Vietnam was becoming embarrassing for the British Government, especially after the U.S. bombing campaign intensified.

In many cases, mediation seems to be undertaken less to influence some specific target among the international audience to the conflict but more to enhance the general reputation of the intermediary for having made a serious effort to bring the conflict to an end. The role of peacemaker remains a creditable one, and the international status of a number of countries has, since 1945, become bound up with the role of intermediary. There is general international recognition that (for example) Sweden, Algeria and Ethiopia have established claims as regular international peacemakers.[11]

REWARDS THROUGH AFFECTING CONSTITUENCIES

The fourth and final arena from which benefits from mediation might accrue is the intermediary's *constituency arena*, broadly defined as those upon whom the intermediary relies generally for support and assistance, as well as specifically for carrying out the intermediary function. This arena might be said to consist of the "internal" audience. Once again, benefits can range from the most symbolic to the most practical. They arise in cases when the intermediary is an international organisation as well as when the role is undertaken by a national government. In the former case, symbolic rewards frequently play a key role in determining whether the organisation attempts to enact the intermediary role. The UN, the OAU, the Arab League and others tend to act as intermediaries in disputes between their members because the organisation itself is publicly committed to objectives such as the maintenance of international peace and security or the enhancement of a sense of unity and brotherhood among member countries. Such goals tend to be threatened by overt disputes between members and thoroughly undermined by lethal conflicts which can threaten the organisation's existence.[12]

Hence, both from the point of view of genuine value commitment and of practical policy, organisations tend to try to demonstrate their commitment to goals of unity and peaceful settlement, as well as preserving their own unity, by adopting a peacemaking role. The reasons for acting as intermediary in most cases are clear. In some, the unity of the organisation has to be repaired by ending the conflict between two members. In others, the lowest-common-denominator policy among divided members is to act as mediator in a conflict where taking sides would be disastrously divisive. Such objectives are relevant whether the situation is one of the NATO secretary general, trying to make peace between Greece and Turkey over Cyprus, or the Arab League acting as peacekeeper and peacemaker in the dispute between Kuwait and Iraq. The practical matter of maintaining intra-organisational unity has already been mentioned in connection with the OAU president's mission to the Middle East in 1971.

The phenomenon of the executive of an international organisation undertaking mediation in order to retain the support and approval of members of the organisation's "constituency" is not unfamiliar, but the use of an intermediary role to buy domestic support, head off internal criticism, buy time and credit or raise domestic prestige is more typical of a government's use of the intermediary role. Governments have frequently taken up the role of honest broker in order to "buy off" domestic pressure to support one side or another—a pressure that can become a major factor in domestic politics for countries where domestic cleavages mirror the external conflict. Often, these pressures relate to external influences and pose serious problems for a government which might best be resolved by adopting an intermediary role.

A variety of such problems arose for African countries during the Nigerian civil war. There was strong domestic pressure on the Ivory Coast government to recognise Biafra, but other West African governments (Benin, Upper Volta and Niger) had substantial Muslim populations and could hardly respond to President Senghor's pressure and abandon the Nigerian Federal Government. In the end all four governments were active in preparations for launching the OAU Conciliation Commission, the Ivory Coast delegation being influential in efforts to make the membership and mandate of that body more acceptable to the Biafrans. Other examples can be quoted of governments trying to preserve domestic unity, increase status and support or (at least) head off criticism at home by adopting a role as mediator.

NATURE AND TYPE OF REWARD FOR MEDIATING

The focus of the previous section was on the source of benefits that might accrue to an intermediary—whence they arose and in what manner. Some of the examples, however, will already have given some insights into our next topic: the nature and classification of intermediary rewards.

Examples quoted in previous sections cover a range of possible benefits deriving from mediation, from the most tangible, such as the restoration of embargoed oil supplies, to the most intangible, such as the enhancement of prestige or the restoration of a sense of stability and security within a region. It has already been implied that one way of classifying benefits is according to whether they arise from the *process* of mediation or from the *result* of the intermediary process (that is, the nature of the final agreement). Another line of thought lies in asking whether the intermediary derives *tangible* or *intangible* benefits and whether these benefits are *immediate* or longer term and hence (to some extent) *discounted* by a recipient.

Another fruitful way of considering possible classification schemes is to recognise that successful mediation produces some tangible and intangible rewards *indirectly*. This phenomenon arises because successful mediation—even the intermediary process itself—can produce "goods" that are generally available to all and cannot merely be confined to the intermediary or the parties to the conflict. A cessation of hostilities while a mediator attempts to reconcile adversaries will benefit others, regionally and (perhaps) globally. A peace settlement may enable others to restore trading links. The restoration of regional peace and stability does not merely serve the interests of a neighbouring intermediary, but all other governments in that region, so that all may well perceive that their external (and possible internal) security has been enhanced.

In short, the intermediary process and the result of a successful mediation may produce (1) *public* "goods" which are of benefit to all and inseparable from the cessation of the conflict and restoration of peace (however imperfect); as well as (2) *private* "goods" which accrue to the parties in conflict and intermediary alone. In many ways, it is the connection between the generally shared values of an absence of overt lethal conflict, linked with the intermediary's production of public goods related to such values, that leads to *indirect* rewards of enhanced prestige and influence, greater trust and status which an intermediary obtains from third parties as a result of assuming the role of intermediary. Even if a mediator fails to help the parties towards a satisfactory settlement, the very activity of engaging in mediation may produce some marginal public "goods" and thus, for the intermediary, some indirect rewards.

Unfortunately, the division of rewards into tangible and intangible, direct or indirect, or public and private suffers from drawbacks inherent in dichotomous classification schemes. We therefore need a scheme which is parsimonious but rather more detailed and for this reason suggest that the kind of benefits derived from enacting the role of intermediary could well be classified as falling into five basic categories, any of which can derive from the *arenas* discussed previously:

(1) *Material rewards*, which may include the restoration or increase of previous transfers of goods and resources between other parties (not necessarily the adversaries) and the intermediary, or the denial of goods and resources to others.

(2) *Influence rewards*, which can include tangible benefits, such as base rights, rights to information or of passage; and less tangible goods, such as promises of future support, greater sensitivity to the wishes of the intermediary, a decline in reliance upon a rival of the intermediary and greater openness to the goods, information and personnel of the

intermediary. (In short, greater interdependence between intermediary and the other party.)

(3) *Support rewards.* If influence rewards involve an increase in the intermediary's ability to have an effect on another party (usually one of the adversaries), rewards of increased support involve a benefit that takes the form of active help and approval for the future actions of the intermediary, whether derived from an external audience or from the intermediary's own constituency.

The line between influence and support is difficult to draw, but it seems worth drawing if only because there seems a common-sensical distinction between an increased *ability to influence others*, which may or may not accompany an increased level of approval, and *assistance from others*.

(4) *Security rewards*, which usually arise from an intermediary's ability to dampen down or eliminate overt conflict (at least temporarily) via a settlement agreement. Whether in the form of public goods for a region or private goods for the intermediary and parties in conflict, the achievement of local peace and stability, plus an enhanced perception of security, is often a benefit that arises unambiguously from playing the intermediary role.

(5) *Status or reputational rewards*, which accrue to a successful intermediary but also to third parties deemed to have made a commendable attempt to bring about a settlement. Such benefits are of particular importance to international or regional organisations, who are often perceived (and perceive themselves) as having some special responsibility for the maintenance and restoration of peaceful relations, and thus face an expectation that they will "naturally" take up the mediator's role.

If this categorisation is useful for considering the benefits that might accrue to intermediaries and a step towards understanding why certain governments or others choose to mediate in particular conflicts, then adding our previous classification of arenas produces a taxonomy highlighting at least two major dimensions of mediator's motivation (the combination is set out in Figure 3.3). Such a framework can be used to throw light on the motives of any and all intermediaries, whether the party in question is a major national government, an international or regional political organisation, or some non-governmental institution such as the World Council of Churches, the ICRC or Society of Friends. Each will have different motives for mediating, but all can have their motives subsumed in this classification scheme.

DANGERS IN THE ROLE OF INTERMEDIARY

Up to this point, we have concentrated on the benefits to be derived from taking up an intermediary role, merely remarking that there may be some costs attached to so doing. However, this should have been enough

ARENA

		CONFLICT & ADVERSARIES	REGIONAL ENVIRONMENT	ALLIES/ RIVALS	AUDIENCE	CONSTITUENCY
NATURE	1. MATERIAL					
	2. INFLUENCE					
	3. SUPPORT					
	4. SECURITY/ STABILITY					
	5. STATUS					

Figure 3.3. Sources and types of intermediary rewards.

to imply that, running throughout the sections dealing with sources and nature of benefits, there was an underlying argument: that for each beneficial aspect of deciding to act as a mediator there might be a less beneficial, often highly costly aspect. In other words, third parties constantly have to calculate the costs of a given course of action as well as its benefits.

Arguments about potential costs are not exactly the reverse of those for benefits. One reason for this may be that, because of predominant values of global society, there is always a tendency to think well of and give the benefit of the doubt to those acting as peacemakers, save in the most blatant examples of calculated self-interest. However, in most cases the arguments about costs bear a strong resemblance to those we have already rehearsed about potential benefits. Costs can be incurred both through undertaking the process of mediating itself and through achieving a settlement, although (again because of the general pre-disposition to think well of the peacemaker) it seems more likely that costs will accrue through an unpopular or unsuccessful settlement than for merely adopting the role of go-between or honest broker. Secretary of State Haig sustained costs from both Britain and Argentina in attempting a balanced approach while trying to mediate the Falklands conflict. Each ally clearly felt that the United States ought not to have adopted this approach, but come out clearly in support of its own position. *Not* choosing sides might have benefits, but also costs, especially when the "sides" are erstwhile allies, expecting support and help from their patron.

Similarly, disbenefits can accrue to third parties in any (or all) of the arenas discussed earlier. Using mediation to "gain an entry" into a conflict or to increase dependence and hence influence on one or both of the parties may backfire and the intermediary be left with less influence, an escalated level of lethal violence and less opportunity of establishing what it regards as a satisfactory relationship with the parties. It can hardly be argued that the UN has established a satisfactory relationship with either the Israeli Government or the Palestinians for all its efforts to bring peace to the Middle East.

Equally, costs can arise from third parties, both regional and international, as well as from constituencies. Reputations can be damaged as well as enhanced; mediation processes can result in decreased as opposed to increased regional stability (especially if they fail). Embargoes can be sustained and even intensified if those imposing them feel dissatisfied with the way in which an intermediary has conducted itself. Costs can also be suffered in the form of diminished support and approval from internal constituencies. Adopting the role of intermediary when there are strong domestic factions feeling that the full weight of governmental or organisational effort should be thrown behind a favoured party can be a dangerous action for the leadership making a choice (although it is likely to be less divisive than backing the wrong side). Similarly, a divided membership of an international organisation can impose serious costs on that organisation's executive for "mishandling" an intermediary initiative or, indeed, for undertaking one at all. Dag Hammarskjhold's difficulties with both pro-Lumumbist and pro-Katangan factions within the UN demonstrate the potential costs of adopting "the wrong sort" of mediation, although in this case the secretary general was able to sustain a sufficient body of support to carry on the UN's effort to bring some form of peace to the Congo.

In short, it is necessary to recognise that, although somewhat asymmetric, there is always a *balance* of potential benefits and costs in undertaking the role of intermediary. Although approval is more readily given than withheld from peacemakers, and becoming an "honest broker" may be the lesser of several evils domestically, nonetheless the choice of such a role always has to recognise potential costs, especially of failure, when deferred problems may return with a vengeance. The adoption of such a course of action is by no means always an easy choice to make.

MEDIATION AS ONE STRATEGY AMONG MANY

Our discussion so far has led to the suggestion that potential intermediaries balance the perceived costs and benefits of undertaking that role before initiating any process that aims (among other things) at finding a solution to a conflict. Moreover, we have suggested that some kind of evaluation process is undertaken by third parties, irrespective or whether they are national governments, international organisations or "private" mediators. (There is a corollary that pressures towards acting as a peacemaker—at least as far as the expectations of others are concerned—will fall strongest on organisations that have accepted some responsibility for such a role, either implicitly, by past behaviour patterns, or by some constitutional commitment.) We see mediation as a *chosen* strategy or response, adopted because some third party considers that the costs of undertaking such a strategy are outweighed by the benefits.

A further implication of our approach is that third parties, at least in theory, have a number of possible "roles" (strategies or behaviour patterns) they might adopt when considering how to respond to some conflict by which they are affected. If mediation is one response, chosen for its apparent rewards when costs have been discounted, so also might be a strategy of direct help to one or other of the parties in conflict, or a decision to remain studiously neutral while letting the conflict run its course.

Such a conclusion was posited some years ago by Oran Young (1967) when he attempted to throw light upon the nature of intermediaries in general by examining the behaviour of third parties at the time of the June 1967 War in the Middle East. "Third parties" according to Young, were "all those actors which became significantly involved in the crisis without becoming totally identified with either the Arab or the Israeli forces. ..." He then identified outsiders enacting the role of *intermediaries* as "those third parties adopting a (more) impartial stance with regard to the opposing sides in the crisis" and went on to contrast them with another type of outsider which he called an *interventionist*, a third party "motivated by some combination of independent interests and partisan interests favouring either of the opposing sides" (Young, 1967, p. 52). Young's analysis implied the existence of three types of third party in situations of conflict, namely, intermediaries, interveners and those "totally identified with either" party to a conflict. In the terms we have used in this chapter, the third of Young's roles might be called an ally or a patron.

By way of conclusion, three thoughts arise from Young's analysis. The first is that it might be more useful (as well as more realistic) to stop regarding mediation and the role of the mediator as something distinct and unique in the responses of others to some intense conflict. Instead, mediation might best be seen merely as one among a number of strategies used to cope with such situations, with third parties deciding which strategy they will adopt (and hence which "role" they will play) on the basis of some evaluation of the relative costs and benefits of adopting one strategy rather than another. In such a framework, questions can be asked about factors affecting such evaluations and choices, constraints on particular third parties in particular circumstances and the manner in which evaluations alter, so that third parties change roles if change will bring greater perceived benefits. Other roles, apart from those of honest broker or intermediary, include that of a thoroughly committed ally, an active intervener, a passive supporter, an affected other or a member of an interested (or indifferent) audience (see Figure 3.4 for a preliminary classification scheme of third-party roles). Each and every one of these

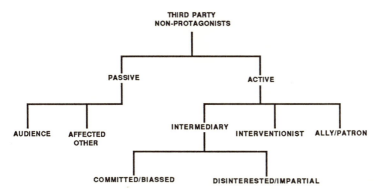

Figure 3.4. Third-party roles in a conflict system.

carries with it a variety of benefits for the party enacting it, well or ill, as well as a number of potential costs. Hence, which role is finally adopted will depend upon the balancing of these costs and benefits.

The second thought is that a fresh way of regarding third parties as potential role players involves asking what range of roles is actually open to them. Baldly, the question is not whether any particular third party can adopt mediation as a strategy (in many ways it seems a strategy easily open to the whole range of third parties, from the U.S. government to the Society of Friends, probably because of the role's relatively straightforward logistical requirements) but what range of other strategies—apart from studied non-involvement—is realistically available. For example, the World Council of Churches or Society of Friends can mediate (or excommunicate?). The OAU or the UN can mediate, or organise a boycott, a peacekeeping force or a condemnatory resolution. The Nigerian government can do all of the foregoing plus (if it so desires) imposing an oil embargo, assisting subversion or, ultimately, organising an armed attack. In short, some third parties possess the necessary resources and opportunities to undertake a wide range of roles, others possess a more limited selection from which to choose. This might be an interesting way of approaching the explanation of which role is adopted in particular cases, and why.

Finally, a third heretical thought is that it might be a gross over-simplification to think that third-party reactions to conflicts can best be analysed as decisions to take up specific roles. Instead of thinking about "interveners" or "intermediaries" and seeking explanations for that pattern of behaviour, it might be as well to treat all third parties merely as entities involved, in a variety of ways, with the adversaries and distinguished by different levels of interaction, degrees of influence on the parties, interest in the outcome, coercive potential, dependence upon the adversaries, commitment to salient values for the conflict and innumerable other factors.

Whichever framework is adopted, however, the final conclusion of this chapter is that it is misleading to think of an *intermediary* role as being, somehow, qualitatively different from other strategies for dealing with conflicts. Rather, it should be considered as one of a range of responses and analysed as part of that range, rather than something wholly unique to itself.

NOTES

1. There is no implication here that intermediaries' aims and objectives can be viewed as constants. The objectives of all parties to a conflict, including third parties, are dynamic. The fact that goals and preference orderings alter over time is one reason for cases in which unacceptable outcomes at one point in time become acceptable later.

2. According to LeVine's (1971) data, the United States, singly or with other Latin American governments, undertook 18 mediation missions between 1870 and 1914.

3. It need not be emphasised that these are highly value-laden assessments.

4. Perhaps one example of this exception that proves the rule might be the mission to Hanoi to act as go-betweens for the U.S. and North Vietnamese Governments carried out by Harold Ashmore and William Baggs in 1966/67. However, at a stretch, it could be argued that the two American individuals represented the Centre for the Study of Democratic Institutions in Santa Barbara (Ashmore and Baggs, 1968).

5. As a less negative example of benefits to be gained from the *process* of mediating (as opposed to successful peacemaking), the very fact that a government or other organisation is engaged in such an activity usually adds to the international reputation both of the government and individual involved in the process. Even in the cynical world of international politics, the peacemaker seems to be respected.

6. The manipulation by Israel of Jewish opinion and pressure groups within the United States during Dr. Kissinger's Middle East shuttle diplomacy and the use of the African radicals—Egypt, Ghana, Guinea—by Lumumba's faction during the 1960/61 Congo crisis are both examples of this last relationship in action.

7. These sources are likely to provide what might be termed medium-term, specific and strategic benefits. In other words, the benefits arise recognisably from the source and can be identified as pay-offs in changed behaviours, material transfers and altered policy positions from specific role players, frequently the conscious targets of the intermediary. On the other hand, there is another, vaguer category of longer-term benefits to be derived from acting as intermediary through some demonstration effect and a learning process by the adversaries, affected third parties and, most particularly, audiences and constituencies. Switzerland's development of a recognised role as a neutral provides a parallel example, while both Sweden and Canada have gone some way towards developing an accepted role for themselves as an international intermediary.

8. In all of these categories it will be noted that we are dealing with what might be termed "strategic" benefits—final rewards of playing the intermediary role. In many cases, acting as an intermediary over one set of issues can bring short-term "tactical" rewards for a more general peacemaking process. UN Secretary General Hammarskjold used an intermediary role to expand the agenda for discussion and begin to deal with wider problems when, in 1957, he was able to use his role in the relatively minor Israeli–Jordanian dispute over Israeli rights to transport fuel into the Jordanian area of Mount Scopus to effect a general stabilisation of that area (Wall, 1981, p. 165).

9. As Rubin points out, biassed intermediaries become parties to a triangular bargaining process, in which part of the interaction involves their trading-off influence on their client (the party they are biassed for) through which they obtain concessions for increased compliance from their client's adversary (Rubin, 1981).

10. Touval argues that, on occasions, mediation can be adopted as a way of restoring purpose to a group of countries engaged in a number of tasks from which the conflict diverts them. This might be termed an *opportunity costs* motivation, as the costs of not achieving even a temporary unity through the lowest-common-denominator process of mediating will be the neglect of more important shared objectives. Touval notes that President Kaunda's motives in proposing the OAU mission to the Middle East contained elements of impatience at the fact that dissension over the Arab–Israeli dispute was diverting African attention and effort from the campaign against the white-dominated laager in the south of the continent.

11. The development and general acceptance of the Commonwealth Secretariat's role as a peacemaker within the Commonwealth underlines the fact that a similar process can involve some international organisations, if not all.

12. The effects of the Western Sahara dispute upon the fortunes, solidarity and even ability to hold meetings of the OAU underline the dangers to regional unity if such conflicts are allowed to grow and thus spread. Sooner or later, members of regional organisations face the problem of taking sides.

4

Acceptance of Mediation Initiatives: A Preliminary Framework

John B. Stephens

A great deal of conflict research has centered on the process of mediation and what factors or tactics speed or hinder settlement of disputes. However, the question of how this process begins has been relatively ignored. While some kinds of conflict have institutionalized mediation, providing specification for when the process can start and who shall mediate (e.g., labour–management disputes, often with arbitration powers to follow), a vast array of conflicts lack such mechanisms. Conflicts not bound by rules for starting mediation are of interest in many ways: when the mediation initiatives are put forward, from what source, who the prospective mediator is and whether the disputants accept or reject the initiative. In short, what are the decisive factors at the "threshold" of mediation?

The present study will focus on one aspect of the beginnings of mediation: the voluntary decision of adversaries in large-scale conflicts to accept mediation to end their dispute. The *voluntariness* of the decision only means that there is not a legal sanction facing the adversary in accepting or rejecting a mediation initiative. Decisions can be heavily constrained, even to where it seems that there is "only one option". This facet will be explored below. Also, *large-scale conflict* refers to two aspects in this work: the size of the disputants (e.g., governments, tribes, religious groups, political organizations) and the importance of the issues to the disputants. While the salience of the issues could differ significantly between adversaries, if one party believes the issues are tied to its fundamental well-being (e.g., resources, security, autonomy), then the dispute meets this second sense of "large-scale". The model presented may apply to various kinds of conflicts, but international disputes, civil strife and intercommunal conflict are of primary interest.

The study is presented in four sections. First, a review of the problem of entry into mediation is considered through relevant ideas of conflict researchers. Second, a model will be created. From a variety of suggested factors, attributes and ideas, categorization will yield a coherent structure for analyzing an adversary's decision whether or not to accept mediation. Thirdly, features of the model will be explored in general and in a particular illustrative case. Finally, a set of continuing issues will conclude the work.

TWO APPROACHES TO THE THRESHOLD OF MEDIATION

In their efforts to produce generally applicable findings about the nature of human conflict, a number of researchers have considered the problem of an intermediary's access to a conflict. As a preliminary, I will briefly review the ideas of two such scholars, Louis Kreisberg and Paul Wehr.

Kreisburg has harnessed a vast array of research and proposes a general model of conflict in *Social Conflicts* (1982). He analyzes intermediaries and mediation by first distinguishing between different roles and purposes of intermediaries generally (arbitration, enforcement, conciliation, training) before focussing specifically on the mediation role. However, his aims are mainly to classify functions and organize existing research on mediation. Concerning the entry into mediation, Kreisburg notes that some conflict types have clearly defined rules of mediation, while others are voluntary or spontaneous, but a concerted examination of the latter type is not offered.

Nonetheless, Kreisburg identifies many factors that are implicitly important to studying the threshold of mediation. First, the need for neutrality in a mediator is seen as essential by some researchers, while others claim it is unnecessary. Kreisburg refines this division by saying that neutrality can refer to intention, consequence, or appearance. He then cites Brookmore and Sistrunk's (1980) laboratory study finding that partiality did not affect a mediator's success, but he does not say which, if any, of the three senses of neutrality the study refuted. This is one important issue to examine as part of the whole question of successful and unsuccessful mediation initiatives.

Second, Kreisburg (1982, p. 271) touches on areas of variation between mediators that are relevant to this study. He states that mediators have their own interests which may be pursued through mediation (see Mitchell, Chapter 3 this volume; and Touval, 1982). If the mediator is also a representative of a power greater than the adversaries, there arises the danger of manipulating any agreement to suit that power's interests more than those of the adversaries. Great Powers' mediation in the late nineteenth century, and U.S. mediation in Latin America in the early twentieth century, illustrate this danger. However, if the interest is maintaining one's career as a mediator, this may produce greater fairness and truer sensitivity to the disputants' needs in order to produce a lasting settlement and engender a positive judgement of the mediator. These interests could exist simultaneously, as might be argued about Kissinger during 1972–76, but this is not explored by Kreisburg. Other motivations for a third party to initiate mediation include moral concern and role obligation (Kreisburg, 1982, p. 275).

A third area is what the mediator brings to the negotiation. He may bring prestige, skills, or personal bonds with an adversary that make an offer hard to reject. Kreisburg cites the conundrum of the "officiality" of the mediator. Persons with a stated position in an organization (e.g., UN general secretary, head of state, leader of a church) may bring greater authority to their efforts, yet may be constrained by protocol or the organizations' policies and principles. On the other hand, a mediator without such a position may have greater freedom to meet with people and suggest concessions but, without an organization's backing, lack sufficient influence with the disputants (e.g., Ramsey Clark's efforts to free Americans held in Iran). Finally, a mediator could bring resources to compensate for concessions made by the adversaries. Thus, the range and level of values available can be expanded and can improve chances for a satisfactory settlement. All the above are cogent dimensions to considering the acceptability of the potential mediator to the adversaries.

Fourth, Kreisburg offers some logical generalizations about the likelihood of mediation taking place. If there is high integration among adversaries, mediation is likely to occur before escalation of a conflict in order to avoid costly and dangerous coercion. Mediation seems more likely when the conflict is between organised entities rather than loosely bounded movements. The organization of a party defines which specific representatives a mediator can approach. Finally, if the balance of the means of coercion is relatively equal between disputants, mediation is more likely. If there is a wide disparity, the stronger party would not be prompted to accept mediation and make concessions. Their superior power should enable them to dictate a more favorable outcome to the conflict (ibid. p. 274).

Lastly, mediators can perform a variety of functions and be drawn into other roles to benefit the disputants. They could first act as a "firebreak", halting escalation while negotiations proceed (ibid. p. 289). Mediators can help strengthen a disputant's representative in persuading his constituency to accept an agreement. A mediator can emphasize the gains each party has made and minimize the impact of what is conceded. Common interests can be stressed and the illusion of rapid movement created by the mediator. Finally, mediators can agree to act in the role of a monitor or guarantor of an agreement, seeing that the provisions of the settlement are adhered to. The UN's work to establish ceasefires and install observers shows this ability to expand, or move between, roles. These possibilities will be considered in the model.

Another study covering a range of conflict levels is by Paul Wehr (1979), who approaches the subject of third-party intervention into conflicts with the aim of producing a specific kind of outcome (non-coercive, positive-sum) and does not single out mediation for particular treatment. He does state that intervenors can be taught how to enter a conflict and offers a "Conflict Intervention Guide" (ibid. pp. 45–50). I shall briefly review the relevant sections from Wehr's guide.

Wehr cites five criteria that a potential intervenor should consider when deciding whether or not to intervene: (1) accessibility, (2) tractability, (3) divisibility, (4) timing, (5) alternatives. *Accessibility* is said to be "sufficient credibility", while *tractability* is judging whether an intervenor is suited to the conflict. Both require much more explanation, but the format is a general guide rather than a comprehensive analysis. *Divisibility* suggests the possible intervention on some issues, but not others. *Timing* is ill-defined; Wehr only suggests there are some constraints (it can be "too early" in some cases and "too late" in others). Finally, *alternatives* queries whether or not non-intervention is better to all concerned. While far too brief, these are fruitful ideas for exploration.

Interestingly, Wehr suggests that entry into a conflict begins with the intervenor sharing a "conflict map" (a checklist or analysis) with the conflict parties and other "influentials" and then depends on two factors: credibility and neutrality. *Credibility* is founded on professional skill and past success, with "good offices or respected people and backing from authoritative organizations outside the conflict situation" as supporting, but secondary, factors. Wehr (ibid. pp. 50–51) claims that strict neutrality is necessary. While an intervenor has an interest in success, improving his credibility and standing must rest on an overriding commitment to a mutually satisfactory outcome and "no commitment to any party in the conflict" (ibid. p. 51).

While there are other works and ideas that could affect this study, Kreisburg and Wehr provide a sufficient overview. Other ideas relevant to the threshold of mediation will be included as the model is constructed.

A MODEL OF ADVERSARIES' DECISIONS ON MEDIATION

The purpose of the model is to promote the understanding of why some mediation initiatives are accepted, while others are rejected. To this end, a division can be made between dependent factors that constitute an adversary's decision on a mediation initiative, and independent factors that help explain such decisions. The first subsection, Dependent Factors, will cite three basic assumptions and then separate the decision on a mediation initiative into two judgements and examine those judgements. One special case of decisions on mediation initiatives will be presented. The second subsection, Independent Factors, will define and organize the factors that influence the two dependent judgements.

Dependent Factors

Assumptions. The following three assumptions are cited to clarify the bases of the dependent factors. While generally unassuming, it is used to be explicit in what is taken as "given" and helps direct the use of the model.

The first assumption is that a mediation initiative's success or failure rests on decisions by the leaderships of each adversary concerning that mediation. Initiatives most often come from a third party, thus an adversary's decision concerns the *acceptability* of such a proposal. Logically, adversaries themselves could suggest a party to mediate, but this occurs infrequently and is not examined by the model, although the central aspect of acceptability would form an important part of an adversary's initiative. Finally, conflicts will be viewed as being between two disputants and a mediation initiative involving one possible mediator. However, multiple adversaries and/or multi-party mediators can be accommodated without major modification.

This assumption leads to a corollary; that the disputants are separate entities with recognized individuals as representatives or leaders. In other words, certain people have a position to act on behalf of the group, not absolutely, but with autonomy and legitimacy. Nonetheless, representatives are often accountable to a leadership group which is far from homogeneous, so the existence of intra-party factions will be considered.

The third assumption concerns the level of antagonism between disputants. Suspicion or hostility between adversaries can range from very low to very high. While mediation is possible, and has been employed, across the range, it seems of greater relevance in situations of significant suspicion or antagonism. At lower levels there is little need logically for an external party to assist disputants who trust one another, since they should be able to negotiate directly. Thus, salient antagonism will be seen as part of the motivation for adversaries to consider mediation.

Two Judgements Comprising a Decision on Mediation. The decision by the leaders of an adversary concerning the suitability of a mediation initiative consists of two judgements: (1) whether the preconditions for negotiation exist; and (2) whether a particular mediator is acceptable. Here, we will simply list the preconditions for negotiations and then argue for two elements of "acceptability" from a variety proposed by researchers. Finally, characteristics affecting both of these judgements will be considered.

Since mediation is a negotiation with an external party added to facilitate agreement, most of the preconditions for negotiations apply to mediation. They are: (1) low or decreasing probability of attaining conflict goals through coercion, (2) decreasing value of conflict goals, relative to the direct costs of pursuing those goals and relative to other goals, (3) some common or compatible interests between adversaries (at least the possibility of a settlement offering mutual advantages over continued conflict), and (4) flexibility by each leadership to consider negotiation.

Added to these conditions is the foregoing assumption that antagonism prevents a direct meeting of adversaries, but might be overcome by using a mediator. Nonetheless, mediation in the abstract still has many uncertainties. The first is whether it is possible for any third party to compensate for the hostility between opponents. Secondly, while a mediator may help moderate an opponent's demand and thus produce concessions, this applies equally to the protagonist. Generally, a mediator constitutes yet another "uncontrollable" and disturbing element to the conflict and must be cautiously considered (see Mitchell, 1981b, pp. vii–ix).

However, mediation is seldom considered "in the abstract" by a party in conflict; the idea usually has a concrete referent. A vast array of concepts has been suggested as the most important elements that define a mediator: neutrality, prestige, salience, persuasiveness, skill, creativity. (This chapter accepts Touval's argument [1982, pp. 12–14] that impartiality is not required in mediators, although it can be one basis for their activity.) The two aspects of the judgement on the "acceptability of the mediator" offered here are the adversary's *trust* in the prospective mediator and the adversary's perception that the potential mediator is *independent* of the adversary's opponents. Some of the preceding ideas of what defines a mediator are subsumed in this formulation of acceptability (persuasiveness, neutrality as one basis of trust), while others will be treated under independent factors (prestige, salience).

A number of comments are needed to understand the position of the two judgements as dimensions of a decision on proposed mediation. First of all, these *judgements are made by the leadership of an adversary*, and the analyst must focus on such judgements and not his own. Although the conditions are seldom transparent, there are discernible reasons for judging one way or another. These influences on adversaries' judgements are the independent factors below.

It is also recognized that often there are differing estimations on the conditions of the judgements within a leadership group. Moreover, the *context of the judgements is dynamic*. Changes within the leadership and especially "in the field of conflict" reflect directly on the possibilities of winning, the cost of the conflict, trust in the prospective mediator and intra-party flexibility. Unless most adversaries presume they can (must) win, it is usually in a period of dramatic change that eventual victory is questioned and negotiations considered. Here it is important to look at the effects of symbolic elements (deadlines, personal loss, or capture of a town) which can all spur a re-evaluation of the conflict.

Finally, trust in and independence of the third party as seen by a disputant can change due to *actions of the third party*. Meeting with the opponents can call into question a potential mediator's independence. Reneging on previous commitments can diminish an adversary's trust in that party. These aspects are explicated below, and an initial framework is set out in Figure 4.1.

A Special Case: "Unavoidable Mediation". This structure is meant to be adequate for the majority of mediation initiatives in large-scale conflicts, but there is one special case where it is bypassed. This is when an adversary judges that the costs of refusing a certain third-party's initiative far outweigh accepting the initiative, even if the judgements on negotiation preconditions and mediator acceptability are negative. An example of this is Alexander Haig's initiative in mediating between Argentina and Great Britain following the Argentine invasion of the Falkland/Malvinas Islands (see Kinney, Chapter 5 this volume). Being an important ally to both parties, neither could reject the offer fearing general disapproval and possible support of their opponent by the United States. Thus, mediation was seen as unavoidable.

However, acceptance in this matter is different, the aim usually being to satisfy the mediator and attempt to condition him to act later as a patron or, at least, not to support one's opponent (Touval and Zartman [1985, p. 9]—in a weaker form). The initiative is "absorbed" rather than "joined" and lacks a strong intention to end the conflict through negotiations. Other illustrations could include some Papal mediation and some UN secretary

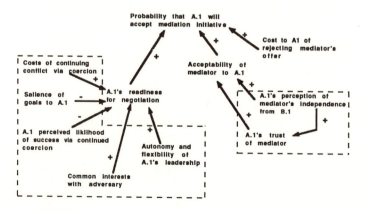

Figure 4.1.

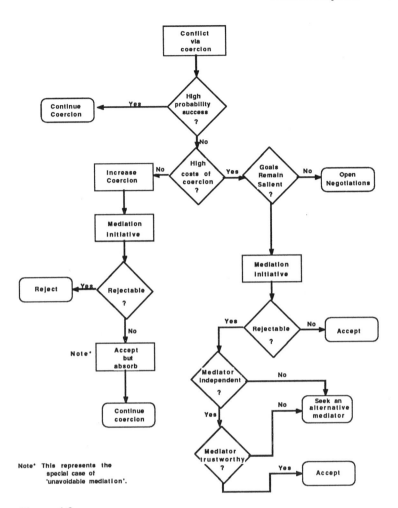

Figure 4.2.

general initiatives, when an adversary's patron(s) strongly backed such an initiative.

This special case is included in Figure 4.2. Here, the immediate question before an adversary's leadership is "Can the initiative be rejected?" and usually arises only when there is a strong presumption that the answer is "No". Then mediation proceeds, but is largely inconsequential as long as the parties believe they could reach their conflict goals without negotiation. Most of the time the mediation initiative can be rejected without prohibitive costs, and the issues can be dealt with in the structure of the analytical framework.

Independent Variables

Given an examination of components of an adversary's decision whether or not to accept a mediation initiative, this section seeks to organize the range of factors relevant to that decision. First, general conflict characteristics and motives for mediation are considered as background factors. The central elements are described as the identity and resources of the prospective mediator, and the nature of the issues in conflict. Evaluation of each of these can be modified by other factors: the potential mediator's actions can alter an adversary's evaluation of his identity and resources, and the history of the conflict can refine and alter the issues being fought over. Finally, the particular circumstances ("battlefield situation" or balance of advantage) an adversary faces when a mediation initiative is taken is an important factor.

Background Factors. Since mediation is considered as part of the conflict, one must explore two areas: the characteristics of the conflict, and the general motivations for mediation. These are necessary parameters to the framework proper. Four groupings are offered for characterizing a conflict: (a) composition of the parties, (b) the prior and prospective relationship between the adversaries and (c) allies to each side of the conflict. Usually seen as a fourth conflict characteristic, the issues in conflict act as a central rather than background factor affecting mediation initiatives.

Analyzing the *composition of a party* can begin with defining the nature of the boundary of that group. Boundaries can be physical, social, religious, ideological, or political. One should consider such a boundary's permeability: the possibilities for moving between, escaping from, or entering into one of the conflict groups. Also, the comprehensiveness of the party (its definition of member's identity and behaviour) can be examined.

This sets the stage for considering *differentiation within an adversary.* Is there specialization of activity within the group? What is the degree of formal or informal hierarchy? Despite the general distinction of this group from its opponent, are there divisions of goals or interests represented by subgroups? Each of these aspects is rather abstract, but will be illustrated below.

An even more difficult problem is trying to characterize the *relationship between the adversaries* in a clear but accurate way. Has there been past interactions and, if so, in what manner—economic, social, cultural, political? Some judgement of the degree of cooperation and confrontation, trust and antagonism, salience and equality or inequality of the previous links needs to be made. Furthermore, what is the likelihood that any relationship remains after the conflict? If groups believe they must continue "to live together" regardless of the outcome of their dispute, constraints to coercion and interest in mutually acceptable outcomes are high. However, such links could also inhibit concessions for fear of looking weak and being forced to sacrifice even greater values in a future dispute.

Finally, present and possible *patrons* are vitally important to adversaries. Some patrons take only a passive role, maintaining the status quo or the control of less important resources. At the other end of the continuum, allies are important for continued or additional means of pursuing the conflict, pressuring opponent(s) to concede. Thus, a protagonist considers the need for such outside help and, equally, denying support to their adversary. Without regressing ad infinitum (patrons, patrons of patrons) an analysis of the patrons of each side is necessary: what support is offered (material, legal, social, moral, etc.) and with what interests and conditions attached? This establishes a basis for considering whether allies would exert pressure on their client to settle, or to reject compromises the client might otherwise accept, and strive to dictate terms later.

Adversaries' Motives. A second set of background factors can be grouped under the heading "motives for mediation". A variety of possible motives for mediation held by an adversary will be considered briefly.

One important motivation for an adversary to accept a mediated negotiation is the expectation that the mediator will influence the opponent into concessions leading to an agreement acceptable to the first party. Consequently, as Touval notes, a mediator "closer to" the opponent can be advantageous to the protagonist. A protagonist tries to use those closer ties between the antagonist and the mediator to bring greater pressure on the opponent than would be possible by a neutral third party or any ally of the protagonist. However, if the mediator makes seemingly unequal proposals to one party's detriment, that party can place the blame for a failed negotiation on the mediator due to unreasonable proposals or hidden malevolence. Although paradoxical, the "added pressure" and "escape hatch" can be unique advantages brought by a mediator.

On a more cooperative level, a mediator's influence can break the spiral or stalemate of coercion and suspicion and introduce proposals without a party's fear of their concession only leading to greater demands by their opponent. Either of the disputants may believe that a compromise solution was possible, but if offered by themselves might only be "pocketed" without an equivalent concession from the adversary. Stemming from these two points and Touval's argument, a mediator can bring resources to compensate for an adversary's concessions. Presumably, the mediator as middleman is willing to offer valued items to the adversaries in exchange for agreement.

Even if these motives are not sufficient, motivation can be defined negatively. Significant opprobrium, loss of support, or punishment could result from not responding to a mediator (short of clearly being prohibitive as in the special case above). The basis for this is the notion that a party's leadership is constrained by "audiences" within or outside their group. At the least, parties need to project an image of flexibility, sincerity for peace, or reasonableness to a wider audience, but sometimes to "doves" within their own constituency. The stronger constraint is support from a patron being conditional upon negotiations or even tied to a particular mediation initiative. That is, a patron's interest in settlement may be forced upon the party directly in the conflict. Similarly, if the opponent is open to mediation, yet an offer is rejected by the protagonist, previously uncommitted parties may act to aid the opponent and/or hinder the protagonist. Even if these concrete actions do not seem likely, a general violation of norms or expectations may be deleterious, if in a more ambiguous manner.

Central Factors: The Nature of the Prospective Mediator. Analysis of the nature of the prospective mediator distinguishes between that party's identity and the resources it brings to the negotiation. There are numerous ways of defining these concepts; analysts offer many ideas which could be set within the categories presented here. Moreover, it is important to see identity and resources as tied to one another, but conceptually different. Identity is holistic, and its components must be treated together, mutually defining and amplifying one another. Kinds of resources can be separated and do not necessarily depend on one another. *Identity* and *Resources* are thus related, but different, aspects characterizing a potential mediator (see Figure 4.3).

Identity can be viewed as consisting of three interlinked components: status, prestige, constituency. *Status* is the nature of the link between the persons who would mediate and their constituency. Is there a formal organization where the mediator holds a clear position, or is there only an informal link by a general background, race, or religion? *Prestige* is the judgement by the adversaries of the potential mediator's authority, skill, or fame. Prestige is not completely general but must be tied to the particular issues and the basic values and characteristics of the parties in conflict. Thus, it can differ significantly between adversaries. Finally, the *constituency's basis*—political, economic, or ethnic—and its division and

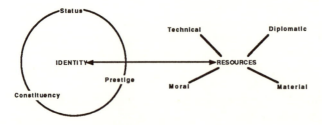

Figure 4.3. Nature of the prospective mediator.

ties to the mediator (e.g., the ability to control the mediator), constitute the third component.

Resources can be separated into technical, moral, diplomatic and material forms. *Technical* resources are communication links, a meeting place, secretarial support—low-level but useful tools for better negotiation. *Moral* resources stem from the potential mediator's perceived authority and worthiness. Mediator approval or disapproval carries weight with audiences who respect the third party's integrity. *Diplomatic* resources involve the potential for action in political forums that could support principles, initiate censure, or promote other assistance for, or persuasion towards, one or more of the disputants. Finally, *material* resources are goods and financing that a mediator can offer to compensate for concessions made in the negotiations.

Central Factors: Nature of the Issues. The other central factor of the model consists of the issues in conflict. However, the nature of the issues grows in complexity as one probes their sources; definition of them by the adversaries and outsiders (including the researcher); their relative importance, both intra- and inter-party; and the tangle of links and presumptions that change as the conflict proceeds. Indeed, in an illustrative conflict one party (the Spanish government) could define the issue as "terrorism", while the opponent (ETA) stated that it is "liberation". Their definitions do not agree, stemming from different perceptions and values. Thus, an important caveat in studying conflict issues is that while one label is convenient for discussing them, each party's definition and explanation of "the issue" must be included. Obviously, one will be led into clusters of issues and values which confound simple explanation.

General typologies of issues have been offered by many researchers. Kreisburg distinguishes consensual from dissensual issues. In the former, parties agree on the basic goals but differ over how to pursue or distribute them. In the latter, different values intersect and interfere. An adversary's aim in this case is to enforce or persuade the opponent of their "better values". Following Ikle (1964, p. 26), issues on the relationship between parties can be extension (continuance of previous arrangements), normalization (following an unusual period of relations), redistribution (of previous arrangements), or innovation (new areas of collaboration). However, the classification proposed here closely follows that of Mitchell (1981a, pp. 43–44); (1) material resources—ownership of, use of, opportunity to have; (2) right and status—legitimacy of behaviour, including the question of the existence of the adversary; (3) attitudes and security.

While a substantive division is necessary, other dimensions are also important. The first is the *saliency* of the issues (how central they are to the group's values, welfare and purpose) and the possible *imbalance of importance* between adversaries. The next aspect is the linkage between issues and *underlying values*—how they became defined as issues, whether some are preconditions to others and whether a hierarchy of issues exists. Thirdly, *issues can change across time*. They can be developed or redefined to be more inclusive or put on different bases. Also, *new issues* can develop from the strategy and tactics of the conflict, introduction of allies, or realignment of factions. All these distinctions can be used to understand the issues in the conflict.

Modifying Factors. Two factors modify these central features. First, particular actions by the third party influence the identity and resources of the potential mediator. One can include past actions or statements that gain the attention of the adversary's leadership, but the focus is on conduct closer to the time and circumstances of the conflict. This enables the model to include "incremental mediation": a third party that becomes involved little by little, moving from a go-between to a conciliator to a mediator. On the other hand, one can point to dramatic moves by a previously uninvolved party that makes it a likely candidate for mediation. As usual, these actions can only be analyzed through the views of the disputants. Indeed, conduct making a party attractive to one adversary may leave their opponent indifferent or dismissive.

One final factor for the framework is important: the path or circumstances of the conflict. These are particular events, tactics, or "battles" of the past and the general balance of resources and goals at the time a mediation initiative arises. The conflict history performs a supplementary role to conflict issues, amplifying the changes in salience, linkage and type of issue. The latter is integral to the judgement of negotiation preconditions for an adversary's leadership. The past tests of strength, results of coercion and restraint and previous offers of compromise do play a conditioning role (along with the overall current balance) for judging the suitability of a mediation initiative. Thus, although relatively clear conceptually, its schematic representation is complex and scope and depth varies in practice. However, to exclude or simplify this aspect seems a greater evil than its inclusion, even in a complex manner.

A complete diagram of the model is displayed in Figure 4.4. General conflict characteristics form a background and are only directly involved when considering factions within an adversary's leadership combining judgements in the decision on whether to accept mediation. However, they form a substratum that influences analysis of a mediation initiative. The central factors—identity and resources of the potential mediation and the issues in conflict—are each modified before being combined to influence adversaries' motivations for mediation and estimation of the current conflict. Finally, the variable to be explained is the decision on a mediation

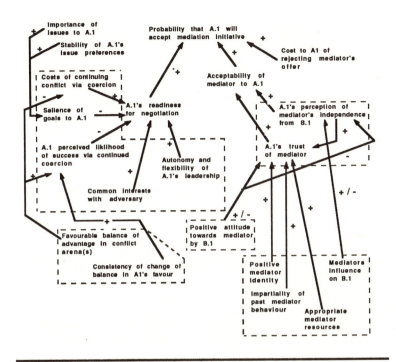

| | Importance of issues to A.1 | |
| | Stability of A.1's issue preferences | |

BACKGROUND 1.Relationship   2. Composition   3.Nature, influence
INFLUENCES   between Parties   and structure   and attitudes of
                 A.1 and B.1   of parties A.1   allies and patrons
                                      and B.1

CONFLICT
CHARACTERISTICS

Figure 4.4.

initiative, stemming from two judgements concerning the negotiation preconditions and the trust and perceived independence of the mediator.

AN ILLUSTRATION OF THE MODEL

Before using a case study to illustrate features of the model, comments on the general aspects of the structure are in order. First, although the "flow" is into a leadership's judgement, this does not imply an objective view of mediation resources or motivations. Each aspect is colored by the concerns and biases of the decision-making group. However, it is not a closed process, existing wholly within the leaders' heads. Moreover, that an analyst can gain access to leaders' calculations and the decision is not a foregone conclusion.

Second, de-emphasis of the personality and influence of a mediator is significant. There are many other elements that influence a start of mediation, and while particular third-party actions can be important, highlighting their relations to other factors is meant to be salutary. "De-personalizing" a third party through grounding a potential mediator in his role, constituency and resources seems a necessary step toward more general, comparable studies. Finally, while many researchers have suggested what factors are important, the model suggests a structure and outline of operation that relates and integrates separate factors. Whether it is accurate or useful can only be determined through application.

To illustrate the framework, the Nigerian Civil War and three mediatory initiatives are now considered. The presentation will necessarily be brief and offers no sustained argument concerning the success of an initiative.

Background: The Nigerian Civil War, 1967–69

The military governor of Eastern Nigeria, Colonel Odumegwu Ojukwu, declared that region the Republic of Biafra on 30 May 1967. This followed a series of steps toward independence countered by increasing sanctions imposed by the Federal Military Government of Nigeria (FMG). The dispute also seemed largely a tribal split—the Ibos dominating the east, the Yorubas the west and the Hausa-Fulani the north. However, there was a combination of factors to consider in judging the composition of the parties.

The boundaries of the conflict were physically and politically declared areas of government. While Biafra began with large proportions of non-Ibos in the southeast and in the Niger River delta, these areas were captured by the FMG by roughly mid-1968. The leadership of Biafra centered on Ojukwu (an Ibo), with only a few advisers exerting influence. In contrast, the FMG was more heterogeneous, with different concerns (some tribal) being important. There was a Supreme Military Council (SMC) composed of senior officers, and a Federal Executive Council (FEC) made up of eleven civilian commissioners. Given the training of the SMC, there was heavy bias toward a military solution to the conflict, partially counteracted by the leader, General Yakubu Gowon, and some FEC commissioners, especially Foreign Minister Okoi Arikpo. This was an important division with the FMG leadership. The relationship between the FMG and Biafra and their respective patrons will be considered within the context of specific initiatives, since they varied significantly during the course of the war.

Issues

The central issue for the Biafrans was security, identified as independent self-government. Since the first military coup in January 1966, numerous persecutions and riots against Ibos outside Iboland brought into question the ability of the FMG to provide Ibos with adequate protection. Broad antagonism, toward the Ibo's education and initiative, led many Ibos to believe that only an independent Ibo state would guarantee their security. There were mass emigrations of Ibos from other areas of Nigeria back to Iboland following the Autumn 1966 rioting. However, once established, issues expanded to include recognition and status of a Biafran government.

The central Nigerian government defined the issue as secession. Biafra's separation could not be accepted because it would doom Nigeria to further fragmentation. Despite Ibo grievances, Ojukwu carried many non-Ibos into Biafra and took offensive military action early in the war, which caused Nigerians to doubt the sincerity of the Ibo claims to security. Moreover, the seceding region held most of Nigeria's oil production and would shatter the national economy if lost. Conversely, Nigerians considered the FMG the only legitimate power dealing with "internal rebels". There could be no question of yielding on this point of authority; it would be seen as an acceptance of Biafra's independent existence.

This account summarizes some general conflict characteristics and the persisting issues of the day. There were many attempts by third parties to persuade the adversaries to change their positions. The Organization for African Unity (OAU) estabished a consultative committee, but its mandate was to assist the FMG and not to act as a mediator. The three mediation initiatives discussed below are not meant to be representative of all the attempts to end the war. They were selected because they illustrate the model's function.

Mediation Initiatives

Dr. Emile Zinsou (August 1967). One mediation offer came from Dr. Emile Zinsou, foreign minister of the neighbouring nation of Dahomey. He approached only the FMG in August 1967. His identity can be classed as having moderate prestige, a high government position (in a small country) and a constituency linked to Western Nigeria, since many Yorubas lived in Dahomey. The resources he could offer were not substantial at a technical level and had moderate diplomatic strength. Dr. Zinsou had shown interest in the conflict previously by leading a peace mission to try to prevent the outbreak of fighting after the May 1967 declaration of Biafran independence. However, his delegation had been refused entry by the FMG.

The circumstance of the conflict mitigated against starting any negotiation or mediation. General Ankrah of Ghana had intervened in January 1967 to provide a forum for the Nigerian military governors to settle differences. Some understandings were reached as a result of the January meetings, but not implemented. Colonel Ojukwu called on Ankrah and three other African heads of state to mediate in April. However, the FMG saw this as an attempt to internationalize a "domestic" problem. The initiative questioned the FMG'S status, and it was regarded as a hostile action. Consequently, when two other African heads of state offered good offices or a peace mission to Nigeria, the FMG response was that no outside mediation would be welcome for an internal dispute. This was later modified by FMG Foreign Minister Arikpo describing how internal attempts were being made and suggesting that everyone wait for his statement at the OAU summit in September. Thus, Zinsou's initiative came during this period of the FMG's efforts to maintain its legitimacy by turning away outside "help".

Moreover, armed conflict was only one month old in early August 1967 and far from conclusive. While Biafran forces had made dramatic gains through the Midwest region, General Gowon had only just announced that the FMG's restraints were lifted and "total war" was to be pursued. Thus, while mediation might have been attractive to the FMG to stop dangerous Biafran advances, it would undermine their diplomatic stand and offer a poor negotiating position. Likewise, the Biafrans might readily accept Zinsou's initiative on those grounds—especially its implied recognition of Biafran autonomy—but the offer was not made to them. Therefore, the case may have been doomed to failure, but at least the model helps analyze the many influences contributing to this rejected mediation initiative.

The Commonwealth Secretary-General (1967–69). The second initiative can be seen as a case of incremental mediation. This is when a third party moves from providing good offices, consultation, or conciliation and slowly changes its role to that of a mediator. It is often a slow process of "facilitative activity" proceeding from low level (carrying messages) to a moderate stage (defining issues, exploring perceptions) to a high, independent role (specific suggestions for action or formulating compromise proposals). Incremental involvement can pose a challenge to the working of the model, but this issue will be discussed in the final section.

Mr. Arnold Smith, secretary-general of the Commonwealth Secretariat, had involved his organization long before the Biafran declaration of independence. He maintained solid contacts with both sides and possessed significant prestige, based on genuine interest in an acceptable settlement. His initial work throughout 1967 was to operate as a channel of communication and advocate talks in a conciliatory manner.

As the head of an international non-governmental organization, Smith's position might be seen to be threatening to Nigerian interests. However, since the secretariat had a broad range of activities which included technical assistance and significant domestic involvement in member states, Smith and other representatives already had a working relationship to build upon. Such activity could provide "cover" for concern on the war. While accepting the need for a united Nigeria, one of his chief deputies was an Ibo and thus helped provide a less biassed image of the organization. Moreover, Smith's identity was tied by a flexible arrangement to a range of states (22 nations in 1967). This diverse constituency allowed for significant autonomy of initiatives, but limited the substance of Smith's proposals. Technical resources were excellent, a flexible diplomatic role was possible and a good material component—as shown by a later proposal for a Commonwealth peace-keeping force (requiring other states' approval and participation)—was present.

Smith's third-party identity was enhanced by actions that developed on a consultative level. The Autumn 1967 talks with FMG representatives produced the idea of Smith proposing a Commonwealth force in talks with Biafra, a good example of using an "external source" for proposals to reduce suspicion. Later, in February 1968, Smith agreed to meet with Biafran representatives outside of British immigration (at Heathrow Airport) to hear and refine Biafran proposals for negotiations. Thus, this initiative and familiarity helped build trust and a judgment of relative independence and quiet assistance to both parties.

The main issues were approached only through procedural and corollary concerns. Conditions for negotiation, cease-fire plans, development of an idea for a Commonwealth peacekeeping force and finally consideration of Eastern Nigerian (Ibo) autonomy within a federal framework built upon one another in implicit bargaining. Thus, conciliation moved into mediation. The latter "began" simply by Smith's role enhancement not being halted. Moreover, the circumstances of the conflict during early 1968 were oscillating around a rough equilibrium. Federal forces were making advances, but only at great costs. Biafran propaganda had mobilized humanitarian concern and put pressure on European governments friendly to the FMG, some of which supplied arms to the FMG. Churches pointed to the starvation of Biafrans and constrained the "total war" previously declared by General Gowon. The FMG feared further diplomatic progress by Biafrans, but knew their blockade had imposed severe limits on Biafra's fighting capacity. Thus, the battlefield balance of advantage and diplomatic conditions combined to make negotiation a greater possibility in the eyes of Nigerian and Biafran leaderships.

Quaker Efforts (1967–70). The third mediation attempt was also incremental. It centered on the Society of Friends, represented by

Professor Adam Curle, John Volkmar and Walter Martin. Its corporate nature and source of concern make it an interesting illustration.

All three members involved had had experience with Nigerian leaders before the war. Professor Curle was involved in a project to establish comprehensive schools in Western Nigeria. John Volkmar headed a group entitled "International Dialogues" which brought francophone and anglophone African leaders together to improve understanding and increase cooperation. Walter Martin had headed the Quaker United Nations Office for two years before the initial approach in 1967. Responding to Friends' concern over the violence and antagonism of 1966, he spoke with the Nigerian ambassador and some Ibos in New York City, asking how they would respond to a Quaker mission to learn about the tribal (and other) problems in Nigeria and have the Quakers report to their respective meetings (congregations). The response was moderately warm from all people queried.

This potential mediator can be identified as a religious, non-governmental actor with each of the three men having a history of proven work and concern. The overriding Quaker interest was in non-violence, understanding and tolerance. Resources were strongly moral and technical, and the trio offered a reliable and discreet communication link. What reinforced this image were the actions and encouragement of the three people involved. Volkmar and Curle visited Nigeria and spoke with a number of leaders in the spring of 1967. They reported that the atmosphere in Nigeria was very bad: deep polarization and antagonism were rife. After secession, the three men stayed in the background as many other third-party efforts went ahead, but they maintained good contacts with many organizations. In mid-1968 Volkmar was urged by the head of state of Niger to try to conciliate. The pivotal process was Volkmar and Curle travelling (in great danger) in and out of Biafra between meetings with General Gowon. Upon returning, General Gowon had increased trust in them because of their courageous actions and because Biafra had not used the Quakers' visit for propaganda, which implied a serious attitude toward this improved channel of communication.

From that point, the trio acted in many forums and private meetings to "educate one about the other" (Adam Curle, personal interview, July 1983). They carried messages between the antagonists, but also discussed perceptions and ideas, while studiously avoiding anything of tactical or strategic importance. Like Arnold Smith, they consulted, developed and suggested. Unlike Smith, their aim was procedural, hoping for mutual actions to reduce antagonism, not to strive for a substantive agreement. By late 1968 the issues had expanded due to Biafra projecting images of mass starvation; indiscriminate bombing by the FMG; and fears of genocide. Ceasefires and relief provisions were the central elements of possible agreement, but both sides only had increased suspicion and hostility. While the situation worsened generally, both disputants valued continued contact through the Quakers to explain and explore, but this channel could not compensate for more powerful, negative factors. This form of "gentle mediation" poses a different challenge to the model's assumptions.

CONTINUING ISSUES AND CONCLUSION

While presenting a framework for analyzing attempts to begin mediation, it would be folly to consider this structure a wholly comprehensive model. Issues and difficulties remain. Four areas of contention are reviewed below: the range of "mediation activity"; the nature of the adversaries' decisions; incremental mediation; and the dynamism of the phenomena which poses a barrier to empirical research.

Contentious Issues

The first issue arises from the aim of bringing a wide variety of mediation initiatives within one model. For instance, Quaker work in international conflicts stresses conciliation, but does touch on consultation and even some small suggestions of action (often procedural and symbolic). Can this strongly moral, non-threatening involvement be compared to a national government's initiative which is usually formal, substantive and interested? This possible dichotomy argues for a range of *types of mediation* where some factors are relevant in one kind, but absent in others. This issue deserves methodological debate, but it seems wise to begin with a model capable of accommodating a range of mediation. Only if significant defects are found in the general framework should alternative structures, tied to a narrower range of possible mediation, be considered.

If there are different kinds of mediation (apart from the special case of the "unrejectable mediator"), there can also be different kinds of decision, rather than the uniformity suggested in the model. This argument is supported by another interpretation of the intentions of the potential mediator, which forms the second issue.

Once making the allowance that a mediator can bring valuable resources to a negotiation, is it not presumed that the "mediator" enters as a new conflict party willing to bargain, threaten and encourage a settlement that meets their own objectives? Even if a primary objective is a settlement satisfactory to the original disputants, how is one to judge if that objective *is* primary rather than a façade for more selfish interests? The ramification for our model is that, if this is a major concern for an adversary's leadership, then their decision will centre on whether the third party's interests complement or hinder their own. Thus, the question they actually face is whether the new party's involvement will introduce an ally or an enemy, and not whether the mediator will facilitate a settlement. The nature of the decision is then quite different from a "decision whether to accept mediation". An illustration of this point could be Biafra's interest in mediation to achieve recognition of its autonomy.

A third issue centres on the consideration of "incremental mediation". The model presumes an initiative from an "uninvolved party", all currently involved parties being aligned with one of the main disputants and thus clearly unacceptable to the other side. However, the go-between or conciliator does not fit into this dichotomy of involvement or non-involvement. Thus, one needs to do two things: (1) understand the initial entry to the conflict by the go-between, and (2) construct a process model for increased, decreased, or a constant level of involvement. In effect, the entry-to-mediation framework becomes a segment of the more general phenomenon of consideration, commitment and action by new parties to a conflict. In the illustrations above, closer examination of Mr. Arnold Smith's involvement would be in order.

The fourth issue concerns the dynamism of the model. While accounting for changes in issues, perceptions of third parties and intra-party factions are important strengths, this complexity can raise two research problems. One is the question of how detailed the analysis must be to include "relevant change". Without some clear boundary, the danger lies in becoming more idiosyncratic in judging on what a decision is based, how issues have developed and the permutations of groups within a leadership body.

A second, practical, problem is access to the necessary information affecting change, especially concerning the leadership's members. It is unlikely that a leader with interests to protect will openly share his assessments or details of internal feuds and resource problems with an outsider while the conflict is still being pursued. Even after the conflict is over, its course and outcome influence future events, and issues and goals often outlive a particular conflict. Access to mapping the division within a leadership group seldom becomes easier. Thus, the complete question is: how can one adequately include the dynamism of the model in concrete research programs?

Conclusion

This study attempted four things. First, relevant work from the conflict research field was reviewed. A variety of ideas and factors were organized into an analytical model to provide a basis for comparing adversaries' decisions on mediation initiatives during a conflict (allowing for one exception to the general structure). The model was then employed to investigate three mediation initiatives of the Nigerial Civil War. Finally, four outstanding issues were presented which could affect the usefulness of the framework. While the issues cited cannot be ignored, the test for their importance lies in utilizing the model and evaluating whether possible criticisms are borne out empirically.

5

Mediated Negotiations in the Falklands/Malvinas Conflict

Douglas Kinney

Third-party mediation of inter-state conflict by nations or international institutions has a sad track record in the twentieth century. Normative international law (and a good deal of recent theory) focusses on the role and character of the mediator as major determinants in the outcome of the situation of mediated conflict. Unfortunately, reality seems to suggest that it is still the two or more conflicting nation-states which determine the outcome of the negotiation and that mediation is, in international affairs, a variant of negotiation, not a separate and more promising form of conflict resolution. Mediation is often, thus, *negotiation via an intermediary*. The two parties still determine most offers and their timing. This is not to deny the creative possibilities for their interlocuter. It only suggests the practical diplomatic limitations on his creativity.[1]

Mediation can be also seen as intervention by a disinterested third party to help resolve a disagreement or confrontation. It will appeal only to parties who, at a given stage, see benefit in neither legal nor military alternatives. It requires that all parties to a disagreement be present or represented. The negotiators from the conflicting parties must have full authority to speak, if not decide for, their side and the power (even by delegation and confirmation) to initial or conclude an agreement. Public commitment to the process is important, and a deadline—expressed or implied—is helpful. There need to be incentives to produce serious

This chapter is based upon research for a work in progress, *National Interest/National Honor: The Diplomacy of the Falklands Conflict*, to be published by Praeger.

bargaining. All of the issues must at least be discussable, if not formally admitted to be negotiable.

MEDIATION: BASIC CONSIDERATIONS

Mediation, therefore, usually requires a mediator to transform a bilateral negotiation into a *mediated negotiation*. A mediator must be desired, or at least initially tolerated, and willing. It is important, of course, that the mediator's intervention be timely and that his role as interlocuter and, indeed, proposer of solutions seen as a valid one. He must be willing to run the risks of failure associated with getting between two parties in a conflict, and capable of disciplining each side in its search for total mastery and a complete "win." He needs to establish a viable form of contact with each of the parties and eventually between them, although it is entirely possible for a good mediation to be completely indirect. The mediator has at his disposal several methods:

(1) The shuttle, in which he travels between parties, usually between their political capitals. This has the advantage of almost instantaneous implementation, depending on distance and the full commitment of the personal prestige of the mediator from the beginning. It allows the mediator to serve as a buffer between the parties' more extreme statements of interests, goals, and minima, a role becoming quite effortless as he literally carries the message and interprets en route.

(2) The summons, in which the parties are convened at a third point (usually the political capital of the mediator) has the advantage of putting parties in a somewhat less independent and autonomous position. By agreeing to assemble they have made a first concession in total dignity and independence. They have tacitly admitted that a solution is desirable and have made the first step themselves in tempering national honor in favor of national interest if their interest lies in a mutually negotiable solution. This can then change the calculus of national honor. Sometimes national honor is *advanced* by the appearance of "reasonableness" resulting from a willingness to talk.

(3) The symbolic convening, in which the parties convene at some third point, a site having distinct (and useful) implications of its own. The mediator can attempt to set new norms and public perceptions by having parties meet in an original and neutral third point, perhaps with some regional significance. He can also convene them in a neutral but recognized forum in which the place/institution itself implies norms and their concession in assembling is even greater.

Parties and mediator must keep a shifting and interacting array of factors in mind. The most important of these include: (a) What is negotiable. (b) How to frame the issues. (c) Felt and unstated needs, and the sensitivity to spot them. (d) The drafting process and principal options. (e) When to negotiate.[2]

The mediator functioning as third negotiator must also create *a process* from the following stages and functions:

(1) *"To lay up alongside"*: The mediator's first challenge is to convince the parties of his credibility as potential interlocuter in their dispute. For a party with whom one does not already enjoy a relationship of confidence and trust, this consists in demonstrating that one's national or institutional interest gives credible reason to seek a mutually beneficial negotiated solution.

While it is tempting to try to guarantee more than that, this can involve extreme short-run costs and potentially wreck a mediation. It can lead to overconfidence, insufficient willingness to make meaningful concessions, or extreme overstatement of initial demands. One party will hold out for an advantageous position given what is assumed to be support from the interlocuter.

(2) *To assess and contrast*: Having established one's credibility as a mediator of the conflict, it is important to work with each side in turn to assess the situation. For each party, one can then contrast how its assessment differs from the other. This includes not only listing stated needs but searching for misstatements of perceived or real conflict.

(3) *To frame and to time*: The mediator needs to sketch for the parties the process by which he would intend to interpret their differences to them and seek agreement. Framing the process for them may imply a time frame, although it is useful to accustom them to the idea that a "renewal period" may be necessary. The time frame itself must remain negotiable.

(4) *To exchange and interpret*: The mediator must begin the exchange of precise, nonpolemical versions of the parties' interpretations of their own interests and needs. At a minimum his interpretation should harmonize the language and format of the two sides' presentations. The mediator must make an interpretation of each side's position to the other with an eye to producing a clearer and, if possible, less adversarial view of the stated needs of each party. Language, of course, bears on the way a suggestion is received by the other party. Style and substance are closely related in the initial presentations of positions.

(5) *To suggest*: Should interpretation fail to produce any closing of the gap in the two positions, the mediator will have to assume a truly active role and suggest positions or tactics that will bring the two sides closer together. The degree of intervention varies with the realism and seriousness of the parties.

(6) *To reframe*: Should a strategy or text from the mediator fail to produce agreement, the mediator is left with the options of reframing the issue, pushing agreement, or disengaging.[3]

(7) *To push agreement*: If it is not possible to reframe the negotiating question, the mediator may want to push agreement. This is at heart his task. The whole non-issue of "biassed mediation" becomes critical in a realistic consideration of the mediator. Even without any influence over one of the parties, it is the job of the mediator (in the end) to convince one party or another to accept that which it states is unacceptable. A truly passive interlocuter may produce agreement where agreement was probable. To produce agreement when none is likely is the challenge to the active mediator. Like the negotiators for the parties, the *mediator* has a variety of tactics, strategies, and gambits open to him in "pushing" agreement.

(8) *To disengage*: When agreement is blocked or nearly achieved but threatened by the tactics or timing of one party, the mediator could give serious consideration to disengagement. This may be necessary not only as a *tactic* (that is, in order to get the parties to return seriously to the negotiating table) or as a *gambit* (to overcome serious but possibly not intentional disingenuousness or delay) but literally as a *strategy* in order to save both the process or the possibility of its renewal.[4]

With the general principle in mind that a mediator is most usefully regarded as a third negotiator with the above range of strategies available, the remainder of this chapter will consider the process of "mediated negotiation" in operation during the Falklands/Malvinas crisis of 1982. Emphasis will be placed upon the mediator's tasks of determining what is negotiable and how best to frame the issues (the *proposals*) or to help the parties frame the issues so that there is a better chance that a compromise may be achieved. It ends by touching upon the delicate issue of *productive* interaction between the mediator and the other parties with whom he is negotiating (*the process*).

FALKLANDS/MALVINAS: THE MEDIATION ATTEMPTS

There were three major diplomatic efforts to mediate the Falklands/Malvinas dispute during the spring and early summer of 1982: (1) by the U.S. Secretary of State, General Alexander Haig; (2) by Peruvian President Belaunde Terry; and (3) by UN Secretary General Perez de Cuellar. Their approaches and working methods were radically different. They worked by shuttle flight, telephone, and alternating sessions with the parties. Their efforts spanned the military stages of the crisis from stand off to full-scale war.

Yet, the striking thing about major attempts to mediate the Falklands crisis was the high degree of participation of the mediators in both the process and the proposals. Each developed a mechanism involving the third party actively, both to implement the interim military and administrative arrangements, and to turn the latter into an on-going search for a more definitive settlement of the question of sovereignty over the Falklands Islands.

A third party comes at a mediation with different stakes and points of emphasis. This can extend even to the question of what is to be mediated. One of the problems in the Falklands/Malvinas conflict was that the mediators all proceeded from the natural goal of the mediator to make or find a settlement. This is not always, ultimately, the goal of one or both parties.

The principle efforts at mediation had several other elements in common, stemming from the combination of the military and territorial nature of the crisis. The shape of any possible settlement involved third parties in three issues: military disengagement, interim administration of the territory, and negotiations to solve the on-going dispute.

Military disengagement involved the end of military hostilities, the guarantee of its finality by mutual withdrawal of armed forces, and an implicit or explicit, concrete commitment not to reintroduce those forces. Arrangements had to be supervised and verified by a third party, but each side wanted to be in a position to act unilaterally if it felt it necessary.

Interim administration of the islands also involved a third party, be it national, multi-national, or international. Proposed third-party administrators were essentially independent of, underpinned, or assisted by the traditional organs of local self-government. Local autonomy, however, was balanced in most proposals by the possibility of increased Argentine access to the Falklands Islands (and dependencies) during the period of interim administration. In other words, proposals suggesting a large degree of local autonomy (suitable to the British/Islanders) included provisions for a large degree of Argentine access (suitable to the Argentines). Conversely, proposals for less autonomy were accompanied by less access.

The question of resumption of the 17 years of bilateral negotiations to solve the on-going territorial dispute centered on the conflict between emphasizing process and purpose. As before the invasion, Argentina insisted that the negotiations were about establishing Argentine sovereignty. The United Kingdom insisted that they were about the future of the Falklands.

DIFFERING AGENDAS, ISSUES, AND PROPOSALS

Thus, the parties had differing agendas and ideas as to what was, indeed, negotiable. The common view of the elements of a solution disguised fundamental disagreement about the heart of the dispute. Territoriality seemed (as it had throughout most of the 17 years of bilateral negotiations) to make the Falklands a zero-sum game. Only consequence changed in the mediation phase of the dispute. The use of force had merely raised the stakes. Indeed, too much weight was to be put by mediators on avoiding further violence. The mediators assumed that this was perceived as a significant benefit by each party.

The United Kingdom sought:

1. A cease-fire and withdrawal of Argentine forces, non-reintroduction to be guaranteed.
2. Restoration of British authority, in whole or in part.
3. Basic guarantees of local rights and institutions.
4. Third-party assistance in implementation.
5. Control of Argentine access and communication at preconflict levels as governed by the 1971 bilateral agreements.
6. An agreement that would not prejudge the final outcome of sovereignty negotiations.

British strategy was increasing and coordinated pressure toward these ends, diplomatic, economic, and, if necessary, military. The balanced use of persuasion and force could be seen in this strategic view as a continuum, the two self-reinforcing and used in tandem. Indeed, at times they are inseparable. The continuum can be visualized as an arrow stretching from Portsmouth to Stanley. With the progress of the fleet in implementation of force, the trade-offs between the use of the two instruments changed. The closer the British came to being able to/having to make an amphibious landing in the Falklands, the less diplomacy was to be depended upon or tactical sacrifices made in order to succeed via pure diplomacy.

In contrast, Argentine goals in its search for sovereignty were:

1. Interruption of British rule.
2. Effective interim control of administration of the Islands.
3. Freedom of access.
4. Involvement of third parties principally to limit British use of force and help secure Argentine gains.
5. Immediate military withdrawal to home bases, preserving and indeed reserving Argentina's geopolitical advantage and ability to use force again with minimum warning time.
6. Widened recognition that decolonization applied and that the controlling norm was territorial integrity.

These steps were to lead to:

7. Negotiations leading to effective Argentine sovereignty in the near or medium term.
8. A settlement formula that would result in permanent Argentine sovereignty at a near (fixed) future date.

Were these unobtainable, Argentine strategy was to seize the Islands by force but defend them diplomatically, garnering world political support to defer British political (and possibly military) counter-measures. Very limited in scope initially, the defensive strategy began to unravel almost before it was implemented. In the Security Council debates in New York, many of Argentina's working premises dissolved in the face of apt British diplomacy.

The Argentine strategy can be visualized as an arrow, spiraling outward from the Falklands. As much would be done as was necessary to hold the Islands. This was seen first as a mere question of deterrence, of putting enough men on the Islands so that there would be no question of any British military response. It was prove necessary, however, for Argentina to go further and further militarily, politically, legally, and financially, in order to maintain a successful defensive posture. The Falklands would eventually come to consume the nation, the government, and Argentine diplomacy.

Each side realized that the arrangements for administration and negotiation were related and trade-offs could, in principle, be made between the two. Argentina, for example, stated openly in Foreign Minister Costa Mendez's letter of 2 April to Secretary Haig that if negotiations were less restricted in aim (Argentine sovereignty) or deadline, concessions on interim administration would be needed in compensation (i.e., Argentina would need more control of the islands and/or more "access").

THE PROPOSALS: MILITARY DISENGAGEMENT

All plans and proposals in the Falklands crisis of spring 1982 called for military disengagement of some kind. A ceasefire was an obvious precondition. Roughly mutual or parallel withdrawal of forces was a common element throughout and the time frames were relatively short, given that neither side had impossible logistical requirements. Most proposals had an explicit or implied commitment *not* to reintroduce forces into the area. Verification was provided for by a third party in most cases. This element was reinforced in the respective negotiations by the call of Security Council Resolution 502 for a cessation of hostilities to take effect immediately and the withdrawal of Argentine forces from the Falklands Islands.

When approached in early April by a mediator, the British government's sense of military provisions in any diplomatic agreement were that these should consist solely of possible arrangements for supervising the withdrawal of Argentine forces in line with Resolution 502. In this sense, military provisions were the only British diplomatic goals at the opening of the crisis: peaceful Argentine withdrawal to obviate the use of force. This was the pure trade-off which the dispatch of the task force envisioned. Argentina, of course, saw any military withdrawal as contingent on a cancellation of all initial British military preparations and a firm and permanent recognition of Argentine sovereignty.

The UN Security Council warned against the use of force in a statement of 1 April by the president of the Council. In Resolution 502 the military provisions called for an immediate cessation of hostilities and withdrawal of all Argentine forces from the Islands, as well as calling on the parties to seek a diplomatic solution. The essence of a "diplomatic" solution on 3 April (when 502 was passed) would have concerned Argentine withdrawal, since no British forces were operating as units in this area.

U.S. Proposals

As the Haig negotiations took shape, the agenda expanded. By 19 April, Argentine officials were formulating a draft with Secretary Haig, which included a very precise formula from the Americans. Beginning on the day after signature, both sides would cease introducing forces into circles of 150 nautical miles from the three island groups. Within 24 hours they would begin withdrawal, Argentina withdrawing half its forces within a week and the rest within fifteen days; the United Kingdom withdrawing to at least 2,000 nautical miles within a week and within fifteen days to their "bases or usual areas of operations." The United Kingdom found the disproportionality of the distances for withdrawal unacceptable, but by 21 April it had clearly accepted that a wider package than just military withdrawal was going to be needed. On 21 April Foreign Secretary Pym told the House of Commons that negotiations and interim administration would have to be part of the package. He was still phrasing the military element, however, as "arrangements for Argentine withdrawal."

In the U.S. proposal of 27 April, the United States called for a cessation of the U.K.'s "zone of exclusion." Argentina was to suspend operations in the same area, also within 24 hours. Each side was to withdraw half its forces within seven days, the Royal Navy to stand-off seven days steaming time at twelve knots. Argentine forces were to be at such a distance or in such a state of readiness that they "could not be reinserted with their equipment and armament in less than seven days." After fifteen days all Argentine forces were to be removed from the three zones around the island groups. British forces were to withdraw to "their usual operating areas or normal duties," which relieved them of the requirement to return to bases at which they might not have been at the opening of hostilities. Both sides were to cooperate with the United States, which undertook to verify compliance with the military measures of paragraph 2 of the U.S. plan. Ceasefire was integrally linked with withdrawal. The U.S. formula for reinsertion time was an ingenious attempt to overcome the problem of geographic distance and achieve military balance. The non-reintroduction was much more specific and was a commitment integral to ceasefire and withdrawal. The strong U.S. role as verifier and guarantor was the underpinning for the Haig military proposals.

In the Argentine response to the U.S. proposal, Sr. Costa Mendez sent a tacit message in his 29 April letter to Haig that Argentina was in military control of the Falkland Islands and saw no reason to surrender that advantage. The power in occupation of the Islands could speak of "difficulties that it is essential to overcome" as it could still so define the question. Costa Mendez spoke of a provisional regime for administration of the islands "as an essential step in the process of separating the two military forces." While stating that it was willing to consider withdrawal in line with 502, the Argentine emphasis was on separating forces and avoiding direct clashes rather than military withdrawal and non-reintroduction. Recognition of Argentine sovereignty and power in an interim administration of the islands had to be resolved in Argentina's favor before "solution of the remaining problems." The remaining problem (in this Argentine order of priorities) would be military withdrawal, which was considered to be the initial prerequisite order of business by both the United Kingdom and the mediator.

In his statement of 30 April, Secretary Haig noted that large-scale military action was likely in the South Atlantic and that his effort to restore peace "through implementation of UN Security Council Resolution 502" had as one basis the call of that Resolution for "an end to hostilities, the withdrawal of Argentine forces from the islands; and a diplomatic settlement of the fundamental dispute." He noted that his proposals had involved "a cessation of hostilities, withdrawal of both Argentine and British forces, termination of sanctions." Adding a new element to the politico-military equation, he noted that President Reagan had ordered the suspension of all military exports to Argentina, cut its eligibility for military sales, and decided to respond favorably to British requests for war material.

Military Aspects of the Peruvian Plan

In the draft Peruvian proposals, military provisions involved immediate ceasefire "concurrent with" mutual withdrawal and non-reintroduction of forces. The schedule was open-ended and was to be set by a Contact Group which was to ensure that the provisions were respected. But there was no provision for enforcement or a guarantor role. (The Contact Group was to "verify" the military provisions.) Clear language was stronger in the interim administration provisions (e.g., "ensuring that no actions are taken in the Falkland Islands, by the local administration which would contravene this interim agreement").

Britain recognized that the revised Peruvian proposals would provide for complete and supervised withdrawal of Argentine forces, matched by a corresponding withdrawal of British forces, with immediate ceasefire to *follow* Argentine agreement to withdraw. The Contact Group would, in the British view, supervise withdrawal. Exclusion zones would be suspended. Thus the Peruvian proposals still required Argentine withdrawal, which Argentina was not prepared to carry out, in exchange for the interim administration and sovereignty provisions.

The UN Proposals and Military Arrangements

The UN secretary general's initiative, put forward in his points of 2 May to the parties, included provisions for military withdrawal by both sides, Argentina from the Falkland Islands and British forces from the area around the Falkland Islands. Britain was already in possession of South Georgia, and the UN effort applied only to the Falkland Islands *themselves*. The military blockades by each side (or zones) were in existence and had to be rescinded. Hostilities were to cease.

In the UN negotiations the British position on May 6 accepted in general terms the secretary general's points, but Britain made it clear that 502 (i.e., Argentine military withdrawal from the Falkland Islands) had to be implemented without delay and that any ceasefire must be clearly linked to the beginning of Argentine withdrawal within a fixed number of days. The secretary general was clear at all times that his initiative was based on, and was an implementation of, 502. Resolution 502 has nothing to say, however, about British forces and therefore about the order, precedence, mutuality, or equality of withdrawal by two militarily engaged sides. The secretary general was quite clear in his statement to the Security Council of 21 May that he believed the implementation of 502 abslutely necessary for peace in the South Atlantic, and he made no indication that the need for Argentine withdrawal was ever in doubt in the UN negotiation.

In the British draft proposal of 17 May, a ceasefire would take effect twenty-four hours after signature. Argentina would then begin withdrawal from the islands, completing 50 percent reduction to at least 150 nautical miles within seven days and all forces within fourteen days. Britain would begin withdrawal at the same time to, at least, 150 nautical miles away (half within seven days, half within fourteen days). As withdrawal began, twenty-four hours after signature, the respective exclusion zones would be lifted and each side would undertake not to reintroduce any armed forces in a zone 150 miles around the Falklands after the completion of withdrawal. The UN administrator was charged with verification of all armed forces in the islands and devising an effective method of ensuring that they were not reintroduced.

These elements of the British final offer on military conditions were not acceptable to Argentina. In the Argentine response of 19 May, Argentina counterproposed the completion of withdrawal within thirty days (i.e., deep into Antartic winter to about 1 July, at which time the logistical operations of the British task force should have become impossible); and full return to normal bases and areas of operations, thus setting British forces 6,000 to 8,000 miles from the Falklands with the sole exception of the patrol ship, *Endurance*. Previously content to secure advantage solely through distanced withdrawal, Argentina now wished to reassert the advantages of her operating capability in Antartic winter and retain her occupation of the islands past Britain's ability to effect the situation. While one cannot judge intentions, this clearly left the capability to default on the military provisions with little expectation of effective British response from a frozen-in South Georgia. Under the British proposal of withdrawing to a distance of only 150 miles, British capability would have allowed the possibility of establishing a major base at South Georgia and beginning to develop the operational capability to maintain naval forces in the area on a fairly large scale. A relative disadvantage would have been the ability of Argentine air to cover the Falklands area from half of the distance facing British forces in South Georgia. Each side found the other's military provisions unbalanced and unacceptable.

In its White Paper of 21 May, Britain noted that in its proposal at the United Nations it had been willing [under Article 2(3)] to withdraw to a distance of 150 nautical miles in exchange for Argentine withdrawal within fourteen days. It had also been willing to comply with international verification under Article 6(4) of the draft agreement. Britain was willing to have aerial surveillance from third parties to confirm all military withdrawals. In its note to the State Department of 26 May, Argentina noted that during the UN negotiations it had proposed withdrawal of forces of both countries on a gradual and simultaneous basis to be completed within thirty days. The phrasing, however, was restrictive on British forces in that it stated that within a maximum period of thirty days "all armed forces shall be in their normal bases and areas of operations." By requiring that at the end of thirty days British forces be in their normal bases and areas of operations, the Argentine draft demanded most British units set sail almost immediately. At the end of thirty days they would thus have been at least a month from being able to return to the area in an operational mode.

Argentine provisions for supervision and confirmation in the UN negotiations were quite specific. Under Article 3, Section 1 they called for supervision of withdrawal by "specialized personnel of the United Nations whose composition shall be agreed with the parties."

British insistence on ceasefire with immediate withdrawal of all Argentine forces was in line with its legal position that it was acting in self-defense under Article 51 of the Charter and was also acting consistently with 502. It viewed the distances of withdrawal of the two sides as totally unbalanced. Britain accepted the principle of UN verification of military disengagement and withdrawal but remained insistent that the only acceptable kind of ceasefire was one unequivocally linked with the immediate beginning of Argentine withdrawal. Thus, moves in the United Nations for ceasefire resolutions were unacceptable to one party. The secretary general told the Security Council on 2 June that the two parties had provided statements on what they would view as acceptable conditions for ceasefire and that there was no possibility of one being mutually acceptable. Britain reiterated in the Council that a ceasefire *not* linked to Argentine withdrawal was inconsistent with 502 and the Council's call (under that Resolution) for Argentine withdrawal. Any ceasefire would have left Argentina in possession of the disputed territory. The Council voted on a draft resolution calling for both sides to cease firing on 4 June. The resolution also called for the simultaneous implementation of 502 and 505. While it received nine favorable votes, enough for passage and for extention, it was vetoed by Britain and the United States and thus not adopted.

While the military provision of the various proposed agreements on the Falklands crisis would seem to have been semiautomatic and a preface to other more "diplomatic" provisions, they provided contretemps of their own and were in a sense the price that Argentina was being asked to pay in the negotiations. In the judgement of Argentina the other elements never outweighed this military price and the settlement was thus impossible. In the proposals, one sees reflected the relative military advantages that each side sought, Argentina consistently pursuing withdrawal to home bases and a longer withdrawal period, Britain seeking—once it had regained South Georgia—to reserve the right to use it as a base from which to ensure compliance with any possible agreement. No compromise proposal succeeded in reconciling these goals.

THE PROPOSALS: NORMALIZATION

Most of the proposals and drafts in the Falklands crisis called for rapid "normalization" of the situation prevailing between the two parties. Nuances of scope and timing, however, were significant.

Argentine thinking during the Haig shuttle called for action as of the date of agreement to end economic and financial measures including restrictions on travel, transport, communications, and transfer of funds between the two countries, as well as the EEC and third-country sanctions. Until definitive arrangements were made permanent, those subjects, as well as others related specifically to the Falklands (residents, property ownership, communications, and trade) would be available on an equal basis to each party.

The U.S. proposal similarly called for the ending of economic and financial measures. The language relating to the Islands was even stronger:

transportation, travel, and trade were to be promoted and facilitated without prejudice.

Similarly, the UN secretary general's initiative called for the rescinding of blockades, exclusion zones, and economic sanctions by each side. The British proposal called for each party to lift economic measures as from signature. Argentina wanted not only the lifting of zones and sanctions but freedom for its citizens to seek residence, property, and work in the Islands as part of normalization. The British saw this as outside of the scope of "normalization" and viewed it, in general, as of far more benefit to Argentina than to Britain as there were few effective sanctions on the economic side against the United Kingdom. Under Article 7 Britain was willing to agree to the reestablishment of communications, travel, transport, and postage, as before the invasion, and viewed this as normalcy, *not* the additional openness to Argentine residents and ownership which Argentina had always sought but never obtained. As in so many other matters, Britain was seeking the status quo ante and enhanced position as compensation for its military withdrawal.

The Argentine note of reply in the UN round stated in Article II: "with effect from the signature of this agreement, each party shall cease to apply the economic measures which it has adopted against the other and the United Kingdom shall call for the same action by those countries or groups of countries which, at its request, adopted similar measures." Argentina went on, however, to call for "freedom of movement and equality of access with respect to residents, work and property" as well as "freedom of communication ... [to] include the maintenance of freedom of transit where the state airline, ... merchant ships and scientific vessels, ... communications, Argentine television transmissions and state petroleum (YPF) and gas services shall continue to operate freely." The British saw such expanded access as changing, in very short order, the operation and character of the Islands.

THE PROPOSALS: INTERIM ADMINISTRATION

Of those proposals and views on interim administration involving third-party control over site or supervision of local government, not all provided for open Argentine access during the period of such administration. Moreover the role of the third party varied greatly.

At the beginning of the crisis, "interim administration" was not envisioned as a diplomatic solution. This last was seen as involving simple Argentine withdrawal or military expulsion of Argentine troops. In either case, there was no clear conception of an interim or transition period. In initial discussions with Secretary Haig two kinds of ideas about multinational or international supervision arose; of military withdrawal and of interim or transitional arrangements. Britain regarded interim administration arrangements as securing freedom for the Falkland Islanders to participate (through elected representatives) in their own governance and to express their wishes about the Islands' future.

The U.S. Plan for Interim Administration

In the Argentine discussions with Secretary Haig, Argentine views, reflected in their 19 April draft, were that interim administration should take a very definite form.

A Special Interim Authority (SIA) would approve decisions, laws, and regulations of the local administration. The traditional local administration (the Executive and Legislative Councils) would add two Argentine representatives on each council appointed by the Argentine government, and one on each council elected by resident Argentines. "The Argentine population whose residence is equal to that of others who have the right to representation will elect representatives, there being at least one representative in each council." There would also be Argentine representatives in the local police who, while under local administration, would be subject to supervision of the SIA. The national flag of each member of the SIA would fly at its headquarters. Among other freedoms, freedom of movement, property, and employment as well as cultural links with the countries of origin were to be guaranteed. Freedom of movement, employment, and property were particularly important to Argentina's view of how the interim period should affect events. The period of interim administration would end on 31 December 1982, and from 1 January 1983 and until full Argentine sovereignty "the head of government and administration shall be exercised by an official designated by the Argentine government."

Thus, interim administration as of 1983 would be entirely Argentine, and the only British role would be as a member of the on-going sovereignty negotiations. The United States would also still be a member of the SIA. Having taken over the roles of head of government and administration of the islands at the beginning of 1983, Argentina would be in a position to pass to the other two members of the SIA only those questions about which there was no disagreement and would in effect take over the Falkland Islands as of the end of 1982. In this case the functions of the third party were not so much to assist Argentina and the United Kingdom, as to simply serve as comfort to the United Kingdom. The Argentine advantages were not counterbalanced. It is not at all clear from the text that (within the SIA) a majority vote of, for example, the United States and the United Kingdom against Argentina would be conclusive. In local government, as Argentine population expanded, Argentina would eventually obtain a majority on the two councils. Thus, while the 19 April proposals submitted to Secretary Haig before he left Buenos Aires might have been seen as workable bases for more negotiations, they clearly contained elements highly prejudicial to British positions and interests concerning local interim administration.

The subsequent U.S. draft retained the SIA with roughly the same role: verifying the execution of obligations in the agreement became verifying compliance. Each party was limited to ten staff for its SIA contingent. Expansion of Argentine representation on the councils was retained. The minimum of one elected and two appointed Argentines on each council was retained, but the suffrage requirement was made more specific: "representatives in each Council of the Argentine population whose period of residence on the islands is equal to that required of others entitled to representation, in proportion to population." Two appointed representatives would serve in the senior Executive Council. The civil service would still be under the direction of the first official below the rank of the governor, who would not be replaced. Most significantly, there was no firm end to the interim administration. This arrangement was to stabilize rather than bring to a head any interim period.

Sr. Costa Mendez, in the Argentine response, said that since provisions in the Haig proposal for "recognition for sovereignty are imprecise, for us it is necessary—if we do not [want] to return to the frustrating situation that prevailed before April 2—to establish mechanisms that give us broader powers in administration of the islands." He called for a provisional regime for administration of the Islands which would overcome the "unfavorable changes" made by the Americans in the drafting of mid-April. Costa Mendez noted that "the number of Argentine representatives involved in the administration of the islands has been decreased, and the opportunity of expanding my country's control in the event that negotiations on the basic issue go on endlessly without a solution has been barred. Thus, we are faced with the real possibility of establishing a predominantly British administration with no fixed expiration date." Missing from the U.S. proposals were the Argentine appointment of the head of government and administration should the target date for negotiations not be met.

Peruvian Proposals

The Peruvian text called for a Contact Group of Brazil, Peru, the Federal Republic of Germany, and the United States to ensure that the local administration of the Islands took no action contravening the interim agreement. Thus, the Contact Group would assume administration of the Falklands in consultation with elected representatives of the Islanders. The Contact Group would assume many key decision-making functions, included in which would be: the applicable law; what the links to Britain would be within government; and the extent of the powers of the governor.

The period of interim administration was defined (as least tacitly) by the responsibility of the Contact Group for "ensuring that the two Governments reach a definitive agreement prior to April 30, 1983." There was no penalty for not meeting the deadline and no turnover to Argentine administration once it passed. Argentina would clearly have to put its faith in the composition of the Contact Group to guarantee its interests during the interim administration period.

UN Negotiations

The UN's proposals included transitional arrangements with a different character. They were to meet interim requirements. Even more strongly than previous arrangements this implied that the period of interim administration was *not* to change the situation. (This prohibition would certainly be consistent with the spirit of Resolution 502.) The length of interim administration was implied by a requirement for negotiations to seek a diplomatic solution for their differences by an agreed date.

In the British interim draft agreement for the UN-sponsored process, a UN administrator approved by each side would be appointed by the secretary general and would administer the government of the Falkland Islands. He would do so in consultation with the Island Councils, with the addition of an Argentine representative of the preexisting Argentine population. On each of the two Councils, UN administration would be "in conformity with the laws and practices traditionally obtaining in the Islands." Argentina would be allowed up to three *observers* in the interim administration period. Interim administration under the British proposal would last until definitive agreement about the future of the Islands was implemented. Britain put heavy emphasis on the fact that the system of Legislative and Executive Councils had been developed in compliance with Article 73 of the UN Charter and thus had a preexisting UN legitimacy.

In the Argentine response, administration of the islands was to have been an exclusive UN responsibility, with equal numbers of British and Argentine advisors. In the interim period, Argentina was to be free to sponsor immigration of its nationals to the Falkland Islands, and they were to have open access to residence, work, and ownership of property. None of this was, of course, in keeping with the traditions, law, and practices referred to in the British draft. Argentina also rejected the provision in the British draft that interim administration should last until a definitive settlement. The two Councils, which represented democratic institutions and freedoms to Britain, represented the continuance of colonialism to Argentina. Britain saw the allowance for one representative from the Argentine population as a concession already disproportionate to the thirty resident Argentines in a population of 1,800 Britons. The Argentine note to the State Department of 26 May proposed that there be only non-Argentine and non-British officers of the Falklands government in all areas, including executive, legislative, judicial, and security. While local law and legislation would be maintained, UN interim administration would use advisors in equal numbers from Britain and Argentina and the two party's flags would fly during interim administration, together with that of the United Nations.

The United Kingdom saw its agreement to a UN administration as a substantial concession. They viewed the falling back from maintenance of administrative links to Britain to purely local self-rule under UN supervision as something that Argentina should match with further flexibility. Particular details were left open-ended and subject to joint decision. Argentina, however, rejected even a local role and required that interim administration should be exclusively in the hands of the United Nations, advised by equal numbers of Argentine and British citizens. In the British view this would leave the Islanders with a UN administration subject neither to local law and practice nor to local political bodies. Purely UN administration, moreover, left no role for the United States as guarantor of either even-handedness or of British interests.

Thus the parties were no closer at the end of the negotiations on the subject of interim administration than when they had begun.

THE PROPOSALS: NEGOTIATING SOVEREIGNTY

While each of the peace plans included longer-term plans for face-to-face negotiations with the aim of resolving the underlying sovereignty dispute, the approaches to these negotiations were varied. All included a deadline or an ideal "target" date with varying degrees of enforcement or penalty. All included a third-party role but again it varied greatly. For example, both the United States, in President Reagan's call, and the United Nations, in Resolution 502, urged *negotiations* on the parties. Resolution 502 specifically called on the parties "to seek a diplomatic solution to their differences."

The U.S. Initiative

Argentina, in its 19 April draft, called for negotiations to achieve a definitive arrangement for Argentine sovereignty. Negotiations would begin within fifteen days and end by the New Year. Argentina would take over executive powers as of January 1, 1983, until full Argentine sovereignty was implemented. Negotiations would remove Falklands from the list of non–self-governing territories and would define their definitive and final status. Both the rights of the inhabitants and territorial integrity were to be considered. The Charter, Resolutions 1514 and 2065, and

General Assembly resolutions on the Falklands were also to be considered. The United States would "help" in the negotiations.

The US proposal referred only to principles of the Charter and "relevant" UNGA resolutions. Rather than *help*, the (tripartite) Authority was to *consult* with the Executive Council and make specific proposals and recommendations to the two governments on a broad range of subjects, including the wishes ("based on the results of a sounding") and interests of the Islanders. "Wishes" and "interests" were to be a factor only for Islands with a settled population, and the sounding was to be agreed "without prejudice to their respective positions on the legal weight to be accorded such opinion. . . ." Were no agreement reached by the end of the year, the United States was to make specific proposals for a settlement and conduct direct negotiations. The parties were to respond within one month to formal proposals or recommendations submitted by the United States.

Britain recognized, as Francis Pym told the House of Commons on 21 April, that any satisfactory negotiation had to deal with a long-term solution to the dispute. Britain said it was willing to consider negotiations proposed under the Haig initiative, but in its view Argentina rejected them by demanding guaranteed sovereignty for a (controlling) role in interim governments.[5]

The Argentine reply to the Haig proposals (in Costa Mendez's letter to Haig of 29 April) said that the negotiations had to clearly result in Argentine sovereignty being recognized in the end, or Argentina needed a stronger hand in temporary administration so as to guarantee the recognition of sovereignty which was Argentina's "unrenounceable goal." Costa Mendez recognized that sovereignty negotiations were necessary, given the "logical impossibility of formalizing their final fate at this time," but the key word was "formalizing." It was on this point that the Argentine reply really constitutes a rejection of the Haig proposal as they regarded sovereignty negotiations. In Costa Mendez's view the negotiations were to be about "recognition of sovereignty." He found "provisions relating to the recognition of our sovereignty" imprecise and therefore proposed the recognition/administration trade-off: "If it were clear that Argentina's sovereignty would be recognized in the end, then we could be more flexible regarding the matter of temporary administration." He stated that the "new element of a virtual referendum to determine the 'wishes of the inhabitants'" to be "in opposition" to UN Resolution 2065 and the Argentine position. Costa Mendez made no comment on the fact that the U.S. proposals had had the question of the wishes of the Islanders apply only to inhabited islands.

In his statement of 30 April, Secretary Haig referred to the call of 502 for "a diplomatic settlement of the fundamental dispute." He noted that the U.S. proposal included "a framework for negotiations on final settlement, taking into account the interests of both sides and the wishes of the inhabitants." He characterized Argentina's position as requiring "assurance now of eventual sovereignty or an immediate de facto role in governing the Islands which would lead to sovereignty." Even in announcing the U.S. decisions in support of Britain, however, Haig said that "In the end, there will have to be a negotiated outcome acceptable to the interested parties. Otherwise, we will all face unending hostility and insecurity in the South Atlantic."

Peruvian and UN Initiatives

The Peru–UN proposal dated 5 May was open-ended on the structure and conduct of sovereignty negotiations. The negotiations were clearly to concern the status of the islands. Parties acknowledged differing and conflicting views on this, but agreed to acknowledge that the "aspirations and interests" of the Islanders were to be "included" (in an unspecified way) in the definitive settlement. The Contact Group was to be responsible for ensuring that a definitive settlement was reached by the end of April 1983. The role of the Contact Group in doing so was unspecified.

The Perez de Cuellar mediation proposed negotiations by the two sides aimed at a diplomatic solution to the sovereignty question by an agreed date. Several potential roles for the United Nations in the on-going sovereignty negotiations were discussed in May 1982: Argentina preferred eventual decision by the General Assembly; Great Britain (and probably the secretary general) envisioned the secretary general providing good offices for an on-going bilateral negotiation between the two parties. During the secretary general's negotiations it seemed for a while that the Junta had approved a formula which would not prejudge the outcome of future sovereignty negotiations. Almost immediately, however, contradictory statements were made in Buenos Aires, and it became clear that there was no such agreement. The secretary general was quite clear in his support of the elements of Resolution 502, including settlement by peaceful means.

In its final offer during the UN mediation, the United Kingdom proposed that no provision in the interim agreement, including those on negotiations, should prejudice the rights, claims, or positions of either party. It also made the negotiations on sovereignty definitive by stating that no acts or activities under the interim agreement would constitute a basis for "asserting, supporting or denying a claim to territorial sovereignty ... or create any rights." The negotiations were to be *real* negotiations. Under Article 8 of the 17 May proposal, they were to take place under the auspices of Sr. Perez de Cuellar and the parties would aim to complete them by the end of the year. Balancing the previous positions of the two parties, no outcome was excluded or predetermined.

In the Argentine response of 18 May, Argentina agreed that the negotiations concerning the Islands' future should be begun without prejudice to the positions, rights, or previous claims of the parties. Argentina did not accept, however, the concept that the outcome should not be prejudged. Nor could Argentina fully accept the provision of the British draft which called for the interim arrangements to last until a definitive settlement could be implemented. Argentina could not accept that the negotiations be open-ended either in outcome or in the timing of the end of negotiations.

The British reply to the Argentine response noted that Great Britain could not accept inter alia the call of the Argentine response for "long term negotiations which led in only one direction." Moreover, the British White Paper of 21 May said that the United Kingdom had no doubts about its claim, but had been willing to negotiate sovereignty at some points without prejudice under successive British governments. It stated that since the Argentine invasion Britain had again been willing to consider negotiations as long as they were not prejudged in their outcome and to set a target date of the end of 1982.

In the Argentine diplomatic note to the State Department of 26 May, Argentina proposed negotiations without prejudice; recognition of divergent positions (but on all three island groups); respect for and safeguarding of the "customs, traditions and way of life of the inhabitants" as well as their "social and cultural links with their countries of origins." Negotiations under the auspices of the secretary general were proposed, and the 31 December deadline was kept as a target date. A single option to extend until 30 June 1983 was added as was reference to specific UN resolutions (in order to comply with the Charter of the United Nations, Resolutions 1514, 2065, and relevant resolutions). The site was specifically given as New York. The secretary general, said the Argentine proposal, "may be assisted in the negotiations by a Contact Group composed of representatives of four states, members of the United Nations. To that end, each party shall nominate two States and shall have the right to a single veto of one of the States nominated by the other." If agreement were reached by the end of the first renewal period, the secretary general was to draw up a report framing the question for General Assembly decision. Argentina thus rejected the British idea of the interim arrangement staying in place until a definitive solution was reached by negotiation. The Argentine re-draft emphasized decolonization and territorial integrity as the basis for sovereignty negotiations.

Resolution 505 of 26 May called on the secretary general to renew his talks, which had included eventual sovereignty negotiations. The Security Council also reaffirmed and called for implementation of 502. Significantly the emphasis was on military ceasefire, not sovereignty negotiations.

PROCESSES AND PLAYERS:
THE CHEMISTRY OF THE MEDIATOR AS NEGOTIATOR

While a mediator's skill in selecting appropriate issues for discussion and compromise and in drafting potentially acceptable proposals is an important element in any successful "negotiation helped by mediation," it is not the only key factor. Also of importance is the interaction between mediator and each of the adversaries, the "chemistry" that may develop positively to help or negatively to hinder the total process of mediation.

In the Falklands/Malvinas dispute, this "chemistry" played a vital role in determining the fate of efforts to head off military violence. We will consider one important aspect of this interaction: relations between the Argentine government and its U.S. mediator. This interaction of the Argentine[6] and U.S. governments was complex and highly personal, and its more interesting aspects lead to as many questions as answers. Whether derived by analysis, or directly stated by the participants, they are highly personal and subjective. They are nonetheless valuable as raw data needing further confirmation, assessment, and tying together for their *relative value in explaining the course of mediation.*

The Mediator and the Junta

Argentine policy makers had taken their case to the OAS on 26 April in order, among other things, to get a more favorable reaction from the United States. They had the impression that they were provided with General Haig's proposal 72 hours after the British (i.e., that they were presented with an Anglo–American document rather than a proposal originating from the United States as mediator). Costa Mendez wanted to discuss this proposal with the Americans but was overtaken by the 30 April U.S. statement and the U.S. decision to back Britain.[7] If they felt rushed and pressured by the series of U.S. statements on 27 and 30 April, they felt betrayed by the logistics and materiel intentions of the United States.

Furthermore, the Argentinians felt that Secretary of State Haig was transmitting a sense of their weakness both to the British as reporter and to the Argentines as a method of influence. He was courteous to the extent of encouraging their sense of grandeur. He was distant yet frank enough that Costa Mendez is said to have said to Haig at one point: "We'll understand if you have to side with Great Britain." The Argentines believed that Haig twice said that he would try to stop the British at Ascension. They are sure, in turn, that they never asked any of the mediators to halt British military actions as a precondition to beginning talks.

The Argentine foreign minister found Haig in need of education on the basics of the "Malvinas" problem. The Argentines felt that they had to educate Haig for an initial two days about the South Atlantic. (No

Americans seem to have had to mention even the most detailed agendas to him twice.) He felt Haig to be rigid, operating from a script—and a NATO script at that. To Costa Mendez, Haig seemed to be functioning not creatively but negatively. Haig (1984, p. 60) felt that Costa Mendez was firmer about guaranteed Argentine sovereignty than were the military leaders.

> The British won't fight. In this judgement, I believe, he had the agreement and not the tutelage of Nicanor Costa Mendez, the Foreign Minister, who was reportedly the main opponent of my advice. On a number of occasions after Galtieri had showed some movement in the negotiations, Costa Mendez met with me privately and demanded what his president had said, hardening the Argentine position and making resolution impossible.

It may well be, however, that one's foreign minister is simply the person that government sends to make retractions and other conveyances of bad news. Galtieri would certainly not like to be in the position of retracting what either the rest of the Junta or the wider groupings of the military senior officers rejected.

This and other confusions may well have stemmed from the American failure to perceive what was a perfectly clear, indeed formal, decision-making system on the Argentine side. Serious decisions required the approval of all flag/general rank officers of all three services. This may be awkward, imprecise, time consuming, and inconvenient in a negotiated mediation, but it was nonetheless the *law of the land in Argentina*. In this and other matters it would have been highly valuable for the American mediators to have had the full and constant participation of the resident U.S. ambassador, who knew his host government well.

Americans and British were prone to use the word "machismo" in discussing the psychology, operating style, and bargaining tactics of the Argentine military government. This does not mesh well with, for example, Galtieri's courtliness or Anaya's tears at the loss of sailors. "Machismo" is a particularly Spanish concept, not entirely native to Argentine society, which is far more pan-European than Hispanic. The Junta's behavior with the negotiating mediator certainly involved bravado, a nearly universal gambit in negotiating. One puts the best face possible on one's situation and outlook. Their collective behavior was indecisive and self-contradictory, neither classic attributes of the Hispanic *caballero* or the military officer. At times it lacked a precision, a most un-Argentine trait. The Falklands crisis produced in the Argentine government not exaggeration but dilution of national traits.

Indeed, serious international crises have a way of bringing into play the full range of human emotion and intellect. A form of machismo was also diagnosed in the Thatcher government and the prime minister herself.

While Haig would directly perceive, the Argentines be repelled by, and the press concentrate on what Haig later called the "icy scorn and iron will of Mrs. Thatcher," (Haig, 1984, p. 60), that aspect of her character and behavior was not inconsistent with her concern (expressed almost nightly to her Permanent Representative in New York) at the impending loss of young lives, should diplomacy fail. Resolve is criticized by no society—public backing for Costa Mendez in Buenos Aires was expressed by dubbing him "the Iron Foreign Minister." If there was anything approaching bloodlust in the Falklands crisis it was in parts of the British press and public reaction to the invasion, not at 10 Downing Street. Determination there had no sense of adventure and heightened experience to it. It was pure political challenge and response.

Some members of the Argentine "team" thought they detected a bias in the mediator, Anaya representing the extreme view that he was simply the agent of British imperialism in the South Atlantic. They saw collusion in his "permitting" the United Kingdom to declare the Temporary Exclusion Zone.[8] They found further cause for suspicion in the U.S. refueling of British units at Ascension. (Indirect or not, the United States was so obligated under the terms of its use of the British island of Ascension.) They viewed Haig's behavior in London as acting as though he had returned home, seeming relaxed and happy. They also thought they detected an increase in his pro-British attitude between his two trips. The press leak of 14 April concerning U.S. intelligence fueled these doubts about the mediator.

The dominant opinion in the Argentine government, however, was that, ideal or not, the secretary of state was Argentina's only serious option for a negotiated settlement with the British once the Task Force sailed. Many conceded that Haig was growing in his command of the issue as the mediation progressed. Anaya and Galtieri felt consistently that Haig changed in his mood with each return to his hotel. He would leave their talks pleased about progress and then return from his hotel shaken and in low spirits. Their assumption was that he was talking by phone with Washington or London and encountering British intransigence.

The Argentines consistently note that Haig never said what Britain wanted except on the last day in Buenos Aires. The Argentine perspective on the mechanics of drafting was that all during April there was no British proposal to discuss. They submitted four or five drafts of which two or three were given to the U.S. team. The Argentines began to feel that this was a one-sided exercise in negotiation in which it fell to them to suggest the solutions, which were then rejected by London or the mediator.

On 18 April, Haig said that he could not take the Argentine draft to the United Kingdom; that it simply would not wash. By his last day in Buenos Aires, he recognized as a "miracle" the result of his request for a "gray" draft, that is, a colorless, low-key, non-polemical text. Yet that text fell flat with the War Cabinet. Apparently perceptions about settlement had not come any closer in the whole Haig shuttle. Haig did not understand why the Argentines could not budge. Was it that the survival of the government depended on their bluffing to the very end; an all or nothing strategy, as regards their own population and the United Kingdom?

Quite apart from the issue of concessions, American assumptions about the urgency of the situation may have been exaggerated, and certainly seemed so to the Argentines. "With the British fleet steaming down the South Atlantic at a steady eighteen knots and the Argentinians daily reinforcing their garrison in the Falklands, the opportunity for negotiations would last only a few days" (Haig, 1986, p. 270). Such an attitude assumed not only that the British were coming all the way but that from the start they intended to prosecute their case militarily. Argentine thinking in the first round in Buenos Aires certainly did not fully accept either point. The timing of the mediator appeared to the Argentine side to be merely one more form of American pressure in favor of the British enemy.

Related to timing was the feeling that this was the only possible mediation and mediator, another view which the Argentines did not share.

It was my opinion, tested in a series of freewheeling staff discussions, that the United States alone had enough influence with both sides to provide an outside chance of success. The United Nations, with its vociferous, anticolonialist coalition of Third World and Marxist members would probably not be able to act quickly enough to be effective, and the debate was certain to digress to issues that would exacerbate a situation that could only be resolved by quiet diplomacy. The OAS was unsatisfactory for similar reasons. [Haig, 1986, p. 270]

Argentina not only *could* but *was* already considering both the UN and the OAS as alternatives for securing its positions. It was precisely the nature of their membership and their way of conducting business that appealed to the Junta. If the Americans could not secure for them what Argentina wanted, Argentina would turn to other mediators. In no sense did they see Haig's mediation as a critical opportunity to be grasped as the sole alternative. War, of course, was a solid alternative in the view of the Junta, not desirable but seeming daily more likely and perhaps ultimately necessary. The resort to force was not, to their minds, the catastrophe which it seemed to the mediator.

The U.S. mediator also appeared more interested in abstract justice and propriety, than was the Junta. His attitude showed clearly in his public statements concerning Resolution 502, which the Argentines took to be biassed, power-based politics. There was, indeed, a sense of chastening which the Argentines found not only improperly judgemental but (in their view) factually, legally, and historically incorrect. Secretary Haig has written that he felt that "a sincere, high-level effort by the United States could do much to strip away the confusing ambiguities of the situation and help to establish who was right and who was wrong" (ibid., p. 271).

Beyond the judgemental preference for the United Kingdom, Secretary Haig held, and may have betrayed, the view that the United Kingdom was "calling the shots." This was certainly not the way the situation appeared in the initial weeks to the Junta. Yet the mediator saw himself essentially as negotiating with the Argentines what was *acceptable* to the British: "It was decided that I would go first to London, in order to know what was possible, before travelling to Argentina and talking to its unpredictable leaders" (ibid., p. 271).

The Process

Less personal were the two systems' readings of each other, a mildly more self-conscious and analytic process.

The Argentines read Haig's consultation process with the British as a successful upgrading by the United Kingdom of the "special relationship." (A case of the British tail wagging the American dog.) Unconsciously grouping the Anglo-Saxons, and misreading a partnership which comes as close to sovereign equality as any in the modern world, the Argentines clung to their hope that the United States would wish to restrain the United Kingdom and be able to do so both militarily and politically. With the Suez analogy in mind, they ignored the modern special relationship of the Trident era and the centrality, in the mainstream politico-legal culture, of the principle of non-resort to force, especially against the interests of major states.

Galtieri's reaction to Haig's method of approach was critical. Two elements of the U.S. approach in particular hardened Argentine attitudes. The first was the insistence on Argentine withdrawal as the key element of what the Argentines saw as the larger, on-going problem. Founded on UN Resolution 502, this American core element was nonetheless seen by the Argentines as enforcement of British interests as opposed to equity.

The second major irritant was the increasingly clear fact that not only did Argentina have to withdraw, but that if it failed to do so, the United States would help the United Kingdom. While the emphasis was clearly on punitive action by the United Kingdom and the cost to Argentina which the United States wished to avoid, the Argentine perception was more focussed on the fact that the United States *would* help, if Argentina did not get out.

These two perceptions led to hardened Argentine positions, including the insistence on the 31 December deadline for the transfer of Argentine sovereignty, and they poisoned both the American and Peruvian peace initiatives. They also led to "fallback think," such as: Even if we lose, we can still obtain the original objective of getting the United Kingdom to bargain seriously.

Foreign Minister Costa Mendez felt that the greatest stumbling block in the Haig proposals was British insistence on consulting the population of the islanders. He read any return to British administration without a fixed date for ending the negotiations as status quo ante, in that the population would clearly *not* choose Argentine sovereignty. He harbored equally grave doubts about the U.S.–U.K. majority vote in interim administration. Argentina was again playing for all or nothing: full sovereignty, rather than a need to trust the U.S. mediator in a continuing process. Thus, U.S. efforts to negotiate an end to the crisis failed, as did the subsequent Peruvian and UN endeavors.

CONCLUSIONS

Negotiating failures in the three principal mediation initiatives of the 1982 crisis call into sharp focus the underlying difficulties for third-party mediation which have given it such a sad track record in this century. In the first instance, Argentina could not take force seriously. The U.S. mediator could not convince either party that there was urgency and a serious penalty for failure to compromise. The United Kingdom could not take seriously the mediator's allowance for the interest and honor of the other party.

In the second, the British could not control force with the precision which the paradigm of trading off force and diplomacy assumes. The mediators were not truly communicating with each other or between the parties, and Argentina was seeking new mediation just as the focus of the crisis was becoming all but exclusively military. (Continuation of tacit bargaining is not the same as continuation of real negotiation.)

In the third, the UN initiative facilitated compromise but could not be turned to agreement due to the timing and growing incompatibility of simultaneously fighting and talking.

Negotiation in three widely varying forms by classic methods exercised by several of the most experienced and influential of third-party institutions thus failed, even with considerable time, to prevent war in the Falklands. The reasons were a complex interaction of *contexts* (universal to territorial violence in the last quarter of the twentieth century); *causes* (specific to the Falklands); and specific *negotiations* and parallel use of force which comprise politico-military statecraft.

The overarching context is the nation-state system, with its emphasis on sovereign autonomy. Sovereignty in turn is focussed on territory, thus putting the latter at the center of international affairs. While the value of territory in national interest terms has declined, its importance to national honor has (if anything) increased. This is particularly true for radical, nonaligned states, many of whom encourage group norms that discount the competing notion of a political "people" in favor of historical (or perceived) "territorial integrity."

The causes remain as complex a barrier as the context of successful negotiation, whether first, second, or third track. The parties to the Falklands crisis shared not only national interests in possession and exclusive use of the territory in question but centuries of what they perceived to be a zero-sum for national honor. Their actions, and even their negotiating strategies, tended to exacerbate rather than ameliorate the problem. They each invoked and, indeed, created domestic political opinion in support of their cause and in turn became prisoners of it at crucial junctures.

The specific negotiations in the Falklands/Malvinas crisis of 1982, and the parallel use of force, have been reviewed briefly. The record suggests that neither direct negotiations between Britain and Argentina nor mediated negotiation involving third parties such as the United States, Peru, or the United Nations had much chance of success while the advesaries' demands remained so far apart. While they continued to misperceive each other's commitment to maintaining "national honor," intransigence was made worse when military strategies were initiated, for these developed a "life" of their own—a dynamic that proved highly inimical to the process of simultaneous mediated negotiation.

NOTES

1. One of the principal such limitations is the constraint on the players not to hurt their standing in the on-going nation-state game. This is one of the more perverse forms which "national honor" takes in limiting nation-state behavior and inhibiting peaceful settlement.

2. Others include: timing, atmospherics, and outside pressures; conflict and power relationships; relative strength of positions; intelligence and the negotiations context; reformulation and re-ordering priorities; risk-taking; trial balloons, re-stated minima and ultima; hidden agenda and the probing process; trade-offs and concessions; win–win and zero-sum solutions; deadlines (real and imagined, substantive and procedural): slow progress, impasse, stalemate, failure; press and public affairs, informative or manipulative; real understanding.

3. "Reframing" may be promising where the parties have come to full realization of the scope and seriousness of their disagreement. It may be, for example, that at that stage they would be willing to freeze the question as previously defined and attempt to make progress by working on subsidiary or other related issues. Sanctions or deadlines that originally appeared firm may have, by this stage, passed or been proven flexible. Serious consideration should be given to not attempting to resolve the main dispute immediately in the terms originally set.

4. While it is generally assumed that any "disengagement" (i.e., an end of the mediation by that particular mediator) represents failure and should invoke all stated consequences, a well-timed disengagement may be the maximizing strategy for the mediator who can foresee any of the following contingencies: (1) that the stated consequences or sanctions cannot or will not be immediately invoked; (2) that an alternative process is in the offing and should, in effect, be deferred to; (3)

that disengagement, temporary or final, should be thought of as a creative option rather than the opposite of success.

5. The objective of "decolonization" was both open-ended as to means and subject to mutual agreement. In the negotiations, the legal positions of each side were protected both by the references to competing principles, and by the specific reservation that the wishes of the plebiscite or poll be without prejudice to the respective positions.

6. And to a lesser degree the British.

7. Victoria Gamba. Interview, Buenos Aires, November 1983.

8. It was a fait accompli, announced *before* Haig touched down in London.

6

The Western Contact Group as Intermediary in the Conflict over Namibia

Vivienne Jabri

The existing literature on the mediation process and the qualities of intermediaries points to the variety of both the patterns of interaction that make up the process and the types of third parties that have occupied the intermediary role. This variety ranges from the International Commission of the Red Cross to Quaker peace missions and, ultimately, to the U.S. secretary of state. A look at the differences in the forms of interaction that make up the mediation process involving these types of third parties raises the question of the validity of placing all these under the rubric of "mediation". Analyses of third-party involvement in the Arab–Israeli conflict, such as those of Dr. Kissinger and President Carter (Touval, 1982), and the Anglo-American mediation between Italy and Yugoslavia over Trieste (Campbell, 1976) have raised important questions relating to assumptions made in theoretical and empirical work on mediation and mediator qualities. The assumption of impartiality and disinterest, originally seen as prerequisites for the intermediary role (Young, 1967) is questioned by these examples. The common theme underlying these works is that these third parties were neither disinterested nor impartial. In the terms used here they were "interested intermediaries".

This chapter provides a framework for the analysis of the tactical decisions made by an *interested* third party occupying the role of *intermediary*. The framework will be applied to the involvement of the Western Contact Group (WCG) in the conflict over Namibia. Given the coalition nature of this particular intervention, the framework will also consider the impact of a *coalition* factor on third-party tactics. The objective is, firstly, to use the WCG as an illustration of the tactics that may be adopted by an interested coalition intermediary; and, secondly, to indicate factors that may influence such a third party's choice of tactics. It will be argued that the involvement of an interested third party as intermediary is best analysed by considering the third party as forming part of (at least) a three-cornered negotiation system, with the third party being one of the negotiators. This focusses attention on the third party's own decision-making processes when interacting with the conflict system. This form of analysis will point to the difficulty of distinguishing, firstly, between third parties which become involved as intermediaries and those which are interveners (Young, 1967, pp. 52–73); and secondly, between the third party and the parties in the negotiation process. It will emphasise the argument that third parties may occupy a number of overlapping roles when involved in a conflict situation. It is hoped that the framework will provide a basis for the systematic analysis of other multilateral and interested intermediary initiatives such as that of the Contadora Group.

THE ANALYTIC FRAMEWORK

As suggested by Touval (1982), the intervention of an interested third party into a dyadic bargaining situation transforms it into a three-cornered relationship or a triad where the third party cannot be assumed to be an outsider. This is the central premise in the framework presented below. It suggests that the third party becomes one of the negotiators in the multilateral negotiation system. Thus, as well as carrying out functions traditionally associated with intermediaries, such as facilitating communication between the parties, clarifying issues and providing a face-saving input for a conceding party (Mitchell, 1981b; Kriesberg, 1982), the third party may also bargain with the parties both to gain concessions facilitating agreement and/or to promote the third party's own interests. Moreover, as Touval suggests, the pattern of interaction between a "biassed" or an interested third party and the adversaries is dominated by the bargaining process not only between the parties, but also between them and the third party.

Third-Party Choice of Tactics

The above discussion suggests that analysis of the decision-making process of an interested third party concerning the choice of tactics must start from the premise that the third party is functioning within (at least) a triadic negotiation system, the third party being one of the negotiators. The third party's tactical input into this system operates at three levels: (1) communication facilitation, (2) proposal formulation and (3) influence to induce concessions.

The interested third party may control the interaction at each of these levels. Thus, apart from facilitating the process of communication between the parties, the third party may also manipulate the process during the provision of information to the parties. The third party may exert an influence on the interaction process by introducing proposals possibly aimed at an agreement between the conflict parties; it may, however, introduce issues that are salient to itself and not necessarily to the parties in conflict. It may bargain with the parties in order to acquire concessions leading to a settlement, but could make settlement conditional upon acceptance of its own stance. It may use varying influence tactics, ranging from persuasion to coercion or rewards, in order to acquire such concessions. All three levels vary according to the content and costs that may accrue from their application. They are aimed at influencing the parties' perceptions of the costs and benefits of agreement as opposed to continued conflict.

The third-party role represents a spectrum of activity ranging from the overt bargaining activity exemplified by Dr. Kissinger's involvement in the Arab–Israeli conflict (Touval, 1982; Rubin, 1981), to the conciliation activity undertaken by Quaker mediators in the Nigerian Civil War (Yarrow, 1978) and the largely facilitative role of the World Council of Churches in the Sudanese Civil War (Assefa, Chapter 8 this volume). Table 6.1 illustrates the behaviour that defines the facilitative and bargaining range of the spectrum of third-party activity.

The third party may start the initiative by adopting a facilitative approach. It may, on the other hand, start in a directive manner having a specific commitment to an outcome and a framework for a settlement process (Kressel, 1972). Moreover, the third party may move from one strategy to the next depending on feedback processes from the negotiation. The third party may, during the course of interaction with the parties, use any of these tactics depending on a number of factors which influence a third party's choice of tactics at any specific point during involvement in the conflict. The following section defines the factors (or independent variables) that may influence a third party's tactical choice during the interaction process.

Factors Influencing Third-Party Choice of Tactics

The starting point for this analytic framework is that, as with parties in any negotiation system, the third party's tactical decisions in interaction with the conflict system must be a process of adjustment and readjustment to the dynamic conditions of the conflict and to the negotiation process. For example, the third party's set of preferred outcomes at time A may well have changed at time B when the third party has considered the negotiating positions of the parties and the situation with regard to the

Table 6.1

Bargaining Behaviour	Facilitative Behaviour
1. The mediator intervenes with a stated commitment to a particular outcome to the conflict.	1. The mediator intervenes with the stated objective of promoting a settlement between the parties.
2. The mediator intervenes with a specific framework for the settlement process	2. The process is open-ended, the mediator allowing the parties to build up the framework.
3. Communication between the parties is not necessarily the priority, emphasis being on communication between third party and the protagonists.	3. The mediator acts more or less as a go-between and seeks to promote communication between the parties.
4. The mediator has almost total control of proposal formulation. These may reflect the mediator's own standpoint on particular outcomes.	4. The mediator helps the parties reach a compromise outcome and seeks to build up proposals based on the parties' positions.
5. The mediator may specify conditions of acceptance of a particular outcome.	5. The mediator does not specify the terms of acceptance of an outcome.
6. The mediator can have his/her own positions on particular issues in the negotiations.	6. The mediator does not express a position on specific issues.
7. The mediator may bargain on specific issues.	7. Bargaining only takes place between the parties.
8. The mediator uses threat and reward tactics to induce concessions towards a settlement and/or towards the acceptance of third party's stance.	8. The mediator aims at persuasion through the clarification of the issues and the consequences of continuation of the conflict.

conflict environment (see, for example, Chapter 11 this volume). This dynamic aspect of the interactional process between third party and conflict system must be taken into account in an analysis of third-party choice of tactics during involvement as intermediary in a conflict situation.

I suggest eight sets of factors that may jointly explain a third party's tactical decisions at any specific time during the interaction process:

1. The conflict characteristics;
2. The negotiation system;
3. The third party's conflict-related interests;
4. The third party's process-related interests;
5. The third party's set of preferred outcomes;

6. The third party's influence potential;
7. Third-party constituency input;
8. The intra-coalition situation (if third party is a coalition).

All eight sets of factors may change during the third party's involvement in the conflict. Moreover, not all factors are necessarily applicable at all points during the interaction process with the conflict system. The eight sets of factors are detailed in Table 6.2.

Influencing Third-Party Choice of Tactics

All of the factors in Table 6.2 are likely to have some impact on an interested third party's choice of tactics. For example, the negotiation system is the source of informational feedback to the third party from the conflict system.[1] Each level of the negotiation system forms an input into the third party's tactical choice decisions so that it may reevaluate and readjust its position during the negotiation process in response to this input. All three levels are subject to change during the interactive process with the third party. Thus, at the start of the third party's initiative, both parties may perceive an equal stake in the settlement process; this, however, may change when one or both of the parties decide that other strategic options would bring greater benefits than negotiation. The third party takes such changes into account when reconsidering tactics in its interaction with the parties.

Coalition Intermediaries and the Intra-Coalition Situation

While the eight sets of factors are applicable to all third parties, the last set is applicable only to a coalition third party. A coalition third party usually brings greater resources and influence potential to the negotiation process than the individual representative third party. Different members of the coalition may be more acceptable than others to certain parties and their patrons in the conflict. Moreover, different members of the coalition may have differential influence with the parties and/or their patrons.[2] A collective stance by a coalition third party may mean greater bargaining power with the parties in conflict. The collective stance made by the Western Contact Group over Namibia was an important factor in the participation of the South African Government in the international negotiations. Another important characteristic in coalition mediation is that the parties in conflict may also attempt to form alignments with individual members of the coalition if they perceive a difference in approach between the participants of that coalition. (This member became an important feature of the negotiations during the later stages of the Contact Group initiative when divisions occurred within the Group).

Coalition third parties may also differ from a single, representative third party in being more susceptible to problems inherent in team mediation. One of these is the potentially cumbersome process of consultation and joint decision-making. This problem may be alleviated if each member of the coalition is highly individualised, as seems to have been the case in the Anglo-American mediation between Italy and Yugoslavia over Trieste in 1954 (Campbell, 1976). However, the process of consultation can even be more time-consuming and cumbersome when different levels of the policy-making machinery are involved. The WCG, for example, functioned at three levels: the New York representatives and senior officials from the foreign ministries; the foreign secretaries; and ambassadors in Pretoria. Another problem relates to coordination of policies and attitudes towards the conflict. Different interests may lead to division and lack of coordination in functioning. Divergent interests may lead to the diminution of third-party credibility, and, therefore, influence potential.

These are important aspects to consider in an analysis of the functioning of coalition factors that may have an influence on the tactical decisions made by the coalition and its members. As Table 6.2 illustrates, these are (1) the level of intra-coalition cohesion; (2) the distribution of influence potential; and (3) the degree of communication and consultation among the members.

The level of cohesion within the coalition is a reflection of the members' level of agreement on the rank-ordering of preferred outcomes to the conflict, as well as the tactics to be used in order to attain the preferred outcome. There may be agreement on the proposals to be presented to the parties and disagreement on the influence tactics to be applied in order to gain concessions towards these proposals.

The distribution of influence within the coalition is also an important factor to consider in an analysis of tactics adopted by coalition intermediaries and their participants. This is defined as "Who has what, in relation to whom?" in the conflict. As suggested earlier, the participants of the coalition may have differential influence with the parties and/or their patrons who may value different resources from each member of the coalition. It may also influence the bargaining behaviour of the parties with the individual members.

The degree of communication between the members of the coalition is defined by the extent to which members function individually in their interaction with the conflict system as opposed to the coalition acting collectively.

It should be pointed out that the above intra-coalition factors have a modifying influence on the individual members' preference sets and their evaluation of their influence potential. They also influence the bargaining process between the adversaries and the members of the coalition. The relationships within the coalition, as with the other factors discussed

Table 6.2

1. *Conflict Characteristics*
>   The issues in conflict
>   Relationships between the parties
>   The presence of factions
>   Patron input
>   Overlapping conflicts

2. *The Negotiation System*

   Inter-party factors:
>   Each party's rank-ordering of preferred outcomes
>   Balance of relative advantage between the parties
>   The parties' options of discontinuing the negotiations
>   The parties respective stakes in the negotiation process
>   The degree of communication between the parties

   Intra-party factors:
>   Whom the negotiators represent
>   The position of dominant factions in relation to the negotiation process
>   Level of support for the negotiating party

   Party–patron factors:
>   A patron's rank-ordering of preferred outcomes
>   A patron's stake in the negotiation process
>   A patron's level of support and commitment to its client

3. *The third party's conflict-related interests*

   These may be linked to any of the following dimensions of the conflict:
>   The issues and parties in the conflict
>   Issues and parties in overlapping conflicts
>   Relationship with other third parties in the conflict environment, e.g. patrons
>   Relationships with intra-party groups or factions

above, are subject to change with time. For example, the dominant member of the coalition at the start of the initiative may no longer be so at a later stage. There may also be changes in the level of cohesion within the coalition as the rank-ordering of preferred outcomes and perceptions of the effectiveness of tactics change. As will be seen in the analysis of the WCG's tactical decisions during its involvement in the negotiations over Namibia, changes occurred in all three of the intra-coalition factors described here. Such changes had a major impact on the functioning of the group.

BACKGROUND TO THE CONFLICT

South Africa came to occupy Namibia in mid-1915, before which Namibia had been a German colony. The League of Nations, against South

Table 6.2 (continued)

---

4. *Third-party process-related interests*

These define the benefits that may derive from occupation of the intermediary role:

> To avoid other reactions, e.g. taking sides
> To influence the outcome to the conflict
> To ensure own control over the settlement process
> To gain future influence with the parties/their patrons
> To exclude other third parties' influence or to compete with it
> To gain credibility for related actions
> To gain prestige and approval for actions
> To go along with one's allies

5. *Third-party set of preferred outcomes*

This refers to the third party's rank-ordering of preferred outcomes to the conflict

6. *Third-party influence potential*
> Material resources
> Status resources, e.g. veto at Security Council, village elder
> Relationships with adversary and other third parties in conflict
> Personal resources, e.g. skill, prestige

7. *Third-party constituency input*

This becomes relevant if the third party's constituency or groups within it are interested in the conflict in which its representatives are involved

8. *The intra-coalition situation*
> The level of intra-coalition cohesion
> The distribution of influence potential
> The degree of communication and consultation among the members

---

African ambitions to annex the territory, placed it within the mandate system. The mandate was placed within the UN Trusteeship system, from 1945 onwards. South Africa refused to comply with the trusteeship regulations, and in 1950 an advisory opinion of the International Court of Justice (ICJ) established that South Africa was not obligated to place the territory under the Trusteeship Council, but that the international status of the territory under the mandate system remained intact. Subsequent decisions authorised the United Nations to receive reports and petitions from the inhabitants of Namibia. These showed that South Africa was violating its mandatory obligations. In 1966, the General Assembly voted to withdraw the mandate from South Africa, a decision which was followed in 1968 by a Security Council decision to withdraw South Africa's mandate over Namibia. In 1971, an advisory opinion of the ICJ ruled South Africa's presence in Namibia illegal. The territory was subsequently placed under the jurisdiction of the UN Council for Namibia.[3] A discussion of the conflict characteristics will show that despite the existence of two major parties to the conflict—namely the South African government whose forces currently occupy Namibia, and SWAPO, the Namibian liberation movement conducting a guerilla struggle against the South African occupation—there are a number of "non-focal"[4] parties involved.

The issues at the start of the WCG initiative in April 1977 were centred around the South African defined "internal settlement" for Namibia in opposition to the UN-defined "process for Namibian independence" as outlined in Security Council Resolution 385 of 30 January 1976. The internal settlement was based on proposals emerging from the Turnhalle Constitutional Conference convened in September 1975. The Turnhalle delegates represented eleven ethnic groups, according to the South African division of the Namibian population. While the South African government claimed this to be an internal Namibian process, evidence indicates that they were in direct control of the proceedings (Totemeyer and Seiler, 1980). By the beginning of 1977, a draft constitution was completed proposing a three-tier system of government, each ethnically based.[5]

SWAPO rejected the Turnhalle process because it was based on an ethnic division of the population. In its "Political Programme" adopted in Lusaka in July 1976, SWAPO stated that it would continue the political and armed struggle until the SAG accepted the territorial integrity of Namibia and the right of its people to independence and national sovereignty. In reference to the Turnhalle process, the Programme states, "SWAPO shall under no circumstances accept the South African plan to impose on our people a weak and fearful confederation of bantustans, a confederation which will be incapable of contradicting neo-colonial orders from Pretoria" (SWAPO 1976, p. 8). It stated that any constitutional talks on the future of Namibia must take place under UN supervision, and should aim at the holding of free elections under UN supervision and control.

SWAPO had, therefore, accepted the UN-defined process for Namibian independence as set out in Security Council Resolution 385. This called for free elections to be held under UN supervision and control and for adequate time, to be determined by the Security Council, "for the purpose of enabling the UN to establish the necessary machinery within Namibia to supervise and control such elections". The resolution called for complete South African withdrawal to be replaced by a transitional UN presence. It also called on the SAG, pending the transfer of power, to allow the free return of exiles, to release political prisoners, and to abolish all apartheid laws, particularly the "bantustans" and "homelands".

The broad issues of *internal* as opposed to *internationally recognised* settlement were manifest throughout the negotiations involving the WCG and evolved into more detailed issues of implementation. Moreover, issues from overlapping conflicts were introduced into the negotiations and had a major impact on the process.[6]

INTERVENTION BY THE WCG AS A COALITION OF INTERMEDIARIES

The issues in early 1977, prior to the intervention of the WCG, were centred around South Africa's escalated moves towards the implementation of an internal settlement in Namibia based on the Turnhalle process. Such moves were opposed by SWAPO, the United Nations and the EEC since they underlined the SAG's non-compliance with SCR 385. This period was also characterised by increasing moves at the UN for the imposition of mandatory sanctions against South Africa. The Security Council debate on Namibia in March 1977 included calls from African and non-aligned members of the United Nations for such action which faced inevitable opposition from the Western members of the Security Council, namely the United States, the United Kingdom, France, West Germany and Canada. The new U.S. ambassador at the United Nations, Andrew Young, had early in February 1977 approached permanent representatives from the other four countries on the possibility of a collective Western approach to the SAG. This culminated in agreement by the five's foreign secretaries, who attended the March Security Council debate, for such an approach to the SAG based on SCR 385.[7]

Continuation versus Settlement of Conflict

The nine governments of the EEC, acting within the framework of European Political Cooperation, had already expressed their opposition to Turnhalle when Andrew Young made his proposal for a collective Western stance on Namibia.[8] The objective of the new Western initiative became clear when the five governments, via their ambassadors in Pretoria, presented to the South African prime minister, John Vorster, an aide-memoire expressing the group's "belief in the necessity for a Namibian settlement in keeping with Resolution 385 and thereby acceptable to the international community". The message emphasised that the activities of the Turnhalle Conference did not meet those standards and informed the SAG that in the absence of an early agreement to pursue an internationally acceptable solution, "the five would be obligated to consider very seriously the measures to be taken".[9] It was therefore clear from the start of the initiative that the objective was to work within the framework of SCR 385. The initiative acquired acceptance in the United Nations because it was based on the UN framework for Namibian independence as expressed in this resolution.[10]

A distinguishing feature of the intermediary role is that the third party has to be acceptable within this role by the parties in conflict. Both SWAPO and the SAG were suspicious of the Western initiative; SWAPO because of Western relations with South Africa, and the SAG because the initiative was based on the UN framework for Namibian independence, the UN being perceived as biassed towards SWAPO. Both parties followed, as Ambassador McHenry stated early in the negotiations, a "dual-track" strategy[11]; that is, they took part in the negotiations while pursuing their original conflict strategies for attaining conflict goals. The SAG continued the implementation of the internal settlement while at the same time escalating the war both in terms of the number of South African troops in Namibia and in terms of intervention into the Front Line States (FLS). (The latter was manifest both directly and through military aid to the rebel movements, UNITA and the MNR, in Angola and Mozambique, respectively.) SWAPO maintained its commitment to the guerilla struggle and expressed this throughout its involvement in the negotiations. Both parties, therefore, accepted the WCG as intermediary, but did not abandon original conflict strategies.

The South African Government's agreement to take part in the international negotiations was due to the collective Western onslaught. The SAG ensured that its options in Namibia remained open by pursuing the internal settlement process while taking part in the negotiations with the WCG (Spicer 1980). It also ensured that its military strategy in Namibia was kept intact. The number of SADF troops stationed in Namibia was increased from 20,000 at the start of 1977 to around 80,000 in 1981, and an attempt was made to localise the occupation by transferring the military command to Namibia, the process starting in August 1977 when military authority in Namibia was centralised in Windhoek whereas previously it had been in Pretoria. This was, in fact, the first step towards the introduction of conscription to all Namibians and the creation of the South West Africa Territorial Force (SWATF).[12] This would suggest, therefore, that the SAG only took part in the negotiations because it was carried out by Western governments closely associated with it and having the capacity to impose sanctions against it.

SWAPO also pursued a local track strategy by maintaining and even escalating Peoples Liberation Army of Namibia (PLAN) operations inside Namibia with guerilla activity averaging once/day in 1979,[13] while taking part in the negotiations with the WCG. Although SWAPO kept up its operations, taking part in the negotiations meant that it had a less costly chance of achieving victory at UN-supervised elections.[14] The negotiations also provided SWAPO with the opportunity of visibility on the international stage and, as such, promoted its legitimacy as a future government of Namibia. SWAPO, therefore, had more of a stake in the negotiations especially since its preference for an outcome was closer to that of the WCG than was South Africa's. However, SWAPO's acceptance of the initiative was also a result of the position taken by the FLS.

Acceptance of the Western initiative by the FLS was of vital importance for SWAPO participation and for WCG credibility within the United Nations. This was recognised by the WCG from the start of the initiative.[15] The WCG initiative, in fact, had the full support of the FLS and Nigeria.[16] Moreover, as part of Young's consultations with other third parties in the conflict in February 1977, he consulted UN representatives from African and non-aligned members, regarding the course of action which was required on Namibia. According to McHenry, these representatives stated that it was necessary to enter some kind of discussions with the SAG, and that the Western members of the Security Council had to do it because they were "the only ones to maintain communication with both groups".[17]

FLS acceptance of the initiative was a continuation of a policy that placed a priority on diplomatic means to solve the problems of southern Africa. The costs to these states of continued South African occupation of Namibia was higher than that for South Africa itself and for SWAPO. This was especially the case for Angola and Zambia, since Namibia was and is used by South Africa as a springboard for continued cross-border raids and intervention. The destabilisation of Angola, both directly and through the South African surrogate, UNITA, cost the Angolan government $7.5 billion in 1982. The estimated cost to South Africa of the occupation of Namibia for the same year amounted to R734 million.[18]

This suggests that acceptance of the WCG initiative was due to the characteristics of the third party itself, and the fact that for SWAPO and the FLS a negotiated solution to Namibia would have meant a less costly means of achieving independence. The collective nature of the initiative meant that South Africa was faced with a united Western coalition, as occurred later in the negotiations. The collective nature of the initiative also contributed to the credibility of the group with the FLS since they could be seen to have more leverage with the SAG deriving from the extensive relationship of the countries involved. Having this relationship meant that they could carry out the function of communications between the parties and could, moreover, influence the SAG into concessions. This was comparable to Dr. Kissinger's acceptance as intermediary in the Arab–Israeli conflict, where the main factor contributing to his acceptance by the governments of Egypt and Syria was the fact that the United States was Israel's major ally and as such could influence it into concessions (Touval, 1982). Western governments with close ties to the SAG have been seen by African leaders as the only parties having leverage on South Africa.

This further suggests that, while the focal parties in the conflict, namely the SAG and SWAPO, reluctantly accepted the initiative and took part in the negotiations while pursuing alternative strategies, the negotiation process and the involvement of the WCG was of importance to the FLS and to the WCG itself, since its members had specific interests both in the conflict itself and in occupying the intermediary role at that specific time in April 1977.

The Tactics of the WCG

The WCG was involved in the negotiations over Namibia throughout the period from April 1977 until the suspension of the negotiations in 1985. After more than a year of active negotiations, mainly through bilateral contacts involving South Africa, SWAPO and the FLS, agreement was reached which shortly afterwards foundered on disagreements regarding implementation. The negotiations finally broke down, however, over issues relating to an overlapping conflict. A review of the tactics adopted by the WCG will illustrate that it adopted behaviour which fell predominantly within the bargaining sector of our spectrum of third-party activity.

The first characteristic identified in Table 6.1 as illustrating bargaining behaviour by the third party stated that the third party intervenes with a commitment to a specific outcome to the conflict. The WCG started the negotiations with a commitment to the implementation of SCR 385 whereby it presented the SAG with the alternative of making moves towards this or facing "strong action" from the five governments. The WCG also had a specific framework for the settlement process. It broadly adhered to the UN-defined framework for Namibian independence ensuring that the proposals put forward to the parties provided for a specific UN role during the transition period and elections leading to the formation of a constituent assembly which would devise a constitution for an independent Namibia. (The proposals formed the basis of the UN secretary general's proposals for implementation accepted by the Security Council in Resolution 435 of 29 September 1978.[19]) The WCG was totally responsible for the drawing up of substantive proposals and had these formulated prior to meeting the parties.[20] It presented these to the parties, who, in turn, attempted to negotiate with the WCG over the details of the proposals.[21] This occurred over the details of the transition arrangements including the nature of the interim authority prior to the elections; the numbers and location of UN personnel and South African residual forces; and the monitoring of South African and SWAPO bases during the transition and election periods. This illustrates that, from the start of the initiative, the WCG had a commitment to a specific outcome to the conflict, functioned within a predetermined framework for the settlement process and was wholly responsible for the formulation of proposals, the details of which became issues of bargaining between the parties and the third party.

Adherence to the UN framework changed when the Reagan administration became involved in the group. This administration entered the negotiations with a declared preference for arriving at a constitution for Namibia prior to the holding of elections (that is, a "Lancaster House model" for Namibian independence). The new administration let its preference for such an arrangement be known at the United Nations when the new U.S. ambassador, Jean Kirkpatrick, privately circulated a document at the United Nations entitled "Proposed Declaration of Intent" which called for "broad guidelines for the constitutional future of the territory".[22] This preference for a Zimbabwe model for Namibian independence was rejected by the FLS, SWAPO and the other four members of the WCG. The WCG did, however, accommodate the U.S. position on this issue by declaring that "possibilities for strengthening the existing plan existed".[23] This again illustrates the third party having their own position clearly specified in the negotiations, regardless of the position taken by the protagonists themselves.

A major feature of the WCG initiative was that the bargaining process between the WCG and the adversaries dominated the entire process. This occurred with the SAG over the transition arrangements, where the SAG preferred a Turnhalle-based interim authority and the WCG rejected this because it was based on the ethnic division of the population. It also occurred with SWAPO over the issue of Walvis Bay. When the WCG presented its first set of proposals to the parties in October 1977, it suggested that the issue of Walvis Bay be deferred to negotiations after independence. SWAPO, on the other hand, insisted that the WCG make a specific pronouncement on this issue, proclaiming the port as an integral part of Namibia. The WCG, despite this insistence by SWAPO, presented their proposals to the Ninth Special Session on Namibia as Security Council Document S/12632 on 10 April 1978. SWAPO rejected these proposals and postponed the negotiations indefinitely following the South African raid on Cassinga on 4 April 1978. One of the factors that led to SWAPO's eventual acceptance of the proposals in July 1978 was the offer made by the WCG that they would support a Security Council Resolution on Walvis Bay stating that it was an integral part of Namibia.[24] Following this acceptance from SWAPO, the Western five submitted their proposals to the Security Council which were accepted as Resolution 431. A second resolution on Walvis Bay was passed on the same day proclaiming that Walvis Bay was an integral part of Namibia.

One of the main bargaining tactics used by the WCG was that of issue linkage. This may be considered in terms of the third party's perceptions of the protagonist's high-priority goals, and making the attainment of these conditional upon a protagonist's acceptance of other seemingly lesser goals. This tactic was in evidence at the Mondale–Vorster meeting in Vienna in May 1977. Mondale presented the WCG's position on the negotiations over Namibia, but issues that were equally under discussion were those of Rhodesia and majority rule in South Africa itself, the last being the issue of highest value to the SAG. According to Mondale's statement, the message to Vorster was that "progress on all three categories"[25] was needed for improved U.S.–SAG relations.

The use of issue-linkage as a bargaining tactic has been most prevalent in the Reagan administration's involvement in the WCG. This introduced the linkage of Cuban troop withdrawal from Angola to Namibian independence, a clear example of a third party using its role as intermediary to obtain concessions towards its own commitment to a specific issue. A major difference between the Reagan administration's approach and that of the previous U.S. government was the priority now being given to the "cold war",[26] a change that had major ramifications on the conduct of the negotiations over Namibia and the functioning of the WCG as a coalition. Dr. Chester Crocker introduced the linkage of the Namibian settlement process to the presence of Cuban troops in Angola in February 1981 in a State Department memorandum later leaked to the *New York Times*. This stated that "African leaders would have no basis for resisting the Angola–Namibia linkage once they are made to realise that they can only get a Namibia settlement through us and that we are serious about getting such a settlement".[27] The emphasis had moved from Namibia to an overlapping conflict, namely that in Angola. The Reagan government sought the removal of the Cuban troops as well as the inclusion of UNITA in an Angolan government. The linkage precondition was taken up by the SAG as soon as it was introduced to the negotiations by Chester Crocker in April 1981 on his first visit to Angola and remained as a precondition for Namibian independence when all other outstanding issues in the negotiations were resolved.[28] The linkage issue became the main stumbling block in the negotiations, despite the fact that this was rejected by the other four governments in the WCG. This will be further discussed in considering the impact of a coalition on the functioning of the WCG.

The use of threat and reward tactics has also been evident in the functioning of the WCG. One of the main threat tactics used by the WCG against the SAG at the start of the initiative was the threat of withdrawal of veto at the Security Council in response to sanctions resolutions. This was used by the WCG at least three times until the presentation of their proposals to the United Nations in April 1978. As stated earlier, the initiative started with a warning to the SAG that in the absence of a move towards an internationally acceptable settlement the five would have to take the "necessary measures". The initial threat was aimed at securing the SAG's participation in the negotiation process. The threat of sanctions was again repeated by the WCG during their talks with the SAG in April 1977—a threat aimed at persuading the SAG to abandon the Turnhalle process. At the end of these talks, the SAG agreed to forego implementation of the Turnhalle proposals. According to Secretary of State Vance, the South African change of position was due to the threat of sanctions made by the WCG. He states, "The South Africans' changed attitude was, in the judgement of many, due to the united Western assertion that we would no longer prevent sanctions unless they began seriously negotiating for Namibian independence under international supervision" (Vance, 1983, p. 277). It has been suggested that the SAG took note of these threats and participated in the process because of this threat (Geldenhuys, 1985). However, when the test of implementation came in October 1978 (when the WCG contemplated sanctions in response to Botha's decision to implement the internal settlement process by holding elections) the five were not willing to do so. Instead, President Carter took the less costly option of offering the SAG better relations if it continued taking part in the negotiations. This was, in other words, a promise of a reward.[29]

While the Carter administration (especially in the first year of its holding office) used the extensive U.S. relationship with South Africa to force the SAG into agreeing to abandon the Turnhalle process for an internationally recognisable process, the Reagan administration was using the same resources in order to reward the SAG as part of its policy of "constructive engagement",[30] such reward being implemented unconditionally.[31] This was manifest in major promotion of military cooperation between the two countries, coupled with consistent diplomatic support for the SAG at the United Nations.[32]

Third parties also use the leverage that other third parties (including allies) can bring to the main parties in conflict. The WCG used the leverage of the FLS in its dealings with SWAPO. The FLS, in fact, often acted as intermediaries between the WCG and SWAPO, underlining the fact that the WCG itself was another negotiator in the multilateral negotiation system. This is also a reflection of a predominant feature of multilateral negotiation systems whereby one or more of the negotiators at different time points of the negotiations act as intermediaries to resolve a dispute between other negotiators (Stenelo, 1972). Following the Cassinga raid in May 1978, SWAPO postponed the negotiations with the WCG indefinitely. Ambassador McHenry held bilateral talks with President Neto of Angola in order to resume the negotiations. The main issues of contention between the WCG and SWAPO concerned the status of Walvis Bay and the location of the residual South African force during the transition period. President Nyerere proposed a compromise: a Security Council resolution supporting SWAPO's claim that Walvis Bay was an integral part of Namibia although not endorsing its legal position. Nyerere urged the WCG to persuade South Africa on the location of its troops and persuaded SWAPO to meet once again with the WCG to resolve the outstanding issues.[33] As pointed out earlier, SWAPO accepted the Western proposals after receiving assurances from the WCG that they intended accepting President Nyerere's proposal on Walvis Bay. As Douglas (1972) and Wall (1981) have pointed out, the third party may bring ultimata from allies to the parties which include tacit threats, promises, or rewards. While the WCG did not specifically present to SWAPO ultimata from the FLS, it is clear that the FLS were used as a pressure route to SWAPO, while the FLS often acted as intermediary between SWAPO and the WCG on substantive issues during the negotiations. Moreover, a third party's ability to persuade a protagonist is enhanced when the proposals suggested actually come from an important ally, as, for example, the proposal for the demilitarised zone on the Namibia–Angola border, which came from President Neto in 1979.[34]

The above sections have illustrated the predominance of bargaining behaviour by the WCG and the directive nature of the initiative. The following sections provide an analysis of the WCG tactics, using the framework presented in Table 6.1. They will include consideration of the factors that may influence third-party behaviour, including (in the present case-study) the coalition situation.

ANALYSIS OF THE WCG TACTICS

This section illustrates the way in which factors shown in Table 6.2 may explain the tactics adopted by the Western Contact Group. As shown in the previous section, these fell predominantly within the bargaining sector of the spectrum of third-party behaviour, especially in the commitment of the WCG to specific outcomes to the conflict, the introduction to the negotiations of issues salient to members of the WCG, and the use of bargaining tactics in order to gain such goals.

The WCG started the initiative with a stated commitment to an outcome and a framework for the settlement process. The outcome sought had to be one that was internationally recognisable, which meant that the framework had to be based on SCR 385 which outlined the UN framework for Namibian independence. The WCG also made the decision to back up this commitment with the threat to the SAG of impending sanctions if it did not forego implementation of the internal settlement and agree to work towards a settlement based on SCR 385. The WCG succeeded in persuading the SAG to take part in the negotiations; but, when the latter decided to hold internal elections scheduled for December 1978 under Turnhalle, sanctions were considered but were not presented to the SAG. Instead, the WCG merely sought South Africa's continued participation in the negotiations. There was, moreover, no longer pressure on the SAG to forego increasing moves towards an internal settlement. Major changes occurred in the functioning of the WCG from January 1981 when the

Reagan administration came to power. These included the introduction of the issue of a constitution prior to an election (a major departure from the previous approach and SCR 435), and the linkage of Namibian independence to the withdrawal of Cuban troops from Angola.

The factors outlined in Table 6.1 are dealt with separately. This does not, however, imply that they act separately or in an individual manner. They are, in fact, interlinked, having a modifying influence on each other. For example, the third party's preferred outcome is modified by its perception of its influence potential, which in turn is modified by feedback from the negotiation system. Moreover, discussing the impact of each factor separately does not imply that the WCG itself (or any other third party) considers each factor in a concerted manner prior to making its tactical choice. The third party cannot be assumed to have perfect information and accurate perception of the consequences of each action. It can, however, be assumed that these factors act in an interlinked manner in influencing a third party's tactical decisions.

The Conflict Characteristics

Conflict characteristics form the background to the negotiation process and may change during any third party's involvement in the conflict. This is especially the case in a long drawn out conflict such as that over Namibia. While the broad issues remained constant, the detailed issues changed during the negotiations and the WCG had to respond. Changes ranged from the relationship of the UN special representative to the South African administrator general during the transition period, to the monitoring by UNTAG forces of South African and SWAPO bases. Finally, they included the question of the rights of the white minority after independence and, ultimately, the linkage issue.

Apart from the issues in conflict, the other important characteristic influencing the WCG's tactical decisions was the fact that the conflict also involved third parties such as the FLS and Nigeria as patrons. Hence, the main opposition against the South African occupation apart from SWAPO's guerilla struggle was manifest at the United Nations where increasing calls for sanctions were made prior to the intervention of the WCG and throughout functioning. This had an impact on the WCG's initial choice of the intermediary role as well as on its choice of tactics. It meant that the Western five sought legitimacy for their initiative at the United Nations. This is evidenced by the fact that the five's proposals ensured a role for the United Nations during the first part of the initiative, on UN acceptance of the process.[35]

The fact that the conflict over Namibia overlapped with others in the region also had an impact on WCG tactics. Members overlapped conflicts.

This was especially relevant in the case of the British government, which had an immediate concern in the Rhodesia/Zimbabwe settlement process, and the Reagan administration, whose primary interest lay in the Angolan situation.

The Negotiation System

The negotiation system provides a feedback influence on a third party's choice of tactics so that it may adjust proposals put forward and tactics used, in response to this continuous input.

At the inter-party level in Namibia, both parties were pursuing a dual-track strategy whereby they took part in the negotiations while maintaining original strategies. The WCG recognised that the internal process was South Africa's preferred option. This had an impact on the WCG's tactics in its interaction with the SAG, reflected in the WCG's consistent use of pressure during the first year of negotiations. When the WCG faced the test of implementing its threat of sanctions in 1978, these were not applied, with the consequence that the SAG maintained its preference for an internal settlement. It was also reflected in the WCG's concessions to the SAG after 1981, with the Reagan administration's concessions of proposing the adoption of a constitution prior to an election.

Adjustment of tactics in response to feedback from the inter-party level and the party–patron level of the negotiation system was also evident in the bargaining process between the WCG and the parties on specific issues in the negotiations. The SAG sought concessions from the WCG on arrangements for the transition period, and SWAPO did so on the location of the residual South African presence and the status of Walvis Bay. Change in the position of the WCG on these issues (more clearly reflected in the WCG's acceptance of President Nyerere's compromise proposal on Walvis Bay) reflects the feedback influence from the negotiation system and the bargaining posture taken by the parties on the third party's adjustment of tactics.

Such adjustment of tactics in response to the negotiation system was especially evident when the proposal for a constitution before an election was introduced by the incoming Reagan administration. This proposal was offered to the SAG in April 1981 and prompted immediate rejection by the FLS and SWAPO. Such rejection of a "Zimbabwe Model" for Namibia led to a modification of this stance to the more limited constitutional guarantees for the white minority prior to an election. The WCG also readjusted its position on the proposal for a dual vote system for Namibia, based on the West German model of proportional representation. This was abandoned in response to opposition from SWAPO and the FLS.[36]

Third-Party Preference Ordering of Outcomes

As suggested in the analytic framework, a third party's conflict-related and process-related interests have a modifying influence on their preferred outcomes to the conflict. It was also emphasised that these may change in response to the dynamic conditions of the conflict.

The WCG entered the negotiations with a commitment to a particular outcome to the conflict and a framework for the settlement process, based on UN SCR 385. This was essential for the credibility of the Western initiative and for its acceptance by the FLS and SWAPO. This preference was evident in the WCG's proposals, which ensured a role for the United Nations in the transition period and in the supervision of elections leading to the formation of a constituent assembly. This preference also led to the WCG's rejection of the Turnhalle process for interim arrangements.[37]

A major factor that led to changes in the conduct of the negotiations by the group was the new rank-ordering of conflict-related interests of the incoming Reagan administration. The emphasis was now on U.S. relations with South Africa, whereas the Carter administration had emphasised relations with important African countries, including the FLS and Nigeria.[38] The new rank-ordering of interests had a modifying influence on the Reagan administration's preference for a constitution to be devised for Namibia prior to the holding of elections. The administration sought changes in Resolution 435 expressing a preference for a Zimbabwe-style model for Namibian independence. This was a major departure from the previous approach as outlined in Resolution 435 which was based on the WCG's original proposals. As indicated above, the negotiation system had an impact on the change in this preference, as did the intra-coalition situation. Another change was the Reagan administration's preference for a linkage of a Namibia settlement to the withdrawal of Cuban troops from Angola and the inclusion of UNITA in an Angolan government. This preference was due to a changed rank-ordering of interests based on the primacy of the "cold war" as a general approach to foreign policy. The overlapping conflict in Angola became the top interest for the new administration. Linkage became a priority and led to eventual open military support for UNITA, following the repeal of the Clark Amendment.[39]

The relationship between third-party conflict-related interests, preference sets, and tactics is also illustrated by the activities of the Federal Republic of Germany in the negotiations. The main interest for the FRG continued to be the presence in Namibia of an 18,000-strong German community, of whom 6,400 were West German citizens. This interest contributed to the FRG government originally agreeing to participate in the Western initiative.[40] It also explained the activism of the West German negotiators, including the foreign minister, Hans Dietrich Genscher, in the formulation of the proposal of an electoral system for Namibia based on the West German model and support for the proposal of a Bill of Rights to replace the Reagan administration's preference for a full constitution prior to an election.[41] The German community as a major conflict-related interest for the West German government is also evident in that it continued to maintain high-level contacts with SWAPO. Sam Nujoma was officially invited to Bonn in June 1982 by the foreign minister, who also attempted to act as intermediary between Nujoma and Chester Crocker in arranging a meeting between the two during Nujoma's visit. The foreign minister also emphasised the importance of developing the relationship between the German community and SWAPO. The aim of this policy was to ensure a level of trust between a future SWAPO government and the German community. Thus, the foreign ministry arranged a meeting between SWAPO and the IG,[42] the main German-speaking interest group in Namibia, at the Geneva Pre-Implementation Meeting in 1981 and again in 1983 when an IG delegation visited Harare.

Third-Party Influence Potential

A third party's ordering of preferred outcomes is also modified by its resources or "influence potential". As in any negotiation system, the resources of the negotiators form an important part of their bargaining positions. A third party's influence potential is dependent on the value attached to its resources by the protagonists and its willingness to use them. A third party may use its resources in an attempt to change the parties' evaluation of the benefits of compliance, as opposed to the costs of non-compliance.

The WCG relied mainly on its extensive relationship with South Africa and on the fact that three members of the group had the resource of the veto at the Security Council. During the first year of the negotiations, the WCG threatened the SAG with the withdrawal of the customary veto at the Security Council in response to sanctions resolutions if compliance in the international negotiations was not forthcoming. The SAG took note of these threats by agreeing to take part in the negotiations, despite the fact that it did not abandon its plans for the internal settlement. As Geldenhuys points out, "while there might have been some element of 'bluff calling' in South Africa's conduct, it is unlikely that Pretoria always dismissed sanctions talk as Western sabre-rattling".[43] The fact that the WCG relied heavily on the joint Western initiative added to its influence with the SAG. The joint Western initiative meant that greater pressure could be brought to bear against the SAG, which could not rely on divisions within the Western camp on the issue of sanctions.[44] The credibility of the Western threat was, however, completely diminished when the test of implementation came in October 1978 and the attempt to gain South Africa's cancellation of the internal elections scheduled for December 1978 was unsuccessful.

The fact that the Reagan administration did not make reward conditional has prompted suggestions that the policy of "constructive engagement" is collusion with the SAG rather than a means of acquiring influence with the Pretoria regime. The fact that the SAG continued its policy of carrying out major SADF operations into Angola while the U.S. administration vetoed condemnation of such action at the Security Council seems to corroborate this interpretation of constructive engagement.[45]

Constituency Input

While the constituencies of the five did attempt to have an input into the tactical choice decisions of the WCG, the impact of this on the actual decisions made is not easily identified.

Groups within West Germany which had direct links to the German community in Namibia attempted to influence the FRG government during the negotiations. The pro-Democratic Turnhalle Alliance (DTA) lobby in West Germany condemned the position of the FRG government in insisting on UN-supervised elections, which such organisations saw as a clear path to SWAPO victory in Namibia and a "selling out" of the German community. This position was mainly taken by the pro-DTA Christian Social Union (CSU). Despite the fact that the CSU formed a coalition government with the CDU in 1982, there was continuity in approach given that Herr Genscher, as leader of the Federal Party, maintained his position as foreign minister. Franz-Josef Strauss, leader of the CSU, was opposed to Genscher's preference for SCR 435 as a basis for Namibian independence and to Genscher's promotion of relations between SWAPO and the German community in Namibia. He also demanded full recognition and support for the DTA, to which his party contributed substantial funding, and the opening of a German consulate in Windhoek.[46] While this constituency does not seem to have had an impact on the overall approach, it may have been influential in West German activism on the formulation of constitutional guarantees for the white minority to supplement SCR 435.

During the negotiations, the British Anti-Apartheid Movement attempted to change the stance taken by the WCG on the issue of Walvis Bay.[47] The final decision taken by the WCG on this issue, however, seems to have been more a result of President Nyerere's suggestion of a compromise resolution at the United Nations than a result of constituency pressure.

Constituency pressure may also come from the negotiator's government "back home". This was an important factor in Dr. Crocker's conduct of the negotiations, where White House influence ensured the maintenance of the linkage issue as an overriding factor in the negotiations.[48]

The Intra-Coalition Situation

The relationships within a coalition intermediary are another important input into the tactical decisions made by a coalition third party and its members. The main intra-coalition factors to consider are the level of cohesion within the coalition; the distribution of influence potential; and the degree of communication and consultation among the members. All three factors changed during the WCG's involvement in Namibia.

The level of cohesion in the WCG was high at the start of the initiative. There was general agreement on the preferred outcome and on the tactics used. All five agreed on the necessity of an internationally recognised outcome and were opposed to the Turnhalle process. They also shared opposition to mandatory economic sanctions against the Pretoria regime. According to Ambassador McHenry, there were no significant disagreements on the proposals put forward during the negotiations when he was involved.[49] This is also reflected in the fact that all five supported Security Council Resolution 418 imposing the arms embargo against South Africa and the resolution condemning the South African raid on Cassinga in May 1978 at a crucial stage in the negotiations. Another indication of cohesion was that the individual participants' interests seem to have been accommodated by the collective group when these arose. When, for example, the WCG was attempting to gain agreement from SWAPO on the interim arrangements in 1977, Dr. David Owen insisted, according to Cyrus Vance's account, that the WCG should not wait until they had resolved all SWAPO's problems and that it should present the parties with a comprehensive list of proposals. According to Vance, Dr. Owen was "deeply concerned with the interaction of the Rhodesia and Namibian negotiations. The Contact Group, he argued, should not push the Namibian negotiations with South Africa so hard that Pretoria withdrew from the process. If they did the Western powers would have no means for avoiding sanctions and our strategy for dealing with the more urgent Rhodesia issue could be damaged" (Vance, 1983, p. 283). The fact that the WCG presented their proposals to the parties as early as October 1977, before agreement was reached, seems to indicate that Owen's considerations were accommodated by the WCG. In this case, the conflict-related interest of one of the participants of the coalition had an impact on the timing of the presentation of proposals to the parties.

Division within the WCG was at its highest after the Reagan administration joined the negotiations. The linkage issue was not endorsed by the other four members of the WCG, who publicly dissociated themselves from the issue despite their agreement to make a reference to it in an official WCG document in July 1982. The fact that there was no specific mention of the issue of Cuban withdrawal from Angola, but a reference to "other regional issues"[50] may indicate attempts within the

WCG to find a compromise formula between the U.S. stance on this and the position taken by the other four. Despite this cursory reference to the linkage issue, however, U.S. negotiators were still the only participants of the WCG involved in bilateral negotiations with the governments of Angola and South Africa. The linkage issue was, in fact, the main factor which led to French withdrawal from the WCG in December 1983.[51] There was also disagreement with the United States on the issue of a Lancaster House model for Namibian independence. This was resolved by "strengthening" Resolution 435 in proposals for constitutional guarantees for the white minority.

Division within the WCG at this stage of the negotiations was clearly apparent at the United Nations. The launch by the SADF of "Operation Protea", on 25 August 1981, brought immediate condemnation at the Security Council, which was vetoed by the United States. The action was, however, condemned by the other four members of the WCG.[52] Such differences in reaction to South African actions between the European members of the WCG and the United States meant that condemnation of South African policies at the United Nations by the European members of the WCG was done on behalf of the EEC and not the WCG. This was apparent during the September 1981 General Assembly debate on Namibia, when Sir Anthony Parsons, U.K. ambassador to the United Nations, speaking on behalf of the EEC, condemned South Africa for its policies inside Namibia.[53]

Division over the linkage issue led to the other members of the WCG acting as intermediaries between the U.S. negotiators and the Angolan government and SWAPO. Moreover, the FLS, specifically Angola, attempted to use the other four members of the WCG to persuade the Reagan administration to abandon linkage as a condition for Namibian independence.

The distribution of influence also had an impact on the choice of tactics by the WCG and changed during the WCG's involvement in the conflict. (This was defined earlier as "Who has what in relation to whom".) At the start of the initiative, the close relationship which was built up between Andrew Young and Don McHenry with Angola's President Neto was of vital importance to the functioning of the WCG and continued cooperation from the FLS. According to the former British ambassador to South Africa, Sir David Scott, the United States (that is, Don McHenry) was the dominant member among the New York WCG. Among the ambassadors in Pretoria, on the other hand, he had greater access to the SAG.[54]

Contact Group sessions with the SAG were still carried out collectively. This changed with the departure of Ambassador McHenry as the main negotiator and the coming to power in Britain of the Conservative government in 1979. The latter became the main member in the WCG to conduct communication with the SAG. The task of communicating the

"Demilitarized Zone proposals" to the SAG was carried out by the British representative at the United Nations, Sir James Murray. This function returned to the U.S. negotiators after President Reagan's accession to power. Improved relations between the new U.S. administration and the SAG, under the policy of constructive engagement, contributed to this. The European members, on the other hand, conducted communications with SWAPO and the FLS.

The degree of communication and consultation between the members of the WCG also changed in the latter phase of its involvement. During the first phase of the initiative, the WCG seems to have acted collectively in its interaction with the conflict system. Proposals were collectively formulated and members consulted if an initiative was taken. However, difficulties in terms of coordination of tactics must have also arisen, as exemplified by Herr Genscher's threat of the inevitability of sanctions at the February 1978 "proximity talks", which led to Foreign Minister Pik Botha withdrawing.[55] The high level of consultation that the WCG started with, however, was greatly diminished in the latter phases of its activity. The U.S. administration introduced new issues to the negotiations including the constitutional proposals and the linkage issue prior to gaining agreement from the other four members of the WCG. Compared to earlier procedures, this was a major departure from previous practice.

Analysis of intra-coalition factors, including the level of cohesion within the WCG, the distribution of influence and the level of consultation among the coalition members, as well as the changes in all three which occurred during the group's involvement, has shown that the coalition structure has an impact on the interactive process between a third party and a conflict system. While the participants of the WCG may have different rank-orderings of interests, the coalition exerted a modifying influence on each member's preferences as well as on their resources. Moreover, the negotiation system itself exerted a feedback influence on relationships within the coalition. As seen above, the WCG functioned less as a coalition once differences in preferences for outcomes arose between the members. A major impact was that some members of the WCG acted as intermediaries between the protagonists and a partner in the coalition.

CONCLUSION

The aim of this chapter has been, first, to illustrate the range of tactics used by an interested third party acting as intermediary; and, second, to indicate factors that may influence such a third party's tactical decisions during its interaction with the conflict system. Given the coalition nature of the WCG, the impact of the coalition structure on the functioning of the WCG was also investigated.

As the outline of the WCG tactics illustrates, these fell mainly in the bargaining sector of the spectrum of third-party tactics. This underlines the assumption which formed the basis of the analytic framework, that an *interested* third party may be considered as forming part of a multilateral negotiation system, with the third party being one of the negotiators. The assumption focusses attention on the third party's own decision-making process whereby interests, preferences for outcomes, bargaining positions on specific issues and resources are factors to consider as influencing choice of tactics. Moreover, the framework also emphasises the interactive and dynamic nature of the negotiation process involving the interested intermediary by including the negotiation system as a feedback factor on the third party's choice of tactics.

Inclusion of the intra-coalition situation as a factor influencing third-party choice of tactics showed that while the members of the WCG were individual bargainers in their own right, relations within the coalition had an impact on the pattern of interaction with the conflict system.

While the analysis on the WCG's conduct of the negotiations has pointed to several factors as being influential in an interested third party's choice of tactics, it has also pointed to problems of assuming a one-to-one relationship between each of the factors suggested and the tactics adopted by the third party. Given the interactive nature of the process, however, it is possible to conclude that these factors jointly influence third-party behaviour at any specific time during its interaction with the conflict system.

NOTES

1. Wall (1981, p. 175) suggests relating third-party behaviour to the "negotiation context"; for an emphasis on the "exchange of information" in the negotiation process see Gulliver (1979).

2. Rubin (1981) provides a comparison of "individual representative" and "collective" third-party roles.

3. Good background sources are Dugard (1973), Green et al. (1981) and Rocha (1984).

4. Kreisburg labels other interested parties in a conflict—such as allies, constituencies and audiences—as "non-focal" parties. See Kreisburg (1982).

5. See Serfontein (1976) and Totemeyer and Seiler (1980).

6. Detailed historic outlines of the Namibia negotiations is found in C. Legum (Ed.), *Africa Contemporary Record* (New York/London: Africana Publishing) [hereafter *ACR*], 1975–76, and Zartman (1985).

7. Interview with Ambassador Rudiger von Wechmar (London, 10 December 1986).

8. The EEC conveyed their views to the South African Government in a demarch sent to Pretoria on 7 February 1977. Mr. Ted Rowlands, minister of state

at the Foreign and Commonwealth Office, stated to the International Conference on Rhodesia and Namibia, held at Maputo on 17 May 1977, that this was sent to the SAG "because of reports that some form of internal self-government might shortly be established in Namibia, based on the recommendations of the Turnhalle Conference", in *European Political Cooperation* (Bonn: FRG Press and Information Office, 1982, p. 105).

9. Statement by the Canadian secretary for external affairs, Don Jamieson, to the General Assembly, Ninth Special Session on Namibia (reprinted in U.S. Department of State Bulletin, Vol. 78, No. 2015, p. 50).

10. Statement by Ambassador Don McHenry before the House Sub-Committee on Africa, 7 May 1979 (reprinted in U.S. Department of State Bulletin, Vol. 79, No. 2031, p. 57).

11. Interview with Ambassador McHenry on "Voice of America", 18 November 1977, quoted in C. Legum, *The Western Crisis Over Southern Africa* (New York/London: Africana Publishing, 1979), p. 16.

12. International Defence and Aid Fund, "Apartheid's Army in Namibia", *Fact Paper on Southern Africa, No. 10* (London), 1982, pp. 16–34. SWATF was established in August 1980.

13. South African estimates of SWAPO incidents given in *Strategic Review* (Pretoria: Institute for Strategic Studies, University of Pretoria), June 1985, quoted in Cawthra (1986).

14. *New Statesman*, 22 August 1980.

15. Ambassador McHenry stated that a "successful undertaking must involve the cooperation of the Front Line States and Nigeria in helping with the negotiation process", May 1979 (reprinted in U.S. Department of State Bulletin, Vol. 79, No. 2031, p. 57).

16. President Kaunda called on the Carter administration to "take the lead" to solve the problems of Rhodesia, Namibia and South Africa (*New York Times*, 6 February 1977, 5:1). General Obasanjo of Nigeria stated (in February 1977) following a meeting with Ambassador Young, "generally we agreed on what should be done" (in Legum, *The Western Crisis*, p. 22).

17. Ambassador McHenry, US–UN Press Release, No. 32, 1 May 1978.

18. United Nations, Council for Namibia, *The Military Situation in and Relating to Namibia*, 1983, p. 8.

19. The Western proposals are printed as a Security Council Document S/12636, 10 April 1978.

20. Interview with Sir David Scott (London, 27 November 1986).

21. Zartman illustrates the process of "formula" and "detail" in the Namibia negotiations in Zartman (1985), pp. 172–211.

22. C. Legum, *ACR*, 1981–82, p. A14.

23. *The Guardian*, 24 April 1981.

24. SWAPO Department of Information and Publicity, *To Be Born a Nation* (London: Zed Press, 1981), p. 242.

25. Vice President Mondale referred to "majority rule for Rhodesia and Namibia and a progressive transformation of South African society to the same end" (*ACR*, 1976–77).

26. For the Reagan Administration's emphasis on the cold war see Halliday (1984).

27. B. Dudes. "The United States and Africa: The Reagan Difference, *ACR*, 1981–82, p. 156.

28. On 17 June 1982, speaking at the Oshivello military base in Namibia, Mr. P. W. Botha stated that the Western plan for a settlement would only be accepted by his government on condition that Cuban troops leave Angola at the same time as South African forces moved to bases in Angola (*The Times*, 18 June 1982).

29. For an account of the foreign secretaries' visit to Pretoria at this stage of the negotiations see *The Times*, 12 October 1978, p. 1h; 16 October 1978, p. 1b; 18 October 1978, p. 8e.

30. The policy of "constructive engagement" was originally adopted by the Nixon administration and is supported by President Reagan's assistant secretary of state for African affairs, Dr. Chester Crocker (see Crocker, 1980, pp. 223–241).

31. For a critique of constructive engagement see Coker (1982, pp. 223–241).

32. Examples of the Reagan administration's military cooperation with South Africa are provided in B. Dudes, "The United States in Africa", *ACR*, 1981–82, p. A160; and E. Brown, *ACR*, 1982–83, p. A278.

33. This is according to an account of the negotiations given by President Carter's secretary of state, Cyrus Vance (in Vance, 1983).

34. President Neto of Angola suggested a demilitarised zone of 30 miles on either side of the Namibia–Angola border in response to South African demands that SWAPO bases in Angola be monitored by the UN peacekeeping forces of UNTAG.

35. One of the main objectives of the New York Contact Group was to gain acceptance of the Western proposals in the form of a Security Council resolution (interview with Ambassador Rudiger von Wechmar, London, 10 December 1986).

36. See account of negotiations over the dual vote issue in C. Legum, *ACR*, 1981–82, p. A27.

37. In Namibia, opposition to the participation in the negotiations and acceptance of the Western proposals had already started in 1977 with the split in the National Party and the departures of Dick Mudge to form the Republic Party. The leaders of the National Party formed Aktur (the Action Front for the Retention of Turnhalle Principles) which was opposed to the reform of apartheid laws in Namibia.

38. The Carter administration recognised Black Nationalism as a paramount force in southern Africa and placed high priority on U.S. relations with important African countries such as the Front Line States and Nigeria. See Study Commission on United States Policy Toward Southern Africa, *South Africa: Time Running Out* (Berkeley and Los Angeles: University of California Press, 1981, p. 356); and Young (1980).

39. The Reagan administration sought to repeal the Clark Amendment, which forbade military aid to Angolan rebel movements without congressional approval. This took place in 1985, resulting in the suspension of negotiations by the Angolan government.

40. The presence of the German community was an important interest for the Federal Republic of Germany. See C. Hill, "French and West German Relations with South Africa", in Barber (1983), pp. 105–118.

41. C. Legum, *ACR*, 1981–82, p. A26.

42. IG: Interessengemeinschaft Deutsch prachiger Sudwester (Common Interest Association of German Speaking South West Africans).

43. Geldenhuys (1984), p. 223.

44. Interview with Ambassador McHenry (Washington, D.C., 11 June 1986).

45. D. McHenry, "New Africa", October 1981; quoted in Rocha (1984), p. 132.

46. R. Hofmeier, "West Germany's Policy in Africa", *ACR*, 1983–84, p. A235.

47. The chairperson of the British Anti-Apartheid Movement, Mr. Robert Hughs, MP, stated in a letter to Dr. David Owen, "We are strongly of the opinion that Britain should insist that the Western proposals should be amended to include Walvis Bay within Namibia" (quoted in *Africa Confidential*, Vol. 19, No. 11, 26 May 1978, p. 8).

48. White House influence on the negotiations was ensured throughout Dr. Crocker's involvement in the negotiations, firstly by the inclusion in the negotiations of William Clark, and then of Vernon Walters and Frank Wisner, both of the National Security Council.

49. Interview with Ambassador McHenry, 11 June 1986.

50. *Financial Times*, 15 July 1982.

51. In April 1983, the French foreign minister, M. Claude Cheysson, speaking at the International Conference on Solidarity with the People of Namibia in Paris, stated that the Contact Group had "ended its labours" and condemned the U.S. administration for its position on the linkage issue; see C. Legum, "The South African Crisis", *ACR*, 1982–83, p. A30. In December 1983, M. Cheysson stated that his government was withdrawing from the Contact Group and suggested that it should be "left dormant in the absence of any ability to exercise honestly the mandate confided to it"; quoted by C. Legum, "The Continuing Crisis in Southern Africa", *ACR*, 1983–84, p. A43.

52. Comparison of speeches at the Security Council in response to South African incursion into Angola. UN Security Council Document S/PV.2300, 31 August 1981, p. 18.

53. *The Times*, 9 September 1981.

54. Interview with Sir David Scott, 27 November 1986.

55. Interview with Ambassador von Wechmar, 10 December 1986.

7

Third-Party Mediation in National Minority Disputes: Some Lessons from the South Tyrol Problem

T. J. Pickvance

THE MOTIVATION TO MEDIATE

Europe is a museum of national minority conflicts which erupt from time to time to disturb the peace of the European Community. In the following pages is posed the question: Are there as yet untried ways of promoting the settlement of these long-standing minority group disputes through mediation of various kinds by agencies created specially for this purpose, either by the Community or by interested unofficial bodies? The answers given in the concluding part of this chapter embody the lessons learned during the exploration of possibilities of peacemaking through "third-party mediation" between the years 1964 and 1972 in connection with the South Tyrol (Alto Adige) dispute, and afterwards in connection with Northern Ireland.

This venture into an entirely new field of personal activity had its origin in three very different experiences. The earliest of these was in 1939 at the outbreak of war when, in common with other active peace-workers, I faced the fact that our efforts had proved ineffectual. Yet, unrealistic as our hopes had been, it was realised that peace time was obviously the peacemakers' chief opportunity, since war causes an almost total breakdown of communications between nations. So the question remained: How can open hostilities be averted in situations of potential physical violence? The second experience was university life, when the question posed itself: Would conflicts be easier to resolve if university disciplines were brought to bear on actual conflicts with the object of understanding their general nature and special features? The third experience cannot be explained briefly. Let it suffice to say that a close study of the doctrines and practice of the Quaker George Fox (1624–91) compelled me to attempt to answer the question: Are they still valid today, for instance, in a Christian approach to a conflict situation in modern Europe?

In 1964 I felt I had to put these ideas to the test, so I cast about for a suitable conflict to try them on, one not too large nor too distant. What follows is the story of how I was drawn into this Austro-Italian affair and, after me, a score or two of other people—British, Danish, American. As a result of my writing to the Austrian Embassy in London, interviews were arranged for me with the political leaders of the South Tyrolese in Bozen (Bolzano) in the summer of 1965. Subsequent events will be detailed in chronological·order, showing how I arrived at answers to the questions I had in mind at the outset.

AN OUTLINE HISTORY OF THE SOUTH TYROL CONFLICT BEFORE 1965

All but the very smallest countries of Europe are mis-called "nation-states", since they are all multi-national, containing as they do one or sometimes several distinct linguistic groups in addition to the dominant group. These groups occupy more or less well-defined homelands, although these may be divided by state boundaries (e.g., the Basque country) or between provinces (e.g., the Ladin area of Northern Italy). In most cases they have been incorporated into the state against their will. They retain a strong sense of national identity and struggle to preserve their language and unique culture against all assimilative efforts. In recent years the struggles for freedom of such minorities have become increasingly violent and have threatened the unity of states, with implications both for the international relations of states and the growth of unity in Europe.

Italian Tyrol, as we know it today, was created by the peace settlement in 1919 when the Brenner frontier was drawn along the crest of the Alps cutting off Austrian Tyrol, with Innsbruck as capital, from South Tyrol or Alto Adige, with Bozen (Bolzano) as chief city. The great majority of the population of South Tyrol in 1910 were German-speaking, according to official Austrian figures and also the Italian Institute of International Studies in Milan. The latter calculated the German language group at 230,000 and the Italian group at 8,000, a ratio of nearly 29:1. By the early 1960s this proportion had fallen to about 2:1. This dramatic change resulted from Italianisation policies begun under Mussolini. In the Fascist era, Italian-owned industries were established in the province with their labour force restricted to immigrants from the rest of Italy, who came in their thousands to settle. These policies were ruthlessly carried through in other spheres. Education in the German tongue was forbidden. The town and villages were given Italian names, and even Tyrolese family names were Italianised. Furthermore, the ancient Tyrolese land laws under which the farmers held their land were abrogated.

This bitter struggle provided a severe test for the Berlin–Rome axis, and in 1939 Hitler decided to resolve it once and for all by giving the South Tyrolese a simple but hard choice: either relinquish all claims to their homelands by becoming German nationals and moving permanently into the Reich, or else remain in the South Tyrol and abandon their German cultural heritage and their bond with their Tyrolese compatriots north of the Brenner. As a result of this "Optants Agreement" of 1939 about 70,000 South Tyrolese left the province for Germany and Austria while the war was in progress. About a third of the optants later returned. But the net result of these major changes, and of smaller ones such as post-war emigration of South Tyrolese in search of work, was that by the 1950s the proportion of the German-language group in the province had fallen to approximately two-thirds. The fears of the South Tyrolese about their future existence as a group are easily understood.

After the Second World War, the Paris Peace Conference of 1946 left the South Tyrolese in a very weak position. It was true that the agreement reached by Austrian Foreign Minister Karl Gruber and his Italian counterpart Alcide de Gasperi contained concessions; education in the German tongue and the restoration of German family names were allowed. But the other provisions were ambiguous and imprecise. The official English text of the agreement was remarkable for containing an obsolete English word, "parification"; thus Clause 1(b) granted "parification of the German and Italian language" for official use. A similar imprecision is evident in Clause 1(d), which aimed at ensuring "a more appropriate proportion of employment between the two ethnical groups" in civil service posts generally. Since "parification" in this context can only mean to make "more comparable" or "more nearly equal", it could be held that the smallest improvement in the official use of the German tongue, or in the proportion of Tyrolese in civil service posts, were fulfillments, in law, of these clauses. The Italian view during the post-war years was that the de Gasperi–Gruber Agreement had indeed been fulfilled, notwithstanding such undeniable facts as that in some branches of the civil service only 1 in 20 of the posts were held by South Tyrolese, who felt that they were entitled to two-thirds of all civil service posts.

Another ambiguity in the text concerned the geographical "frame" within which the Tyrolese would exercise the promised concessions. In the Autonomy Statute that eventuated they found the province bound up with Trentino, the province immediately to the south, in a new Region whose powers were exercised by a Council in which their representatives were in a permanent minority of 2 to 5. As many of the legislative powers that the

Tyrolese considered vital to their interests were vested in the Region, they made the transference of these to the provincial government one of their main objectives.

The de Gasperi–Gruber Agreement was manifestly so defective in these and other respects that Gruber insisted on the delegates from South Tyrol assuming responsibility for accepting or rejecting it. Reluctantly, a majority voted to accept.

For the ensuing struggle for a greater measure of autonomy during the decade that followed, the political parties in the province united in 1945 to form the South Tyrol People's Party (SVP). Austria gave what support it could, notably by having the matter placed upon the agenda of the XVth United Nations General Assembly in 1960. But negotiations with a series of weak governments in Rome, who were beset by other difficulties which they felt to be more urgent, yielded no tangible results. Impatience mounted. Extremists had begun to use dynamite in the 1950s, and violence against property reached a climax on 10–11 June 1961 when electricity pylons around Bozen were demolished. Eighty percent of the electricity supply to the province was cut off, and as more than ten percent of Italy's electricity was generated in the Tyrolese Alps, the Italian government at last realised it had a serious problem in this border province.

Within three months, on 1 September, a government commission of nineteen representatives of national political parties and of the South Tyrol People's Party was set up. What years of political action using democratic methods had failed to achieve had been accomplished within months by fewer than a hundred young Tyrolese men trained in Austria in the use of explosives. Another success that the men of violence could claim was the setting up on 7 September of a sub-committee of seven of the Political Committee of the Council of Europe to consider the South Tyrol question.

The "Commission of 19" was expected to report within months, but progress was exceedingly slow for various reasons. Its deliberations were interspersed with talks between the foreign ministers of Italy and Austria; general elections in both countries caused delays; differences of opinion between the more moderate Austrians and the SVP, and between the more moderate and the more nationalistic Italian representatives in the Commission about the extent of the concessions to be made to the Tyrolese, all took time to resolve. Furthermore, terrorists' attacks upon people and property adversely affected public opinion in Italy. In 1963 the Commission's sittings were suspended. A visit to Rome by Struye, the Belgian chairman of the Council of Europe's sub-committee, occasioned their resumption—a pointer to the importance of European opinion.

After two hundred sessions, the Commission completed its work later in 1963, but its report was not published until April 1964. Important though the Commission's work had been in bringing leading Italian politicians to adjust their minds to the existence of a resolute minority group, settlement was still a long way in the future. The government of the day did not feel obliged to accept all the Commission's recommendations, and Austria did not feel that some of the concessions went far enough, so they took the question up at international level.

THE SEARCH FOR INFORMATION

That was the state of the dispute in 1965 when I first became interested in it. The first move, mentioned above, resulted in Frau Dr. V. Stadimayer, the Innsbruck government's expert on South Tyrol and herself a native of that province, arranging for me to meet Dr. S. Magnago, the leader of the South Tyrol People's Party, and his deputy, Dr. F. Volgger, in July 1965.

A report of this meeting, made to the Quaker Peace and International Relations Committee in London the following November, brought a decision to send a mission of three to Austria and Italy in February 1966. The stated aims of the visit were to "express goodwill and friendship to Italians and Austrians" and "to increase European Quakers' understanding of the situation in Alto Adige–Trentino, by studying the factors (social, economic, political, etc.,) in the 'South Tyrol problem'". The mission, which was asked to report back to the Committee, consisted of Finn Friis, formerly a Danish diplomat and member of the League of Nations secretariat, Leslie Metcalf, the Quaker International Affairs representative in Vienna, and myself.

With the visit in prospect we wrote to Ambassador Guidotti at the Italian Embassy in London, who was well acquainted with the problem and who had already offered to supply literature for a study of the question. He asked for preparations to be made for our visit at a time of political difficulty in Rome. When we arrived the following February we discovered that arrangements had been made on both the Austrian and the Italian side for us to meet a wide range of people representing many shades of political opinion in Vienna, Innsbruck, Bozen (Bolzano), Trento and Rome. Cooperation was friendly and complete on both sides. We were able to interview fifty-five people, mostly individually, ranging from foreign minister and senior civil servants to representatives of university students.

Some early impressions of this first visit remain strongly with me. To the Tyrolese we were welcome as evidence of international interest in their difficulties. The psychological situation of minority groups needs to be understood. They are usually small populations of tens of thousands to at most a few millions. They are often isolated geographically, not infrequently in mountainous or less accessible areas where their ancestors may have taken refuge in the face of pressure from other tribes many centuries ago. Rarely do they have protector nations who can champion their cause. They feel impotent and forgotten, so ardent patriots turn to violence to draw attention to their plight. Journalists come and go. We were the first organisation of any kind that had made an extended visit to study the question on the ground. Our presence was in itself an encouragement to the Tyrolese.

The Italian case was very differently motivated. Although they, like every country with minority problems, do not invite international attention to what they always argue are internal matters, they too had a case to present. They could maintain that the de Gasperi–Gruber Agreement had been fulfilled, although in spirit it certainly had not. But their real case was at a much deeper level and rested upon historical and strategic grounds. They had entered the First World War under the secret Treaty of London in order to liberate Trentino, the last portion of Italy to remain under Austrian rule. It was their fourth war of liberation in a century. By securing the Brenner frontier in 1919 they had gained control of the pass through which Germanic tribes had entered the peninsula since time immemorial.

The sympathies of liberal-minded people are more easily aroused for smaller nations suffering injustice at the hands of larger ones. It was well to realise that fifty years earlier our mission might well have come to study "the Trentino question", viz., the grievances of the Italian-speaking majority in Trentino who were still under the Austrian yoke—although this was much lighter than the one borne later by the South Tyrolese.

Immediately we began interviewing we were in difficulties, the extent of which only became apparent later. Languages were the most obvious. The student or would-be mediator in national minority questions is faced with the need to master pairs of languages—German and Italian, Spanish and Basque, French and Flemish. Reliance upon interpreters is therefore inevitable. After some years of experience during which, as I realised afterwards, points were misunderstood or missed altogether, I came to the conclusion that the language difficulty can be both exaggerated and underestimated. A good general knowledge of a language is certainly not adequate for a detailed study of a conflict. Even an excellent knowledge is insufficient if it does not include the political vocabulary in both tongues and also the special terms which spring from the local laws and culture of the linguistic minority. Ideally, we needed on our side of the table a native British interpreter with an excellent knowledge, as defined above, of Italian or Tyrolese German, with his Italian or Tyrolese counterpart on the other side, each monitoring the other.

A further difficulty is the similarity of key words. It has often been said that between the British and the Americans is the barrier of a common language. Between the peoples of Europe are vocabularies with super-ficially similar words with different meanings—such as democracy, Liberal, academic, state, nation—which add greatly to the task of real understanding. In other words, an acquaintance with the culture of each country is as indispensible as familiarity with the language of politics.

But it was not so much accuracy of translation of questions and answers as knowing what questions to put that constituted the chief difficulty. This was inevitable since we had come to inform ourselves, not to attempt to mediate. Mediation presupposes a thorough knowledge of the questions at issue.

No completely satisfactory way of becoming well-informed is possible. In national and international politics the customary method is to be briefed by experts. But the most impartial briefing is limited by the knowledge and understanding of the experts, who frequently disagree. No one may realise at any given time what are the significant events and who are the significant actors in the situation. Only in the hindsight of history are such judgements possible. Nevertheless, history also teaches that some politicians achieve the stature of statesmen—people who understand what really matters in the long run.

From the literature available to us in 1966—some of which was not entirely free from propaganda—we could only acquire a knowledge of the main events of the past. It became clear only in 1970 when Dr. A. Alcock's *History of the South Tyrol Question* (Alcock, 1970) was published how inadequate our preparation had been. In 1966 we were face to face with men who had played important roles as much as twenty-five years earlier. With Alcock's information we should have understood why names such as W. von Walther, F. Volgger and A. Podesta, to mention only three, were included in the list of people we were to meet. Much of the information we needed had appeared in the press when it was current news, and we required a knowledge of political history at that level. Thus, to turn from one conflict to another would necessitate gaining the services of a fresh team of individuals. In the light of our experience, one way of acquiring valuable insights from within the situation is to put the question: Can you name anyone on the other side who writes with sympathy and understanding about your own point of view? The answers may produce some rare and helpful individuals.

As one becomes acquainted with politicians and officials, mutual trust grows and one receives more-or-less confidential information. We learned early in our visit that Tyrolese leaders had no expectation that the Brenner frontier would be changed. So the cry of the Austrian annexationists, "Ein Tyrol", was always unrealistic all through the period leading up to the settlement. But it was not politic to draw attention to the fact that the borders of Austria were fixed by the four-power treaty. Although the demand for re-unification is now muted, it played a part in the struggle and still expresses an unextinguished hope.

As events which led up to the situation in South Tyrol in 1965 became clearer to us, it was necessary to revise our ideas about the identity of "decisionmakers"—the key figures in the situation. It has already been noted, with regret, that unsophisticated violence used against property achieved more in a few months than years of frustrating political action through normal channels. We have also noted that violence used after 10–11 June 1961 was counter-productive, because it was used to justify delays in the negotiations through its effect on Italian public opinion. So, to the politicians and officials whose decisions are implemented by governmental action, must be added all the unofficial citizens who act upon their decisions and so change in some degree the course of history.

Inevitably, when one enters upon a project, some preconceived ideas prove to be erroneous. Anyone familiar with the Northern Ireland scene, where religious attitudes feature so prominently, would naturally expect the Catholic Church in Italy to be a bridge and a strong reconciling factor between the two language groups. However, early in our visit we learned that in the Mussolini era the Tyrolese priests became centres of resistance to Italianisation, because they were among the few cultured people who could transmit Tyrolese culture in the German tongue after it had been proscribed in schools. This was specially the case in remote mountain villages. This information, coupled with reports that Italian priests had been among the worst Italianisers in the Fascist era, drove home the first lesson about the nature of national minority problems, namely that whatever factors are operative in such situations—and there are many— religion is not the most fundamental of them. It is drawn into the struggle and made to serve either side. Catholic church leaders in 1966, therefore, needed to be very circumspect when they made public statements, since these were always open to misinterpretation as political statements supporting one side to the disadvantage of the other.

The necessary revision of my estimate of the role of religion raised larger questions. How many factors are at work in national minority conflicts? Which are the more powerful? Can one be singled out as the most fundamental? During the years that followed, these questions recurred (see Pickvance, 1975). I concluded, having become acquainted with a number of such disputes, that there is a similarity of attitudes displayed by minority groups everywhere, and a similarity in the sentiments expressed, sometimes in identical words. Even in South Tyrol the fears of the Italian language group, who were in a minority of 1:2 in the province, were expressed in the same phrases as were the fears of the Tyrolese who were in a minority of 2:5 in the Region, and 1:200 in Italy as a whole. Minority group psychology is an easily recognised phenomenon.

THE AGREEMENT

We must now chronicle the main events following the completion of the Commission of 19's work early in 1964. Deadlocked political situations have the nature of log-jams on rivers; the problem is not how to gain movement everywhere but how to release a relatively few number of logs so that the current can get them all moving again. One such log-jam was caused by the Tyrolese demand in 1957 for full provinical autonomy for South Tyrol, with separation from Trentino. This was quite unacceptable to successive Italian governments, who foresaw the possibility of the province declaring itself Austrian. Once the Tyrolese withdrew this demand, the task became largely one of transferring enough powers from the Region to South Tyrol.

Negotiations to this end were begun early in 1964 at foreign minister level. On the Austrian side, Bruno Kreiski was in charge until January 1966. He was followed by Lujo Toncic-Sorinjand and, from January 1968, by the experienced Kurt Waldheim. Their opposite numbers were first Guiseppi Saragat and then, from January 1965 until the completion of the settlement in summer 1969, by Aldo Moro. These men, with Sylvius Magnago as leader of the South Tyrolese, were the chief architects of the Agreement eventually achieved.

The Agreement comprised two sections (see Alcock, 1970, pp. 434–49). The first section was the "Package" of 137 clauses, the great majority of which were concessions to the Tyrolese demand for more autonomy. Part VIII included four Articles which created "internal guarantees". These involved setting up a permanent commission as a means by which representatives of the Tyrolese could bring any future grievances before the Council of Ministers in Rome. This constituted the first safeguard against a recurrence of serious disharmony.

The second section is of great importance. It defined a procedure for guaranteeing the implementation of the "Package", and also met the Tyrolese demand for a form of international guarantee. But the most interesting procedure, and the one most capable of general application in the settlement of similar disputes, is the procedure itself. For want of a better name it was called an Operational Calendar. "Calendar" is used here in its sense as a list. It was a list of political acts each of which was to be completed before the next was carried out. This step-by-step procedure was to be followed by the Austrian and Italian governments in turn, separately or jointly. The underlying logic was that each step was made politically possible by the taking of the preceding one. The Calendar established an acceptable order of priorities. It was not exactly a time-table, for only one step had a time limit. It was an agreed way out of an impasse.

The principle of the Calendar will be illustrated by the first and eighth steps. First in order was "the provisional signing of a Treaty changing Article 27(a) of the European Convention for the Peaceful Settlement of Disputes in so far as relations between Austria and Italy were concerned". The European Convention, as agreed by the signatories, applied only to future disputes between them. Under the proposed new Treaty, Austria and Italy agreed that the Convention should also apply to this long-standing dispute. This served as a form of international guarantee to which the South Tyrolese could have recourse, through Austria, if the "internal guarantees" referred to above failed to resolve any serious difficulty.

The final signature of this Treaty is No. 8 in the Calendar. The eighth step is made possible by No. 7, which is the first vote in the Italian Chamber and Senate on the changes in the Italian Constitution which formed part of the Agreement. Under the Constitution, a change in it requires two votes in the Chamber and the Senate, each with a specified large majority, with an interval of six months between them. So after the first vote on the new Constitutional Law in the Chamber and Senate (No. 7), Austria and Italy can sign the Treaty (No. 8), which had earlier been initialled. Then can follow Parliamentary approval of the Treaty and the second vote of the new Constitutional Law; these together comprise No. 9.

The Calendar requires completion of all its steps before both countries can declare the dispute resolved. This gives assurance to the South Tyrolese that the concessions made to them under the Agreement will not only pass into law but be implemented before Austria will join Italy in declaring the dispute at an end.

On 22 November 1969, at a crucial Extraordinary Congress of the South Tyrol People's Party, the "Package" and the "Operational Calendar" were accepted by a 52.9 percent majority. A week later, in Alcock's words, "Moro met Waldheim at Copenhagen and it was decided to set the Calendar in motion. ... Events moved at an unprecedented pace in the South Tyrol question ... within a month of the Extraordinary Congress, one-third of the Calendar had been carried out". Three years earlier we had been assured by people in the province that this clash between Germanic and Latin cultures was incapable of resolution.

DISCUSSION DOCUMENT AND FOLLOW-UP

After our mission of three had reported to the Quaker Peace and International Relations Committee in 1966, the extensive notes of our interviews with fifty-five people in Austria and Italy were combined and circulated to our Study Group. We had then to decide whether a further good will mission should be sent or that some other action should be taken. Repeating the visit seemed pointless. Perhaps a report on it should be prepared? The Italian Ambassador had hoped for one, and a similar request came later from the Austrian side. But the Study Group felt that more was needed. A political problem requires a concrete political plan. Could we produce any sort of proposals that would be a useful contribution to a peaceful outcome?

In 1966 we were aware that the negotiations described above were in progress. But we also knew that terrorism organised by Austrian extremists was continuing and that a successful outcome of the negotiations was not assured. In the circumstances we decided to attempt to produce a "discussion document". Since only the representatives of the parties to a dispute can work out a political settlement, our document would only present ideas, comments and suggestions of the kind that concerned people can make from outside the struggle, using such insights and expertise as we had.

After some of the ideas that we eventually submitted had emerged, Leslie Metcalfe and I visited Austria and Italy again in May 1967 and sought the advice of individuals, officials and others who were well disposed to our efforts. We had found that as trust developed some officials would give us their personal views in confidence. This exercise completed, I returned to England and produced further versions of the discussion docment before its final form was approved. In the production of the final version, specialists from many university disciplines were consulted, together with many with long practical experience of international questions. The document analysed the South Tyrol problem as a "double minority" problem, not dissimilar to the Northern Ireland problem. So our purpose was "to suggest ways of helping to solve the Alto Adige problem by creating the conditions of peace by terminating the threats that both ethnic groups feel to be aimed at their existence by removing their causes".

At that time we only had the terse and sometimes obscure German text of the Package which had been conditionally accepted in 1967. Recalling how much anger had been caused by misunderstandings due to obscurities in the text of the de Gasperi–Gruber Agreement, it seemed important to draw attention to points in the Package that were open to different interpretations. It was already evident that some South Tyrolese were unrealistic in their readings of ambiguous passages. Our discussion document was dispatched in time for a meeting called to clarify the text of the agreement.

Once the discussion document had been dispatched, attention could be turned to other possibilities. In the Summer of 1968 new possibilities opened up with the retirement to South Tyrol of an American Quaker couple of Austrian extraction, Adolf and Christa Furth. Previously we had considered the possibility of a work camp in which young people of both groups could participate. This idea had quickly been abandoned when we discovered that neither young nor old crossed the social frontier. At that time both groups disapproved of mixed marriages because they led to assimilation of one or the other partner. We were also told that adult Tyrolese who crossed the boundary might be disciplined. However, events beyond the boundaries of the South Tyrol began to change that. The occupation of Czechoslovakia by Soviet forces and the resistance that followed, together with the repercussions of the revolt of students in

France, led to the youth of both language groups breaking away from the discipline of their leaders. The atmosphere was conducive for a work camp, and the Furths together with a local schoolteacher made arrangements for the summer of 1969, which was the first occasion when the young of both language groups met and worked together in South Tyrol. At the same time the Furths, together with the schoolteacher Stelio Danese, brought together a mixed study group of adults which in 1969 published a report that created a minor disturbance in Tyrolean circles. The main proposal of this report, which was incorrectly referred to as the "Pickvance *papier*" was the establishment of a teachers training college where the language of instruction was bilingual. The proposal was criticised not on educational grounds, but for its feared effects on the Tyrolese.

WHAT CAN THE MEDIATOR DO?

In this final section I propose to answer the following questions. What conclusions may usefully be drawn from this exercise into third-party mediation? Furthermore, how might they be given practical expression?

Lurking behind both questions is an assumption, viz., that a third-party mediator is competent to make realistic practical proposals. From the very beginning it was asked: How can you hope to understand a conflict in a foreign country when you have not lived in the actual situation? At the time I had no reply, other than that I felt obliged to carry through this venture, and that the sceptics might prove to be right. My answer would now be very different. I should question their own assumption, which is that living within a conflict situation necessarily gives one an understanding of it that enables one to see how peace could be achieved. I have found no evidence to support this view and much to refute it. It may be dismissed summarily by referring to Northern Ireland, where politicians of undoubted intelligence and life-long familiarity with the province have propounded solutions ranging from rule from Dublin, a federal Ireland, devolved government for the province, direct rule from Westminster, to independence from both Westminster and Dublin. As for methods, some advocate violence to change the status quo and others to maintain it, while others repudiate its use altogether. The list of incompatibles could be lengthened considerably. However, one cannot avoid the conclusion that living within a situation does not guarantee either understanding or wisdom. On the contrary, the evidence supports the view that most people who have spent the whole of their thinking lives in a tense situation feeling that their national existence is under constant threat, develop defensive, belligerent attitudes and find it difficult to adopt a flexible, objective frame of mind.

The spectator sees most of the game, and if the spectator is an experienced student of the game, he may have a better understanding of what is happening between the opposed sides than they have themselves. But he has no means of influencing events directly, and no one has any obligation to consult him. Even if his own national group is involved, the mediator remains outside the decision-making group of politicans and civil servants who are officially handling the situation. In a country foreign to him his difficulties are compounded. So the basic questions become: How can the experience and wisdom gained from minority group struggles in the past be made available to political leaders on both sides in disputes today? Furthermore, how can the minds of leaders on both sides be schooled so that the lessons learned can become part of their shared perceptions of their common task of achieving a settlement?

An example may clarify this, in that the problems and the solutions to those problems are not unique. One of the common demands by minority groups is for their due proportion of state and semi-state jobs, and politicians need to know the practical difficulties of meeting this "obvious" demand for justice. But, as Alcock points out, one assumption made in the 1969 Settlement was that the language groups would remain as distinct as they had hitherto been. Thus, it was expected that the candidates at elections would continue to declare themselves as members of either the German or the Italian language groups and that they would represent their respective interests. In other words, it was assumed that voting would continue along tribal lines in the province.

This assumption was basic to the working of the Agreement because the allocation of jobs in provincial and communal (local) administration was to correspond to the proportions of the representation of the two language groups in the Provincial Parliament. This arrangement was made to meet a South Tyrolese demand for justice on this point. In the event the very success of the Settlement frustrated that intention. What happened is that the release of tension between the two groups encouraged mixed marriages, which had hitherto been under a social taboo. So some prospective candidates began to describe themselves as German *and* Italian, or neither, and were therefore disqualified. Also, the political left put up candidates who represented the left and not the views of either community. Successful candiates of this kind distorted the proportions in which the state posts were to be allocated.

The efforts of the politicians to ensure a more just and equitable distribution of these posts were frustrated by other unpredicted and unpredictable developments. The unexpected has happened; the South Tyrolese have not filled vacancies when they occurred. That not enough suitably qualified Tyrolese candidates might sit for and pass the competitive examinations that are customary in Italy for administrative positions, had been seen and provided for. In that event a member of the Italian language group might be given a vacancy, but not for longer than a year. What had not been foreseen was that the Tyrolese would no longer want these government posts!

This state of affairs was brought about by changes in the economy which transformed the job prospects of the Tyrolese. Agriculture, which was almost entirely in their hands, was a depressed industry in the 1960s, but in the following decade, thanks to EEC subsidies, it was flourishing. Also, tourism, encouraged by the provincial government, poured money into the province in the 1970s, with tourists coming especially from Germany and Austria. The Tyrolese preferred these more lucrative occupations to the comparatively poorly paid jobs in state administration, where salaries and pensions were not keeping pace with the inflation caused by the boom industries. Thus it came about that the Italian group, who owned so much of the older once-prosperous industries now in structural decline, and so many of the once sought-after posts in administration, were now in their turn the more depressed group.

The lesson to be drawn from this regarding future agreements in other cases is that, while the principles of justice may be "settled", constant adjustment may be needed regarding the application of those principles. Thus, according to a post-1980 census, the number of German speakers increased by over three percent while the number of Italian speakers dropped by nearly four percent, a trend that, if continued, would lead to a very different population distribution to that existing at the time of the Agreement. For example, the fact that the demand for justice in the allocation of state posts is a constant feature of minority disputes should serve as a reminder that where there is salient population change, measures should be incorporated into the settlement allowing flexibility and review where necessary.

It is often the case that those involved in a conflict consider it to be unique, while the observer with comparative experience will see commonalities between conflicts. Hence, the experience of the observer can prevent the politician from reinventing the wheel. An example can be taken from this case with respect to the way in which the Tyrolese demand for an international guarantee was met. We have seen how from 1964 the foreign ministers of Austria and Italy sought to satisfy this condition. The situation remained deadlocked for two years until it occurred to someone that by a simple alteration of the European Convention for the Prevention of Disputes, which was eventually incorporated into the Package Deal, Austria would still be able to give a measure of protection to the Tyrolese, should the necessity arise, even after the dispute was declared settled by both countries. Conceivably this might offer a way out of other intractable situations.

The mediator can make a useful contribution, but what are the best methods by which leaders can be helped? During the ten years when I was in contact with people involved in the South Tyrol dispute, and afterwards from 1971 when I was making similar visits to Ireland, the idea was growing in my mind for the need for a permanent European organisation or institution for national minority group problems. For a number of reasons I became convinced of the value of having an independent, prestigious institution in Europe to assist politicians in dealing with such disputes.

What is suggested here is not the creation of an academic centre for the theoretical study of these conflicts, although comparative studies of them would be one of its essential activities. Nor would it be a body controlled by representatives of the linguistic minorities in Europe, valid though the principle of a senate is, where each constituent group, whether large or small, is equally represented.

The simplest way to define the concept is to outline the functions the proposed body would have. Perhaps its most reassuring role would simply be to exist as an embodiment of international recognition of a special type of political problem, and as implying recognition of the right of nations, small or large, to maintain their own identity and culture. Its main functions would be advisory and educational and its mode of operation such that it would command the support of European Community finances. Its special field of enquiry would be comparative studies, paying particular attention to the causes of increased and decreased tension, and the success or otherwise of measures taken to solve disputes. The primary purpose would thus be practical rather than theoretical. Since the expertise in all the fields of knowledge required for this work would be beyond the capacity of the permanent staff, it would operate mainly as a research and organising centre.

How might such an international body operate? Its educational task might be stated in the following way. Party political methods being what they are, ministers come and go, and some politicians find themselves elevated to ministerial rank and confronted, perhaps overnight, by duties that may not be of their seeking. Consequently reliance upon instruction and advice from permanent officials must necessarily be heavy. If, therefore, civil servants and rising politicians of the main parties on both sides could share the same opportunities of discussing the nature of national minority problems, the chances would be increased of the deeper understanding of the subject thus acquired having an influence at party and cabinet level.

As to feasible methods of achieving this end, perhaps the simplest would be the well-tested model demonstrated by the international seminars for diplomats arranged by the Society of Friends (Quakers), each of which lasted for several weeks, in the period following the Second World War.

Diplomats in the earier stages of their careers who have attended them have attested to their value in forming friendships across international divisions between people who might one day have to deal with one another in senior positions. Similar opportunities might be provided specifically for civil servants and politicians of host-nations and their minority groups. Those attending the seminars would thus get to know their opponents' point of view in a wider context and become acquainted with the attempts, successful and unsuccessful, that different countries have made to settle such conflicts. Participants would then be in a position to decide how much of this information might be relevant in their own countries.

Could the institution lay a more direct role in mediation? It might sponsor international teams of experts to study different conflicts over a period of years at the depth we have shown earlier to be required. From their comparative knowledge of majority–minority disputes they might be able to suggest ways of promoting settlements. But quite apart from their labours as applied social scientists, their existence might be at least as influential as an embodiment of a new spirit of conciliation in Europe and of the growth of the idea of common political rights. From our experience in Austria and Italy, it would seem that the formation of friendships is not the least of achievements in this field of work.

To summarise: Our exploratory work done in connection with the South Tyrol dispute from 1965 onwards may be treated in hindsight as a pilot study in third-party mediation. It could be followed up in a variety of ways, such as those described above. Conflicts are not unique, and expert input plus the development of comparative understanding among political actors on a continuing institutional basis might well lead to the possibility of settlement of many of the majority–minority problems in Europe today.

8

World Council of Churches Mediation and the Sudan Civil War

Hezekiah Assefa

This chapter presents an analysis of the mediation of the Sudan Civil War (1955–72) which provides many insightful lessons on how non-political, non-governmental international organizations could play a mediatory role in internal wars which have international dimensions. The Sudan Civil War was waged for 17 years and claimed over 500,000 lives and more than a million refugees before it was settled by the Addis Ababa Agreement of 1972. The war was between the two regions of the Sudan: the predominantly Muslim and ethnically arabized-African north, and the animist or Christian and negroid south.

The roots of the conflict go as far back as the late 1700s when the Sudan was under Turkish–Egyptian rule and when the southern part of the country was exploited as a source of slaves and raw materials. Southerners perceived the northern Sudanese as partners of the Egyptians and the Turks in this exploitation. In the late 1890s, the British took over control of the Sudan from the Egyptian rulers and began administering the north and the south as separate entities, recognising their differences in ethnicity, language, culture, and stages of economic development. The policy of separate administration accentuated and widened the divisions between the two regions. When the British decolonization process started, there was even discussion about granting independence to the north and the south as separate states, or, at least, joining southern Sudan to Kenya or Uganda, also British colonies. However, ten years before the Sudan was to gain independence, the British reversed their policy of separation which they had practiced for several decades and decided to grant independence to a unified Sudan. During the few years before independence an attempt was made to involve the southerners in the decision to join them with the north. However, they were basically used as a rubber stamp to give legitimacy to a decision that had already been made by the colonial officials and the northerners in Khartoum. The efforts to gain the consent of southerners to the union reportedly involved a great deal of pressure, manipulation, and trickery (see Beshir, 1968, p. 65; Wai, 1981, p. 43; Albino, 1970, p. 26).

The union was fraught with problems from the start. In the Sudanization process to replace the British civil servants with Sudanese nationals, only 6 out of 800 positions were given to southerners, the highest being an assistant district commissioner (Beshir, 1968, p. 72). A series of blunders on the new Sudanese government's part, and many unfavorable incidents, led to further tension and misunderstanding between the north and the south. Riots, demonstrations, and general unrest ensued in the south, and both southerners and northerners were killed.

Under colonialism, the British had created a contingent in the Sudan Army called the Equatoria Corps, primarily composed of southerners and located in the south. The purpose was to create a counterbalance to the predominantly Muslim element in the Army (O'Ballance, 1977, p. 39). During this period of tension, northern politicians persistently demanded that northern troops be sent to quell the disturbances in the south, as it was feared that southern soldiers in the Equatoria Corps might refuse to shoot at their own people. A detachment of northern tropps was sent to the capital of Equatoria province amid considerable southern apprehension. As the first group of northern soldiers arrived, many southern civilians, afraid of what the troops might do, took their families and fled the capital. In the meantime Khartoum ordered the transfer of some detachments of southern solidiers to the north. It was rumored that these detachments were going to be disarmed. As was feared, the southern troops refused to obey the transfer orders and mutiny broke out on 18 August 1955. The mutineers broke into ammunition stores and began hunting and killing northern officers. The shootings were accompanied by looting, and great panic ensued. The violence that started at this point continued and was met by northern retaliation which left many people dead.

The soldiers that were involved in the mutiny fled to the bush, formed bands, and started intermittent raids on villages and government installations. Out of these bands grew a secessionist guerilla movement that came to be known as the Anya Nya. Eventually, under the command of Colonel Joseph Lagu, a southerner who had deserted the government's army, the guerillas were transformed into a united and effective insurgency with a political wing known as the Southern Sudan Liberation Movement (SSLM). In the meantime, the conflict between the insurgents and the government was escalating and drawing in the neighboring governments, regional powers as well as the super-powers. Ethiopia, Uganda, Israel, and various Western governments and organizations, as well as the Vatican, supported the insurgents, some with material, training, and arms. The Soviet Union, Egypt, Libya, Algeria, and other Eastern European countries supported the Sudanese government.

By the end of the 1960s, the Sudanese government had changed many times, either through parliamentary elections or military coup d'etats. Each regime had different solutions to the southern problem, ranging from outright military suppression to attempting a negotiated settlement. In 1969, Colonel Gaafar al Numeri took power in a coup and declared that he would end the Anya Nya insurgency by granting autonomy to the south. However, the conflict only escalated further, the consequences were yet more devastating, and the end of the war was nowhere in sight.

CONFLICT RESOLUTION EFFORTS

Various mediation efforts were attempted over the duration of the conflict. By the mid-1960s, President Kwame Nkrumah of Ghana and later President Milton Obote of Uganda had offered their good offices to mediate the civil war. However, their offers were rejected on the grounds that the conflict was an internal matter.

By 1970, the Movement for Colonial Freedom (MCF), which later changed its name to Liberation, became actively involved as an intermediary. The MCF is a London-based organization affiliated with the Labour Party, having the backing of about 140 Members of Parliament and about twenty-five large national trade unions in Britain. As its name suggests, it had been actively involved in educating British public opinion to support the independence of many British colonies. The MCF had little contact with the Sudan after its independence in 1956. However, by 1970, the problem of southern Sudan began to gain attention in the West, largely due to a propaganda publication of the SSLM called the *Grass Curtain*, and that became the pretext for the MCF's involvement in the conflict as an intermediary.

The *Grass Curtain* had claimed that many atrocities were being perpetrated on southerners by the Sudanese government. Some MCF members demanded an enquiry into the claim in order to condemn the Sudan government for its human rights violations. As part of the inquiry, the second secretary of the Sudan Embassy and the editor of the *Grass Curtain* were invited to make presentations at an MCF conference to explain their views of the Sudan situation. After the presentations, however, the conference resolved that the "MCF should endeavour to use its good offices to bring about some kind of rapprochement between exiled Southerners and the Sudanese government."[1] Following the conference, informal discussions were encouraged between the presenters to the conference through Barbara Haq, the MCF's secretary, as the facilitator.

Gradually, more and more people from each side were drawn into the process. The MCF organized two fact-finding missions to the Sudan composed of parliamentarians, politicians, and trade unionists who met with Sudan government officials and some southerners. The Sudanese minister of southern affairs, Joseph Garang, came to London to continue dialogue with the SSLM representatives. However, for several reasons, the talks seemed to go nowhere. First, Garang, an ardent communist, strongly believed that the southern problem would be solved only when the south became socialist. According to some observers, this was not something likely to happen in the short run. Secondly, Garang's primary objective was to co-opt the intermediary organization to the side of the Sudanese government and use the situation to improve its image, which was being tarnished by the publication of the *Grass Curtain*. He seems to have succeeded in his second objective, being able to get prominent British politicians to endorse the Sudan government's position and give press releases unsympathetic to the southern movement. In November 1970, an article by Haq, published in the *Nile Mirror*, condemned the SSLM representatives in Europe as CIA agents. That dealt a death blow to the intermediary effort of the MCF.

THE ROLE OF THE WCC AND THE AACC

As relations between the MCF and the SSLM deteriorated, communications between the Sudanese government and the SSLM came to a standstill until the task of the intermediary was assumed by the World Council of Churches (WCC) and the All Africa Conference of Churches (AACC). Along with other humanitarian organizations which were working to alleviate the suffering of the victims of the civil war, the WCC had acted as an aid giver in the Sudan conflict for several years. In addition, its affiliate organization, the AACC, had sent a goodwill mission in 1966 to observe the conflict and the condition of religious freedom for the southerners, and to investigate the expulsion of all foreign missionaries by the government.[2] The AACC had planned a second goodwill mission soon after. For various reasons the trip was delayed until 1970. By that time the war had escalated, the number of refugees and victims of the war was mounting, and there was stalemate in the battlefield. The WCC, which had been providing humanitarian assistance for the refugees for some time, now felt the need to provide relief to the victims in southern Sudan also. Therefore, it began to assess how much and what kind of aid was needed. A group within the WCC, led by Kodwo Ankrah, argued, however, that aid could not be effective without peace and that the opportunity provided by the aid assessment should be used to explore peacemaking possibilities in the Sudan. Thus, the long-standing plan for a goodwill mission by the AACC was resuscitated to include a team from the WCC which would be involved in relief need assessment as well as peace exploration. Meanwhile, the Commission of the Churches on International Affairs (CCIA) of the WCC commissioned a researcher along with a CCIA staff member to study the origins, issues, development, and status of the conflict and prepare a report.

The joint WCC/AACC team got itself invited to the Sudan by the arrangement of the Sudan Council of Churches. Among the team members were Dr. Leopoldo Niilus, the director of the CCIA of the WCC; Canon Burgess Carr, the executive secretary of the Commission who had just been appointed general secretary of the AACC; and Kodwo Ankrah, the African secretary for the WCC Interchurch Aid Commission. They met with government officials and explained the WCC's plan to provide aid to the war-torn areas if a way to reach the affected people could be found. They also offered the good offices of the WCC for exploratory peace talks between the government and the SSLM. The government was receptive to the aid but insisted that it should be sent only through Khartoum and under government inspection. Concerning the proposed talks with the SSLM, it expressed willingness to open contacts with groups "who had influence on people in the south and amongst the refugees"[3] and offered to discuss the details of regional autonomy that Numeiri's government had offered to the south in 1969. Possibilities for a cooling-off period during the talks were also explored.[4] The intermediaries also gave the government a copy of the report of their investigation into the background and issues of the conflict for the government's examination and reaction to the document. They asked for feedback concerning the extent to which the report had captured the government's perspectives in the conflict.

Around the period when the WCC began its involvement as a third party, it passed two resolutions in its Central Committee meetings that might have enhanced its credibility as an intermediary. One resolution urged international bodies and member churches to press governments to "assist the efforts of free African states to attain and preserve their independence and unity." This no doubt had a great appeal to many newly independent African countries, including the Sudan. Another resolution that was passed earlier was called "Program to Combat Racism," and this called for humanitarian and educational assistance to liberation movements in Southern Africa. In a continent where the churches were traditionally perceived as agents of colonialism and institutionalised racism, these resolutions, which actively sought to foster African causes and concerns, greatly enhanced the image of the WCC in the eyes of many Africans.[5]

Also, at the time the WCC/AACC began their intermediary involvement, the Nigerian Civil War suddenly came to an end with the defeat of the Biafran insurgents. A very well organized consortium of Western churches, called Joint Christian Aid (JCA), had provided relief assistance to the Biafrans during the war. When the war ended, the consortium was left with a great deal of material, money, and transportation equipment that had been earmarked for Biafra. The JCA was, therefore, considering shipping it to another disaster area, the southern Sudan, to assist people in the SSLM-controlled territories.

There was a tremendous concern in some circles that the shipment of relief directly to the SSLM would further exacerbate the war since, by assuring the insurgents of a supply of food, medicine, and other necessities, the SSLM would use its own resources to buy arms. Moreover, there had been allegations that the JCA, during its involvement in the Nigerian Civil War, had served as a cover for arms reportedly supplied to the "rebels" by Portugal and South Africa. Therefore, there was a similar concern that the JCA's proposed shipment of relief aid might serve as a conduit for arms shipment to the Anya Nya. Burgess Carr, having heard that a JCA meeting was scheduled in New York to approve the plan of sending massive relief aid to SSLM, attended the meeting and presented reasons why this massive aid was ill advised. He pointed out that giving aid to the Anya Nya at that time would only succeed in circumventing the reconciliation efforts that were being undertaken by the WCC and AACC. He then obtained a reluctant agreement from the consortium to suspend the plan temporarily until peace explorations were given a chance.[6] Carr then went to President Numeiri and urged him to expedite the peace process on the grounds that too much delay might result in more external aid going to the SSLM, which would strengthen the insurgency and extend the war endlessly.

Meanwhile, due to the increased publicity of the southern situation in the European media the Sudanese government sent a delegation to Europe to improve its image by explaining its proposed policy of regional autonomy for the south and to solicit relief aid. This delegation hoped to counter the effect of the SSLM propaganda in Europe and to ensure that whatever aid was given would be channeled through the government. The WCC was one of the organizations contacted for aid. It responded to the request by stating that it could mobilize many church donor agencies to send relief through the government if peace were established and it could be assured that the aid would reach those who truly needed it. Since most of the would-be recipients had fled from the government or lived in the Anya Nya controlled territories, it was clear that aid sent through government channels would not reach all of the victims. However, the intent of the WCC's response was to underline to the Sudanese government that peace was a prerequisite to giving meaningful aid.[7] During this trip, the Sudanese delegation communicated to the WCC that the government had read the WCC's background report and found it "fair and objective." According to Nilus, "they recognised the validity and relevance of our basic descriptions and thesis although they had some criticisms to offer."[8]

On the mediation front, it was decided that AACC would contact southern leaders residing in southern Sudan and in Ethiopia. The WCC was to do the same in Europe. The purpose was to communicate to the exiles the discussions of the intermediaries with the Sudanese government and assess their views concerning possible peace talks. Through Mading de Garang, the SSLM representative in London and the editor of *Grass Curtain*, the WCC was able to approach General Lagu, the Anya Nya commander. The WCC also helped organize and pay for a trip by two SSLM representatives in Europe to travel to Zaire, Uganda, Kenya, and Ethiopia, where many southern exiles lived. The objective was to discuss the proposals for peace talks, to gather the views of the various factions, and, if possible, to formulate a consensus position concerning the negotiations. Apparently, there was a great deal of uneasiness among some people within the WCC about dispatching this mission. One group worried that the Sudanese government might interpret this action by the WCC as helping to unify the various factions in the Southern movement, thus creating a more formidable enemy for the government in case the negotiations failed and the war continued. They feared that the Sudan government might view the WCC as an ally of the SSLM, and the latter's neutrality as an intermediary might be in jeopardy.

Once General Lagu heard about the govenment's willingness to talk, he wanted to meet the intermediaries to get a clear understanding of their plans and assessment of the seriousness of the government's intention to negotiate. In the meeting the intermediaries assured Lagu that, from their perspective, Numeiri and the ministers they had talked with seemed to be in earnest in their quest for negotiations. But, if the intermediaries sensed any intent to exploit the mediation either to score propaganda points or to use it as a strategy to divide the SSLM, they would tell Lagu and withdraw their services. Such a declaration reportedly assured Lagu of the sincerity of the mediators as well as of the negotiation process.[9]

The two SSLM representatives in Europe travelled to the various countries where there were concentrations of southern exiles. They explained the government's proposals and came back with a report which recorded the opinions of all the leaders and groups consulted. The report indicated that there was a fair amount of support for starting negotiations, and, with the exception of a small group in Ethiopia and Zaire, the idea of negotiating within the framework of one Sudan was acceptable "if the Khartoum authorities are serious about finding a permanent settlement to the conflict."[10] However, regional autonomy was rejected as a basis for negotiation, and the majority preferred a loose federation. There was consensus that aid should not be sent through Khartoum.[11] Also, the SSLM responded to the WCC's background report on the origin and process of the conflict and characterized it as "showing understanding of the situation and as objective." They pointed out some pieces of information mising in the report.

After gathering SSLM's views, the intermediaries returned to Khartoum and reported their findings. At this meeting with the government, they were able to work out an agreement which authorized them to arrange an informal, preliminary, and confidential conversation between some SSLM representatives and a few Sudan government officials in Addis Ababa for 8 November 1971.

The WCC then communicated the date of the planned exploratory meeting to General Lagu and asked him to nominate his representatives for the talks. The WCC also worked out an arrangement to defray the cost of transporting some of the distant delegates to Addis Ababa. In the meantime, the WCC and the British Council of Churches made plans to help the SSLM representatives retain and pay for constitutional lawyers to provide legal advice for the forthcoming negotiations. The British Council of Churches and the Barrow and Geraldine S. Cadbury Trust in Birmingham contacted prominent lawyers to help the SSLM and paid for their services. Sir Dingle Foot, a former solicitor general for the British government, agreed to be the legal advisor. The lawyers tried to familiarize themselves with SSLM's thinking about the type of federation or autonomy that might be acceptable. According to the lawyers who prepared the document for the SSLM, they were asked to draft "two alternative schemes, one for a federation comprising four states and one for a federation comprising only two states."[12] This seems to have been a negotiating strategy in that if the four-states plan was not acceptable to the government, then they would fall back on the two-states plan.

The planned preliminary talks took place on 9 November 1971. Burgess Carr, one of the intermediaries, who by now had assumed his position as the general secretary of the AACC, became the facilitator for the meeting. The government delegation included some southerners, which apparently became a source of irritation to the SSLM representatives who insisted that the southerners be on the SSLM's side instead of the government's. The atmosphere was reportedly hostile, and Carr had to intervene several times to pacify tempers. His strategy was constantly to remind the parties the principal purpose for which they were meeting. He also brought to their attention the urgency of getting down to the task of negotiating since further delay in the peace process was only protracting the agony and suffering of their people caught in the war. Several social gatherings were also organized by the intermediaries in order to relax the hostility and the discomfort between the delegates and to open up informal talks between them.

A bitter argument arose over the issue of whether the talks would take place under the framework of regional autonomy or loose federation. The intermediaries then intervened and began to present for the parties' approval a series of draft proposals which were debated and reformulated until a version was finally reached that was acceptable to both parties.[13] Several informal conversations developed and resulted in establishing personal relationships between the contending delegates. A message was sent by the leader of the Sudan government delegation to SSLM's General Lagu through his personal representatives which reiterated the sincerity of the government in entering into negotiations and invited full and earnest participation by the SSLM. A date for the official negotiations was set for 20 January 1972 in Addis Ababa, presumably under the chairmanship of Emperor Haile Selassi of Ethiopia, who was one of the most respected leaders in Africa.

While preparations for the 20 January meeting were under way, the Sudanese government began a diplomatic and military offensive aimed at "improving its bargaining position." As soon as the WCC received news of the military offensive, it sent a telegram to President Numeiri stating that the attack was contrary to the negotiations under way and that, if it did not stop, the intermediaries would withdraw "since they cannot render their services under these circumstances." The president telegrammed the WCC and reassured them that the recent clashes were not an attempt to escalate the fighting or to impede the negotiations, and requested the WCC to continue its peacemaking efforts.[14]

In the meantime, the Sudanese government was also trying to organize a conference for all donor agencies willing to give aid through the government for the purpose of coordinating their assistance. The WCC was invited to participate, but it made its participation contingent on the outcome of the January negotiations. "We made it clear that our member bodies are anxiously awaiting to see what the January negotiations may bring, and that if the meeting fails, WCC will lose credibility and its ability to control some of the activities of its member bodies in relation to their activities in the southern Sudan."[15]

THE ADDIS ABABA DISCUSSIONS

The SSLM was not able to get its delegation ready for the 20 January meeting, so the start-up date for the talks was postponed until 15 February. When the delegates arrived in Addis Ababa for the formal talks, the SSLM representatives found out that Emperor Haile Selassie was not going to chair the negotiations. It is not clear whether the emperor had undertaken to be the mediator and changed his mind or whether it was a misunderstanding by the parties who thought that by offering his good offices he had agreed to be chairperson.[16] A breakdown was already becoming imminent. It was very important to the SSLM that the negotiation be chaired by a prominent head of state because it would give the talks international recognition. Also, their legitimacy and prestige would be enhanced if another government chaired the meeting rather than if the delegates from each side took turns to be chairperson as the government delegates suggested. The SSLM delegates thought that they were tricked by the northerners into coming to Addis Ababa for the negotiations when actually no one had agreed to sponsor the negotiations. Thus, they were ready to leave. The intermediaries eventually persuaded the emperor that the negotiations should not be allowed to fail merely because of a lack of a sponsor. Haile Selassie then reassured the SSLM that the negotiations would take place under his auspices, that he would send his foreign minister to open the first session, and that his personal representative would attend and report to him on all the subsequent sessions. Even after this reassurance, a dispute arose as to who would chair the day-to-day negotiations. Carr suggested that a committee be formed of members from each delegation and that he and the committee work together to find an appropriate chairperson for the negotiation sessions. In the subsequent meeting the parties agreed to name Carr as the "moderator" for the formal negotiations and the deadlock was broken. The rest of the intermediaries—Leopoldo Niilus and Kodwo Ankrah of the WCC, and Samuel Bwogo of the Sudan Council of Churches—were seated as observers along with Nebiyelul Kifle, the personal representative of Haile Selassie.

The formal negotiations were opened with a speech by the Ethiopian foreign minister. Then the moderator began the sessions with a sermon based on the story of Nehemiah, which drew from the traditions of the Old Testament and the Koran. He challenged the parties to forget the past and join hands to rebuild the Sudan as Nehemiah had rebuilt the war-torn walls of Jerusalem.[17]

The first order of business was to settle the question of the media. It was agreed that there was to be total secrecy of the discussion and proceedings, and that if information had to be released to the press it would be by a written statement agreed upon by both parties and submitted by the moderator. Once the procedural questions were settled, the Sudanese government presented its draft proposal of regional autonomy for the south, with explanations for all the articles in the draft. The next day, the SSLM responded with their reaction and proposals. The SSLM had earlier obtained a draft of the government's proposal and had time to prepare their counterproposals. They reportedly "tore the government's proposal to pieces. . . . It was a day where everyone was getting it off their chests with accusations and counteraccusations. The intermediaries listened and the moderator called for brief adjournments whenever tempers flared."[18]

After the general presentations, an agreement was reached to divide the issues into political/human rights, economic, and military/security issues. A smaller group of representatives from each delegation was chosen to take the SSLM's and the government's documents and identify the areas where there were points of agreement and disagreement. The points of disagreement were then to be presented to the plenary session for debate and negotiation. In the meantime, the intermediaries arranged social gatherings for informal interactions and discussions among members of the opposing delegations. While the smaller group worked on the compilation of the position papers, the intermediaries traveled between the hotels where the delegations of the two sides were staying to explore how the various delegation members perceived the differences and how they thought the gaps could be bridged. After the documents were compiled, an agenda was agreed to proceed first with the political/human rights issues, then the economic, and lastly the military/security issues. It appeared at that time that it might be easier to come to an agreement on the political/human rights issues than the economic or the military, and the plan was to deal with the most agreement-prone issue first.

The human rights clauses as drafted by SSLM's lawyers were accepted by and large by the government delegates. However, the creation of an autonomous regional government that satisfied the needs of both delegations became a source of a great deal of controversy. There were many moments when the discussions were heated and the moderator had to call for an adjournment and consultation. Sometimes, during this break, the intermediaries would prepare drafts that attempted to reconcile the proposals of the two sides. To aid this effort, the intermediaries had confidentially contacted the Organisation for African Unity (OAU) located in Addis Ababa and solicited the expertise of its staff for advice and guidance on some of the problems that arose during the negotiations. Particularly, the deputy secretary general for political affairs of the OAU, Mohammed Sahnoun, who had a lot of experience in international negotiations and diplomacy, provided much guidance when the intermediaries contacted him in impasse situations. Sometimes he helped them prepare a compromise draft, which the intermediaries would then take back to the parties. "With the compromise draft before them, the negotiators would have something concrete to look at rather than dispute in the abstract and sometimes they even adopted the compromise draft with some modifications."[19]

When the political and human rights issues were eventually resolved, Carr asked the delegates to pray silently together. Then the negotiators continued with the economic issues. During the discussions, whenever specific issues of disagreement arose, members from both delegations, who either had special training in economics or worked in that domain, were selected to work together to identify the problems and prepare a working draft for debate and negotiation by the larger group. It is reported that the atmosphere in some of the smaller groups was becoming very cordial and cooperative. Sometimes, in the debates, some northerners took sides with the southerners against their own delegation and even made arguments on behalf of the SSLM concerning what was fair and what was not. The moderator made the prayers part of the procedure and would ask all the members to stand up and pray every time negotiaion over a major issue was concluded in an agreement.

As expected, the military/security issue was the most difficult. The questions of what would happen to the Anya Nya after the end of the war, and how the military security of the south would be safeguarded from the north in the future, were very important issues for the SSLM and became very controversial. The SSLM wanted the entire Anya Nya insurgents (an estimated 10–15,000 soldiers) to be absorbed in the Sudan army and stationed in the south. The government wanted to keep a combined force of 15,000 troops in the south, 4,500 of these to be from the Anya Nya. The idea of keeping northern troops in the south was unpleasant to the SSLM. Even if northern soldiers were to be kept in the south, they wanted them to be restricted to the barracks in one location. The negotiations over this issue lasted for days. The intermediaries tried many ways to break the impasse: adjournments, private and small group consultations between the intermediaries and the parties, consultation with OAU advisors. However, they were unable to move closer to agreement. On the fourth day of deadlocked negotiations, the SSLM delegation's spokesperson moved the meeting be adjourned indefinitely since they were unable to resolve such an important issue. To the intermediaries' surprise, the leader of the government delegation also agreed with the indefinite adjournment.

The moderator refused to act on the motion and instead resorted to another strategy. He and the other intermediaries contacted Emperor Haile Selassie and asked him to use his prestige and influence to break the deadlock. Haile Selassie agreed to see each delegation separately the next day. He then offered a proposal whereby the Anya Nya would constitute 50 percent of the Sudanese army in the south and gave the SSLM his personal guarantee that no reprisals would be taken against returned Anya Nya fighters, a source of major concern for the SSLM. Haile Selassie had leverage over both the Sudanese government and the SSLM and neither party could afford entirely to ignore his suggestions. He was unofficially harboring Anya Nya fighters and allowing Ethiopia to be used as a training ground as well as a conduit for aid from other supporter governments to the Anya Nya during the war. Thus, his displeasure with the Sudanese government's intransigence in solving the southern problem would have serious repercussions on the Sudanese government as this might encourage Haile Selassie to help the Anya Nya even more openly. The SSLM, as a beneficiary of the emperor's support, would also have to pay attention to his suggestions, since alienating him might result in the termination of his support to their movement. After Haile Selassie's proposal, both delegations consulted their superiors and accepted the concept of a 50–50 composition of the army in the south. However, when translating the concept into numbers and determining where the troops were to be located, the controversy arose again. Through several behind-the-scenes negotiations, an agreement was reached where 15,000 military and paramilitary troops would be located in the south: 6,000 troops from each party would constitute the military and the remaining 3,000 paramilitary forces would be composed of Anya Nya returnees. The troops were to be located where the government desired. This arrangement was finally found acceptable to both parties and the issue resolved after many days of bitter and hard negotiations.

At that point, the moderator said that he got up and started praying aloud. He was crying as he prayed and other members of the delegation were crying too. One general reportedly stated that he was crying out of remorse for the killing between brothers that had taken place for all those years.[20] The final draft of the agreement was prepared and initialled by the leaders of each delegation on 27 February 1972. The ratification ceremony was scheduled for 12 March 1972.

President Numeiri informally ratified the agreement on 5 March, ordered a cease-fire, and started preparations for the implementation. However, the interim period was too short for the SSLM since there was difficulty communicating the agreement to all southern exiles, and it asked for the extension of the ratification date by two weeks. "A great deal of explanation and reassurance was needed among southerners . . . who had been accustomed to despair and found it difficult to believe the good news of the peace settlement" (Wai, 1981, p. 160). Also, a very vocal minority in the exile community had apparently criticised the agreement and objected to its ratification.

A surprise was thus waiting for the intermediaries when they arrived in Addis Ababa for the ratification of the agreement. On 26 March, Joseph Lagu, the leader of the SSLM, came to Addis Ababa accompanied by another southerner, who had not participated in the negotiations, and an Israeli escort. He stated that he was in Addis Ababa not to ratify but to renegotiate the agreement, arguing that his delegates had exceeded their mandate. Some Sudanese government officials had already arrived in Addis Ababa for the ratification ceremony. There was a flurry of intense discussions between the intermediaries and Lagu to dissuade him from his argument that his delegates had exceeded their authority, since the claim was unfounded. They tried to persuade him that the Sudanese government officials were there not to renegotiate but to ratify and that this hard-earned peace settlement must be given a chance. The Ethiopian government had served as the conduit of exchange of messages between the SSLM delegates and Lagu and, therefore, was able to produce copies of telexes which showed that Lagu had been informed about the negotiations step by step and that he had given them his approval. Lagu then reportedly abandoned his argument and demanded to see Haile Selassie to reconfirm the guarantee for the protection for returning Anya Nya insurgents. The guarantee was reiterated and the Addis Ababa agreement was ratified formally by both parties on 27 March 1972. Lagu then left for Khartoum with the intermediaries. Thus came the end of the 17-year-old civil war that had claimed over 500,000 lives and created millions of refugees. After the ratification of the agreement, thousands of refugees started returning. The intermediaries were then involved in supervising the ceasefire and the resettlement of the refugees, and in the disarming of the combatants.

LESSONS: THE INTERMEDIARIES

There are many lessons to be drawn from this experience. The first and most important one concerns the type of organization that could play an effective intermediary role in internal wars. One of the problems that impedes external conflict resolution efforts in civil wars is the position taken by many incumbent governments that the issues of the conflict are internal affairs and any involvement by outsiders violates their sovereignty. In the Sudan civil war, the presidents of Ghana and Uganda had separately offered their good offices to mediate the conflict, but their offers were rejected by the Sudanese government on the grounds that it was an internal matter and would have to be solved internally. International organizations such as the United Nations, or other multinational, political organizations such as the OAU have also been found to be ill-suited, since they tend to politicize the process and, by openly interacting with the insurgents, they might confer on them de facto international status. Thus many governments have resisted third-party mediation efforts and have reluctantly felt that force is the only arbiter of their conflict even though the material and human costs are immense.

On the other hand, the assumption of the role of the intermediary by a non-political, non-governmental, international organization could circumvent some of these problems. The intermediary involvement of such third parties would not necessarily confer international political status on the insurgents and would not threaten the sovereignty of the incumbent governments as much. This might make governments more willing to accept mediation as an alternative to their pursuit of a military solution to the conflict. In the Sudan case, the fact that the intermediaries were an international humanitarian agency was a factor in their acceptability as mediators.

In the context of the Sudan, the World Council of Churches' infrastructure was effectively employed and could be similarly used in peacemaking even in other circumstances. In the Sudan case, the WCC used the channels of its regional council, the AACC, which in turn used the channels of its member council, the Sudan Council of Churches (SCC), to open avenues for conciliation and to identify the significant actors, the important concerns or issues, and appropriate entry points. The Sudan Council of Churches had access to the local players and helped in providing the pretext for the WCC/AACC visit. The AACC had access to the neighboring governments and regional international organizations such as the OAU and reinforced the SCC's efforts on the national and regional levels. The WCC is composed of many churches and denominations from over one hundred countries which are organized on the basis of national and regional councils. It has the potential of reaching conflicting parties all the way from the leaders to the grass roots, as well as their supporting governments. This infrastructure seems to provide an invaluable access and information base that is rarely available to many organizations and could be usefully harnessed for peacemaking.

Moreover, the fact that the WCC is a humanitarian organization was an added benefit. Humanitarian agencies such as the WCC, the International Committee of the Red Cross, or Oxfam could have an important mediatory potential. In conflicts which entail large-scale human suffering, humanitarian agencies have a great advantage over many other organizations in obtaining acess to the conflicting parties. They are often called in by at least one of the parties to provide relief or rehabilitation; or, if they take their own initiative, their humanitarian mission makes their approach less suspicious. Such access could provide peacemaking opportunities for these organizations. They could use their presence to observe and study the conflict at close range, to get a better idea of the viewpoints and concerns of the protagonists, to identify key actors and decision makers, to monitor the process of the conflict, to assess the outlooks for peaceful regulation or even resolution of the conflict, and to identify the possible entry points for mediation. Their demonstration of concern for the people's welfare and their willingness to wrestle with the difficult task of providing rehabilitation and aid under dangerous circumstances could help establish the integrity of these organizations and provides them with a good basis for beginning intermediary activities. In view of these possibilities, it might, therefore, be a worthwhile idea for such humanitarian organizations to dispatch unofficial observers, along with their relief and rehabilitation aid, to war-afflicted areas in order to study the conflict and to explore the feasibility of peacemaking.

Even though these organizations manifest the desirable attributes for playing an intermediary role, one might wonder whether they have the necessary skills and resources (as listed in Young, 1967; Wehr, 1979). It is true that not many have the resources to exert significant leverage on the parties, to supervise truces, etc. The Sudan experience, however, shows that these resources could be used by proxy. The WCC was able to utilize Haile Selassie's resources (meeting site, transportation and communication facilities, and leverage over the parties to break deadlock) and the expertise of the OAU staff by coopting them into the process, either formally or informally.

With regard to requisite skills, even though organizations like the WCC are not usually thought of as the reservoirs of expertise in mediation and diplomacy as are international political organizations such as the United Nations, the WCC was able to make up for its deficiency by using team mediation. By putting together people with different but complementary skills they were able to create the requisite skill and knowledge base that no one mediator could have possessed. As a matter of fact, the team approach provided an opportunity for an expanded range of ideas, options, and strategies to be considered in order to cope with problems that arose during the mediation. The team itself represented the spectrum of positions expressed in the conflict. Burgess Carr, the secretary general of the AACC, a Liberian, was more identified with the ideal of preserving the unity of African states, and the Sudanese government could feel that its position in the conflict could be well understood by the mediators. Kodwo Ankrah, a Ghanian and the WCC's refugee secretary for Africa, had worked for several years with southern Sudanese refugees, and was known and respected. He had a first-hand experience of their suffering. Thus he commanded a great deal of trust from the SSLM, and his presence in the team was an assurance that their position would be understood and well represented among the intermediaries.

In terms of their skills, the mediators also complemented each other. Carr is a very charismatic person and an eloquent orator. He "has a presence of mind to take quick and appropriate steps and to take advantage of opportunities that arise during the negotiations. He had tremendous contacts in many African government circles. He is gifted with the ability of cutting through confusing arguments and getting to the heart of the contentions."[4] Kodwo Ankrah, even though quite a humble person, enjoyed the great respect and trust of both parties and had the skills to evoke empathy between the parties. Dr. Leopoldo Niilus was a trained lawyer, and as director of the Commission of the Churches for International Affairs of the WCC he was involved in many international issues and had sensitivity to the international dimension of the conflict. He had a great skill in analyzing problems and foreseeing difficulties. Moreover, he is a person of wit and humor. "When the parties locked horns or reached a deadlock in their negotiations, Niilus would either crack a joke from his endless catalogue or tell a pertinent story that might either make the parties laugh or give them some insights into their intransigence."[22] His witicisms are reported to have kept up the spirits of the negotiators at times when the negotiations were encountering difficulties. It would be quite difficult for one person to possess all of these important characteristics and skills. However, by utilizing a team, the required skills and characteristics of the ideal mediator could be approximated.

LESSONS: THE PROCESS

While the above lessons revolve around the characteristics of the mediator, there are also lessons concerning approaches and strategies used by the intermediaries in the Sudan conflict that can provide valuable lessons for emulation. One is the method of inquiry into the conflict utilized by the third parties before their mediation began. They undertook a study to identify the origins, development, issues, and the status of the conflict, and the resulting report was shared with the Sudanese government and the SSLM for feedback and clarification. Interestingly, both conflicting parties felt that the study was fairly objective and a good representation of the conflict as they saw it, and filled in the elements that they thought were missing. The report had many beneficial results. First, it established the intermediaries' credibility by persuading the parties that the third parties were informed and objective and did not have their own hidden agenda. Second, it gave the parties the opportunity to hear their own positions and concerns, as well as those of their adversary, restated by an objective third party whom they trusted. This, no doubt, should have given them more insight, if not empathy, into the positions of their adversary which, until then, they might have considered totally unreasonable. Third, it would have enabled the parties to discern which issues were central and which were peripheral, thereby allowing the negotiations to focus on the important aspects of the conflict.

Another strategy was the intermediaries' empowerment actions. In a negotiation situation, it is imperative that some equality be maintained lest the negotiations be lopsided and the process be exploited by the stronger party. Even though the SSLM was able to create a stalemate on the battlefront, it was not an equal bargaining partner to the government at the negotiating table. It lacked negotiation skills, experience, and resources when compared to the Sudanese government representatives. The intermediaries intervened to fill this gap for the purpose of making the mediation process fair and credible. They financed the transportation needed by SSLM representatives to travel where southern exiles were to discuss and forge a united position concerning the negotiations. They retained prominent lawyers to draft position papers for the SSLM and to advise them during the negotiations. They even "leaked" information to the SSLM concerning the government's thinking on the question of southern autonomy. In the absence of these empowerment actions, merely offering one's good offices between two unequal parties would have resulted in being used by the stronger party. In the Sudan case, the mediators were of the view that, in situations of imbalance, the mediator's concern for balancing and producing a fair result should outweigh his strict adherence to impartiality. In the circumstances of obvious inequality, the mediator, by his impartiality, would be playing into the hands of the stronger party, or, by his passivity would be ensuring the imposition of injustice.

Moreover, several lessons could be learned from the strategies used by the mediators in the conduct of the face-to-face negotiations. One was the manipulation of the agenda in such a way that the less controversial issues were negotiated first. This approach had the benefit of building goodwill on the part of the contenders, giving them a sense of accomplishment, confidence in the process, and, in general, a willingness for give and take. Another was the control of the communication process during the negotiations. When discussions strayed to irrelevant recriminations, the moderator kept the parties on course by constantly reminding them of the primary purpose of the negotiations and the consequences of unnecessary delays of a peace settlement to the suffering of the war victims. When exchanges became very emotionally charged and deadlock appeared imminent, the intermediaries would break up the sessions and undertake informal, behind-the-scenes negotiations with each side to explore where their common areas lay and to develop a compromise draft for the parties. During the informal consultation periods, they would try to explain and interpret to the parties the arguments and concerns of their protagonists. Most importantly, they would ask the delegates what arguments they would make or what position they would take, if they were in the place of the contender. The intent was to help the parties develop empathy and consequently a more open mind to accommodate the interests of their adversary. In the Addis Ababa negotiations, there were reports of members of one delegation taking sides on certain issues with the opposing delegation, sometimes against their own, which suggests that there was a great deal of empathy at least on some issues.

After the informal consultations during the breaks, the intermediaries would present the parties with a more concrete draft proposal, which would reconcile the divergent positions, for the parties to work on, amend, or modify. This strategy seems to have helped a more focussed discussion than debates in the abstract. It also seems to have made agreements more likely since the parties would have something more objective and concrete to work with. They could look at the compromise draft as a fall-back position if their own became unattainable.

Moreover, whenever problems appeared insoluble, the intermediaries broke up the larger negotiating body into smaller committees where people of the same professional background and experience considered the issues and proposed solutions. In such smaller committees there might be more willingness to consider issues on their own merits and, possibly, to evaluate alternatives, using the same professional standards. This might enhance empathy and even cross-party loyalty that can foster agreement.

Another strategy that probably was unique but interesting about the 1972 Addis Ababa negotiations was the atmosphere generated by the intermediaries for the peace process. Prayer sessions were made part of the process. Sermons were given by the moderator that capitalized on the common denominators between the Bible and the Koran. There seems to have been a constant appeal to the transcending common humanity of the contenders, which might have made the issues that divided them less significant. This process might be unique to that negotiation but illustrates what some theorists call "emotional healing" which, if attainable, is the most appropriate context for conflict resolution.

LESSONS: THE IMPACT OF MEDIATION

Finally, the Sudan case illustrates a more general theoretical point about the role of mediation in conflict resolution. Some have been quick to point out that the success of mediation is highly dependent on factors outside the mediator, such as stalemate on the battlefield, the nature of the parties and the issues, and the cost of maintaining the conflict. They argue that, if the right situation prevails, the role of the mediator is minimal in contributing to the success of the peace process. This might be true in some cases. However, one is liable to arrive at such a conclusion for the wrong reasons. One reason why the mediator's contribution is dismissed as marginal might be because the observer may not have had adequate information to assess the role of the third party. Mediation processes are, in most instances, secret and informal, principally because of tactical considerations. In most cases, the number of participants is small and the documentation minimal. Even where available, documents are confidential and incomplete. In addition, documents cannot capture certain aspects of the personal and affective interactions between the intermediary and the conflicting parties.

In doing research, even if the investigator is able to talk to the mediator, the latter may be hesitant to divulge confidential transactions and relationships for fear of breaching trust and of jeopardizing his or her future effectiveness by inhibiting other conflicting parties from seeking his or her good offices. Moreover, as Yarrow points out, the intermediary is inclined to attribute most of the credit for a successful mediation to the parties, while renouncing publicity for oneself (Yarrow, 1978). The attitude of the WCC about its role in the Sudan peace process is a good example. In its annual report, the role which its CCIA played in bringing about a negotiated settlement in the Sudan conflict is briefly described. The report concludes: *"The WCC has been hesitant to claim too much for itself in relation to these activities and that is proper."*[23]

For all these reasons, the goals of the researcher and the mediator may not always be congruent. The researcher may not be able to secure adequate information about the personal aspects of the mediation process in order to assess properly the role played by the intermediary in bringing about the final product of negotiation. Particularly, the affective process is what makes mediation unique and difficult when compared with other third-party conflict resolution mechanisms such as arbitration or adjudication. Unfortunately, however, there is no easy way for the researcher, especially an outside observer, to capture this aspect conveniently. Consequently, he or she might tend to magnify the cognitive and visible elements of the peace process at the expense of the affective and behind-the-scenes elements. Under these circumstances, therefore, it is tempting to dismiss the contribution of the intermediary as nonexistent or trivial. These problems demonstrate the need for extreme caution in arriving at such conclusions since there is the danger of making such a claim for methodological rather than substantive reasons.

NOTES

1. Barbara Haq, "Statements on Activities of Liberation (MCF) on the Question of Resolving the Problem of Southern Sudan" (April 1972, unpublished ms).

2. AACC, *Missions to the Sudan* (WCC Archives, Geneva, pp. 25–27).

3. Summary of the Proceedings of the Meeting, 15 May 1971 (WCC Archives, Geneva).

4. Ibid.

5. Colin Legum, "Fighting Ends in Sudan After 17 Years." *The Times* (London), 26 February 1972.

6. The JCA and some Western religious organizations saw the Sudan Civil War as a religious conflict and felt strongly that they must come to the rescue of Christian southerners, who were being persecuted by the Muslim north. Because of this attitude, they were at odds with the WCC's cautious policy toward interference with African internal affairs.

7. K. Ankrah, interview.

8. L. Niilus, interview.

9. L. Niilus, ibid.

10. Report of M. Garang and L. Wol-Wol's mission to Africa, 30 August 1971 (WCC Archives, Geneva).

11. Ibid.

12. Hatchet, Jones & Co. "Memorandum for Submission to the Conflict Research Society," 21 November 1973 (London, unpublished ms).

13. Minutes of Meeting, 11 November 1971 (WCC Archives, Geneva).

14. Ibid.

15. Kodwo Ankrah, "Memorandum to Alan Brash," 22 December 1971, Geneva (WCC Archives, Geneva). The implication of this statement seems to be that if the Sudan government and the SSLM did not succeed in reaching an

agreement in January, member bodies might start to give aid directly to the Anya Nya, and that the WCC could do nothing to stop it.

16. Some have pointed out that Haile Selassie might have been unwilling to chair the negotiations, since he was fighting an insurgency of his own with the Eritrean Liberation Front, and any significant gain by the SSLM in a negotiation he chaired might become a precedent, forcing him to make similar concessions to the Eritreans.

17. The substance of the sermon was recited to the author, and it is interesting for its emotional and inspirational content.

18. Kodwo Ankrah, interview.

19. Canon Burgess Carr, interview.

20. Carr and Niilus, interviews.

21. Niilus, interview.

22. Kodwo Ankrah, interview.

23. *WCC Annual Report*, Geneva, 1972.

9

The Role of Third Parties in the Negotiation of International Agreements

Andrew Williams

Other contributions to this volume demonstrate the slow but steady development of a body of theory that goes some way towards explaining the process of medition. The concern of this chapter is to present certain thoughts about the mediation process based upon observations by the author, who was associated with the Centre for the Applied Study of International Negotiations (CASIN). This centre was established in 1979 in Geneva, Switzerland, and has as its objective the analysis of the process and substance of negotiations, particularly at the international level. It aims to do this by bringing together different actors in the international system in a variety of different combinations and circumstances, but always with the aim of promoting a dialogue. This has proved very successful, and the past few years have seen the organisation of a whole series of seminars, workshops and informal meetings on topics ranging from Mexico's debt problems to East–West cultural relations. It is intended here to concentrate on a discussion of one particular case by looking at the problems encountered in the negotiation of a Code of Conduct on the Transfer of Technology in the United Nations Conference on Trade and Development (UNCTAD), and by positing one way of seeing the CASIN's modest role in this as what might be termed a "mediator".

It must be said at the outset that CASIN is attempting in a limited way to break down the barriers between "theory" and what is here called "practice". Many essentially nonsensical divisions exist in the study and practice of international relations, usually introduced to clarify certain concepts and the differences between philosophical currents. The problem is that these categories—"realism" and "idealism" being two good examples—have become encrusted onto the literature as a new orthodoxy. More seriously, both from the point of view of the historian of international politics and from that of the practitioner who tries to make some sense of this same international politics, we run the risk of incorporating these categories in our decision making with the worst possible results. Moreover, there is an almost structural tendency in the study of international relations to assume that the world began at Yalta, and that a mythical world existed before called the League of Nations. Without in any way presuming to write off the enormous body of literature (mainly American, it must be added) that seems to fall into this trap, there does appear to be a need to make sure that the growing body of mediation theory does not fall into the same errors. The first suggestion of this chapter is therefore that a sense of history should not be forgotten in the analysis of subjects such as that addressed in this symposium.

The ultimate justification for this assertion derives from a common-sense belief, backed up by observation, that what can be loosely called mediating "styles" or "approaches" draw much more from deeper historical traditions of such action than they do from a sole interpretation of the world since Morgenthau.[1] This may go some way to clarifying the problems thoughtfully posed by Ian Clark. One of these is that "the regulatory processes that have characterised the international political process occupy an uncertain twilight zone between underlying power configurations and the resultant political outcomes" (Clark, 1980, p. 4).[2] Clark expresses a healthy realisation of what the French call *la longue dureé* in the great tradition of F. H. Hinsley (1963), while at the same time being well aware of the recent stimulating work—for example, on "regimes"—by authors such as Keohane and Nye (1977). These approaches are self-consciously ahistorical, mostly taking *Politics Among Nations* as their point of departure. Clark has the merit of going much further, at least to Rousseau and Kant.

THE SWISS TRADITION AS INTERMEDIARY

Having implied that we are all part of an historical process at least two hundred years old that will not submit itself meekly to categorisation as "realist" or "idealist", it must be demonstrated that CASIN's present work fits into some kind of perceivable historical tradition. This tradition is physically embodied in the existence of the Swiss state, a state that has had to pursue its own version of "hyper-realism" since its inception. It is also represented by the great organisations of "idealist" impetus—the International Committee of the Red Cross, the League of Nations and its present successor, located not by accident on Swiss territory. The Swiss have attempted to build a particular mix of morality and power politics into their political culture which has perhaps no parallel. The recent debate on whether Switzerland should enter the United Nations thus assumes a particular importance and interest and has resulted in some debates worthy of study.

Why have the Swiss developed the tradition of mediation for which they are justly famed, and how has this manifested itself over the past century or so? How has this tradition become linked with the presence of the international organisations in Geneva? What probably new synthesis will this lead to? Finally, what does this show us about the nature of mediation, its limits and possibilities?

Many writers on Switzerland have stressed the mediatory nature of Swiss society. One of the most famous, the Frenchman Andre Siegfried, wrote that the Swiss as a nation are the "result of a balance of forces between a triple centrifugal cultural attraction and a triple centripetal political attraction". The cultural attraction is out towards France, Germany and Italy, and political attraction derives from a "certain view of political associations" (Siegfried, n.d., p. 121) which positively encourages regional particularism at the expense of centralisation and yet stresses joint interests across these differences. In such a system the political discourse can often seem very dull compared to the ideologically charged debates of Switzerland's neighbours. Orson Welles' famous line about all those hundreds of years of peace having led to the cuckoo clock is a fairly typical example of anti-Swiss rhetoric. But in many ways Switzerland cannot afford to let disagreements get out of hand. She is in a perpetual state of delicate equilibrium that requires a studied neutrality and a sense of compromise in both domestic and foreign relations.

As Siegfried also shows, this neutrality does not imply a disinterest in European or world affairs. The Swiss are passionate believers in a balance of power in Europe, to stop any of their neighbours getting too strong. They are as keen on such a balance as the British, and this fact possibly explains some of the traditional Anglo-Swiss feelings of understanding reinforced in the case of international Geneva by a common Protestant tradition (ibid., pp. 58–60).

Mitchell suggests in his work that one of the most widely accepted "implicit analogies" used by the student of international politics is the "domestic" analogy, where "assumptions that underlie many solutions to intra-state problems are unconsciously transferred to the inter-state level" (Mitchell, 1981b, p. 5). The Swiss seem to be a particularly good example of this. There is a fairly vast literature on Swiss efforts at arbitration, mediation and good offices, which has been usefully summed up by Dr. Raymond Probst, then chief of section of the Departement politique federale (DPE), now called the Departement federal des affaires étrangeres. (Probst, 1960). Probst also stresses the role played by Switzerland in the development of the system of international conferences, and especially the Hague Peace Conference of 1899 and 1907. Some cynics might say that to put faith in such instruments is the last resort of the politically impotent, and the history of the League of Nations gave some back-up to this theory, it being obvious that the "petite entente" was by far the greatest vocal supporter of collective security, since they had no objective security of their own. But the Swiss have for long considered that such instruments were the most sensible approach to the defusing of external threats. Not that they have avoided other back-up measures, such as their militia army, one of the largest per capita in the world, or their mountain redoubt, built by public subscription on a vast scale during the Second World War, but dating back much further in some of its practical realisation. They have thus been fervent partisans of uniting "realist" and "idealist" postures in their foreign and defence policies for most of the modern period.

On the other hand, this wish to participate in the institutionalisation of mediation has not always been totally successful and has on occasion led to major problems. Swiss historian Pierre du Bois has investigated a selection of cases, principally from the two world wars of the century, that shed some light on the problems inherent in this posture.[3] He stresses the fact that the Swiss have always had to make sure of the maintenance of their internal cohesion, based on linguistic differences as well as on fiercely guarded distinctions between federal, cantonal and communal power structures, which even today require a permanent internal mediation over particular projects. (The building of motorways is perhaps a good example of this at the moment. One commune, Bex, was able seriously to delay the completion of the national motorway system through its opposition to disruption of its territory.) In time of war until 1918, however, one major risk of splitting Switzerland into its respective linguistic constituencies lay with the danger of linguistic identification across national frontiers. Thus the French-speaking part of Switzerland (la Suisse romande) tended to feel in all ways more sympathetic towards the French predicament in 1914, and the German-speaking part towards that of Germany. Of course, a proviso to this must be made, due to the (also widely held) fear by both French- and German-speaking Swiss of absorption into a larger and therefore self-consciously superior-feeling sister culture.

1914–18 was particularly damaging to the ideology of a Switzerland united against all foreigners, which has been the country's founding myth since William Tell. The relative difficulty in deciding who was the "baddy" and who was the "goody" in the First World War, something historians are still arguing about today, complicated the internal stresses of this period for the Swiss. Added to this was the difficult balancing act of what to do about a changing Europe and the presence of a new Russia after February 1917. This new Russia was greeted with a cautious enthusiasm by a Swiss administration that tended to favour the German cause but also had no desire to see a more extreme regime installed in Russia. It was, after all, the Swiss who had allowed that "plague bacillus of Bolshevism", Mr. Lenin, to leave in a closed train for the Finland station. This might explain why one of the federal counsellors, Arthur Hoffman, acting on his own, attempted to mediate between Kerensky and the Germans to obtain a unilateral peace in the East and to ensure a stalemate leading to peace in the West, with neither Germany nor France emerging victorious. The attempt was a failure, neither Kerensky nor the Germans being interested, although perhaps it was in Kerensky's long-term interest, as history was to prove. This failure shows several things. The mediation attempt by Hoffman was not at all impartial, but was done for definite reasons of his perception of domestic Swiss self-interest. It was a failure because the parties that were supposed to be brought together actually resented the intrusion. It must be added that the action in this case resulted in Hoffman having to resign his post.[4]

1939–45 has other examples, also described by du Bois, that merit a similar analysis. The then president of the confederation, Pilet-Golaz, had kept a distrust of Bolshevik Russia as a result of his country's various difficult relations with the USSR since its inception, a feeling shared by many other European politicians, it must be added. The impending defeat of Germany, for which Pilet-Golaz seems to have conceived a certain alarm due to what can only be seen as his partiality for the Fuhrer (probably because of Hitler's anti-Bolshevik rhetoric and actions), led him to the desperate idea in 1943 of providing himself as go-between to procure a cease-fire in the West so as to allow the Germans to finish off the Russians. The Russians got wind of this through their allies and were most annoyed. The Germans were also offended by Pilet-Golaz's affront to the image of an invincible Third Reich, and the mediation was, as a result, a failure, Pilet-Golaz being forced to resign. Yet again the mediation was in no way impartial nor asked for by any of the parties.

No such attempts have been made since 1945. A much more discreet approach has been followed, one that has proved its worth in countless actions by the Red Cross. A couple of examples will suffice to demonstrate this reliance on old methods. The first of these is the good offices undertaken in the Algerian crisis by Olivier Long, later director-general of the General Agreement on Tariffs and Trade (GATT), whom the Front pour la Liberation Nationale (FLN) asked to act as a go-between for themselves and the French government. His activities contributed to the Evian talks and the resulting independence of Algeria. In another case a representative of the International Committee of the Red Cross (ICRC) was asked to intercede to assure the release of three plane loads of hostages taken by the Palestine Liberation Organisation (PLO) in 1970. He did not succeed in obtaining their release. The two cases are in stark contrast to the quoted war-time experiences. In neither case was the mediation forced on either party; in neither was the internal stability of Switzerland in any way involved.

It is tempting to draw the conclusions that Gilbert Winham thought the average academic would make (although he does not himself). Were the Swiss in the earlier cases in fact becoming not "mediators" but "negotiators", if we define mediators as "disinterested" and negotiators as "parties to the conflict" (Winham, 1977)?

As Winham points out in one case study that he has examined, that of the multilateral negotiation of the GATT Kennedy Round, the then director-general, Eric Wyndham-White, does not fit into any neat category of either mediator or negotiator, taking the normally accepted definitions of either. The fact is that any mediator is "interested" in that he engages his personal or institutional reputation. The problem is that it is often very difficult to tell whether the parties to a conflict really want a settlement. This can be due to internal differences or because of the desire to find simultaneously an excuse to blame the other party or even the mediator for failure, and to give their cause better publicity.

Have the Swiss changed their tactics in negotiation/mediation because of a change in their perceived world view? This might be seen to be the case. Can we observe the development of a new kind of Swiss attitude, one that internally relies on a militarily almost impregnable Confederation based on popular support, and externally on a far more circumspect enthusiasm for ideologically based regimes and the projection of a solid internationalism, one that has little of the extremes of "idealism" attached to it? This is the view of the author, who has, however, a limited knowledge of Swiss society. Post-1945 policies have to be seen in a wider context of a reevaluation both of Switzerland's place in a changed Europe and world and the realisation that small states can have a big impact if they know where to place their dynamite, which means doing it with intelligence and care.

CASIN AND THE CODE OF CONDUCT
ON TRANSFER OF TECHNOLOGY

The work of a small Swiss-based organisation like CASIN may illustrate this to some extent. It has set up a number of courses intended to communicate to international civil servants, diplomats and industrial executives some of the insights available from academic work on negotiation and mediation. CASIN has also developed a particular interest in the global "North–South" negotiations in UNCTAD. For all these reasons it was delighted to be approached by UNCTAD to help, in a very modest way to be sure, to act as a forum in one of the "intractable" problems—that of the negotiation of a Code of Conduct on the Transfer of Technology,[5] in line with General Assembly Resolution 37/210 of 1982 which allows for extra UN consultants to facilitate the preparatory work on the code.

This negotiation, still in progress, demonstrated the vastly increased level of complexity inherent in multilateral negotiations where there are large economic resources at stake. Until recently (in many peoples' minds still) the ideological differences involved in these essentially North–South discussions made any progress impossible. Oversimplifying somewhat, developing countries believed that they had been exploited by colonial powers for decades, and that the technological advances in the North were therefore already paid for. The North's line was that technology had a high cost attached to it, and that it must be paid for by acquirers, poor or not. This was also tied to the problem of patent rights and their defence.

This kind of philosophical difference meant that by the time of the 1979 UNCTAD conference at Manila, a near stalemate had been reached in progress towards a code. Joan Spero's standard text (Spero, 1981, p. 210) says as much.[6] On a wider level the initial idea of making UNCTAD into a platform for the promotion of the economic rights of the developing countries and the brave hopes of a New International Economic Order seemed to be dashed at least temporarily. However, perhaps this was but a temporary reverse, UNCTAD being a "victim of its own success" over the past twenty years, where a whole host of subjects had been discussed that would have been unthinkable before 1960.

CASIN can be seen as having been requested to use its "good offices" rather than to act as a mediator. But what did this mean in practice? A first role was in the organisation of informal consultations among interested parties about issues which were still outstanding. These issues could be mapped quite easily by examination of the number of brackets extant in the different versions of the draft Code.[7] A second was in an analysis of the different positions held by the various actors in the negotiations—suppliers and recipients of technology in particular—and the likely direction in which they were to move on outstanding issues. A third was to formulate recommendations on the basis of as wide a range of informal contacts, consultations and expert groups discussions as possible so that, finally, this accumulated expertise would be put at the disposition of those servicing the fifth session of the Code conference to be held in late 1983.

Meetings were held in spring and autumn of 1982, with another one in July 1983, interspersed with the above-mentioned informal contacts. The membership of these meetings was made as diverse as possible, the aim being to have all parties concerned present. On the other hand the meetings were deliberately kept numerically limited to encourage an informal atmosphere. This atmosphere was further enhanced by taking the participants out of their usual environment, whether it be UNCTAD or a foreign ministry.

Every effort was made to ensure representativity. From the beginning there were experts present from a key cross-section of countries from North and South, as well as, on occasions, from the East Bloc. It is important to stress here the bringing together of parties that normally do not discuss questions of this kind in an informal and systematic way. The institutional framework of UNCTAD does not easily allow for the organisation of informal gatherings, and even less does it allow for contacts between governmental officials and representatives of organisations outside governmental circles. This effectively excluded a large number of potentially vital actors in the international system—trade unions, multinational companies and non-governmental organisations, being the most obvious examples.

The meetings were deliberately kept informal, usually being held in restaurants. Although the North–South dialogue is conducted in a relatively dignified manner in Geneva, it was thought wise to have these meetings in an unthreatening environment where some form of "controlled communication" might be possible. The meetings were chaired in a very loose way by the director of CASIN, whose role was not to direct the discussion but to make sure that everyone was able to express an opinion. The agenda was in a sense the Code itself, in that the aim at every meeting was to remove a few more "brackets", or at least to discuss how this might be done. The number of participants was never more than a large dinner party, no formal notes were taken and nobody was committed to anything. Certainly there was no reference, as seems to have been the case with John Burton's method, to academic ideas on negotiation, misperception and the like. The practitioners present would probably have reacted very badly to such ideas, it was felt, even though some of them were clearly introduced (at least tacitly) by the chairperson.

What could be expected from these meetings? It was possible, even at the end of 1982, to define the main areas of division and to see a good deal of common ground even on issues of dispute. The 1983 meetings consciously tried to increase the number and the range of participants, including those seen as major critics of a code which would (after all) affect them the most in practice. It was hoped that this would better define the negotiating parameters and continue the process of breaking down psychological, and therefore real, barriers.

No-one wanted or would take responsibility for a failure to produce a code. If there was to be a code, it was to be a "meaningful instrument". But what did this signify in practice? To put it in simple terms, what was to be expected from a code, what were to be its effects and objectives, and how should it be used? On a more imminent level, what were the minimum assurances or safeguards that would be acceptable to Group B (the North) or the Group of 77? None of these questions had easy answers, since they would undoubtedly involve major economic structural change in the internal system, but at least they had now been postulated.

As for the role played by CASIN, a new definition would seem necessary. It has not acted as a direct mediator, certainly not as an arbitrator, and it is not a negotiator. Fisher seems to have found the term that fits best, that of "third-party consultant". Fisher defines this as one who "analyses the basic relationship between the parties rather than by encouraging or imposing specific settlements on substantive issues" (Fisher, Ronald J., 1983, p. 302). This is not quite the same thing as mediation as defined by Wall (1981), whose model includes far more actors than are involved in a third-party consultation such as that in which CASIN is engaged. One element that would seem to indicate a third-party consultant role for CASIN is implied in Fisher's distinction that this consultant "must establish greater trust in order to encourage the sharing of the participants' feelings and perceptions regarding the basic relationship" (ibid., p. 305). The transfer of technology discussions cannot have an outcome in the sense meant by conventional mediation theory, since the stakes are not only perceived as being too high (especially by the industrialised countries) but also because the questions involved are too diffuse. Even to come to truly understand the opposing point of view is, therefore, a major breakthrough.

Fisher does not mention this, for obvious reasons, and neither does he include what could be termed analogous situations in his list of cases of third-party consultation. On the other hand, many of his cases are ones that might usually be defined as insoluble. In his "community" list, that is to say in black/white confrontations in the United States, Catholic/Protestant confrontations in Northern Ireland or Jews/Arabs in Israel, all the conflicts are insoluble in the sense that they require major changes of group psychology. These are not quite the same as old-fashioned inter-state or industrial disputes. In these we can search for points of disagreement (ie., what is *not* negotiable); in the former we have to find what *is* negotiable. "Precious little" is the honest reply, since the process of negotiation means accepting some common ideology of discussion. These far more difficult discussions are going to become more, not less, prevalent.

On another major point, CASIN's experience seems to at least partly agree with Fisher's formulation. This is when he puts emphasis on the nature of third-party identity. There is, as he says, not much disagreement that the third-party consultant must have "adequate personal and professional expertise as well as specialized knowledge regarding conflict processes", although what can be termed "adequate" is not defined and is perhaps undefinable. He also points out much disagreement about the consultant's need for a "degree of knowledge about the parties and their relationship" (Fisher, Ronald J., 1983, p. 321). This must obviously depend a great deal on the particular case, but CASIN's experience perhaps shows that too much initial knowledge might have been detrimental, whereas bringing the intelligent, but not specialised, eye to a very complicated issue can have the effect of facilitating the process of partial agreement.

SUCCESS OR FAILURE?

The notes drawn up by CASIN after the first meetings showed at least some clarifications of differences. The main problem was defined as being that of whether the Code should be legally binding or not, the South wishing it to be so, the North not. This seeming impasse was circumvented by an agreement that it would not be binding, at least to begin with. This is not the total climb-down by the South that it would appear. A morally binding code could be claimed to be at least as effective as a non-binding code, because it embodies a clear intention. No code is a total defeat for the South, a non-binding code signed is at least a partial victory. As in many such discussions there is not a zero-sum game situation since there can be no winners and losers either at the moment or in a different time scale. The problem of harmonisation of national with international legislation was also agreed upon as a key factor. This may be included in what has widely been called the "re-entry factor". How can an agreement be accepted by a society that may not have had its mind changed in the same way as its negotiators?

The great fear of some industries and governments is that they will later be accused of not having asked for enough or having given in too easily. But this sometimes means that they are loath to get involved with private fora where they will possibly be lulled into what they see as a false sense of security or of unreality. They must appear as extremely committed to their position, if only to placate their own constituent galleries. There is also a fear of letting such vast enterprises as a code of conduct on the transfer of technology be decided in an international organisation far divorced, as they see it, from their world of "practitioners" and "reality".

There is still no fully mutually acceptable code extant. Many of the original brackets look less entrenched in the document as it goes through its various incarnations, but many of them are still there. What can be said to have been achieved? On the general level it must be said that the so-called dialogue is not what it once was at the time of Ambassador Mohammed Bedjaoui's book (Bedjaoui, 1979). On the other hand it still exists, because it is doomed to do so. The transnational corporations

(TNCs) are going to become more, not less, significant actors; inter-dependence is a reality. Secondly, the institutional framework for this dialogue has changed, internally at least. UNCTAD is now far less influenced by the Prebisch model than it was, however much the United States might say the opposite. What might be termed a de-ideologisation of UNCTAD has and is taking place: the albeit-limited admission of the previously vilified TNCs is one example of this. Thirdly, the TNCs themselves seem to have changed. They now accept some kind of UNCTAD interference, even if it is with a bad grace, because increasingly they also accept the reality of interdependence, and the need for new markets.

In such disputes a great deal has to be changed in opponents' core value systems and here CASIN has made some contribution. This ties in well with the "problem-solving" techniques of the Centre for the Analysis of Conflict. There is in the North some sign that the core values of our capitalist system are in fact changing, that there is a growing acceptance of the necessity of interdependence for the most realistic of motives, the need to sell and buy. Unfortunately it may well need the 1980s equivalent of the 1929 crash of the Creditanstalt to make the lesson sink in. In much the same way as it was once wrongly accepted that money supply was in some way fixed and that one country's gold loss was another's equal gain, it might one day be easy to freely exchange technology.

The international system is going through one of its periodic and necessary crises. Interdependence has always existed, as Switzerland proves, as the first murmurings of Europe may be said to demonstrate. It is essential that those interested in mediation should not be dissatisfied too greatly with the advance of the craft, since historical forces move at a very slow absolute rate in terms of human lifetimes, but that the long-term view shows very distinct movement, if not always in the direction initially envisaged.

This chapter has tried to come to grips with a number of problems and the possibility of a third party playing some role in helping, to use Burton's phrase, to "settle" a series of objective conflicts that cannot be "resolved" since they are structurally grounded in our present economic system. The majority of discussion in this volume is about situations where open conflict (in the sense of violence against individuals) is a constant threat. The usually hushed portals of the United Nations do not see much real violence, but the discussions therein do represent millions of human destinies nonetheless. The parallel posed here is that of a diverse and divided polity, Switzerland, that has managed to devise methods of internal conflict resolution that it sees as partially transferable to another debate in another forum. As this endeavour is the aim of all the writers in this volume, it is hoped that the chapter will help generate some discussion about the future of such attempts.

NOTES

1. Morgenthau (1948). This work and its five subsequent editions is the key proponent of the major "realist" paradigm of current international relations.

2. Clark is here referring to the body of work known as "regime" theory in the field of international organisation.

3. Some of Pierre du Bois's work on this topic was apparently published in the *Laxenberg Papers* during 1984. The author saw an early draft of this work in manuscript.

4. Cf. *Documents Diplomatiques Suisses, Vol. 6, 1914–1918* (Berne: Benteli Vorlag, 1981), especially documents 301, 303, 316, 318, 320–322, the last being Hoffmann's resignation.

5. The "state of play" on these discussion in 1980–81 when CASIN became involved is usefully summarized in Pedro Roffe, "UNCTAD: Code of Conduct for the Transfer of Technology—Progress and Issues under Negotiation", *Journal of World Trade Law*, March–April 1980, pp. 160–172. An UNCTAD document on "major issues outstanding" (TD/CODE TOT/27, 17 November 1980) is also useful.

6. For the UNCTAD definition of the question before UNCTAD V, see "Technology: Restructuring the legal and juridical environment: issues under negotiation, Items 13a) and 13b) of the provisional agenda" (TD/237, United Nations, 29 January 1979).

7. For example, UNCTAD, "Draft International Code . . . as of 10 April 1980" (TD/CODE TOT/33, 1981).

8. For a useful summary see Banks (1984b).

10

South African Initiatives: Contrasting Options in the Mediation Process

Hendrik W. van der Merwe

This chapter shares the attitude of the editors of this volume that mediation should be regarded as an understandable and analysable process. It contains reflections on my experience over recent years and on ongoing and some unresolved conceptual, ethical and strategic issues concerning conflict and the accommodation of conflict in South Africa. In many circles South Africa is seen as a classic case of irreconcilable interests where disagreements can only be settled through major and somewhat cataclysmic confrontation and violence. In such an atmosphere mediation, conciliation and negotiation have become dirty words.

In this chapter I argue that it is essential, and possible, to remain positive and constructive about the prospects of a negotiated settlement in spite of numerous obstacles, including prevailing violence. A constructive approach requires a mode of thought quite contrary to the popular despair reflected in the common phrases such as: "There is no room for mediation"; "It is too late for conciliation" or "We don't want conciliation until we have justice". The mediator or conciliator could not ask for a greater challenge! Conflict resolution (or mediation, for that matter) can be both an art and a science. As an art, it refers to those given personal dispositions, behaviour patterns and specific actions which come naturally or spontaneously to the mediator. As a science, it refers to those methods and techniques which are analysed, described and shared in the scholarly world, and those skills acquired in a formal learning.

The author gratefully acknowledges financial assistance from the Human Sciences Research Council in the form of an overseas grant for senior researchers.

While my training as a sociologist at the Universities of Stellenbosch and California introduced me to some of the fundamental writings, it was only during the past five years that I started reading about conflict resolution and management. From my experience in mediation on community, regional and national levels, I seem to have learned some universal lessons which I have attempted to report within some of the conceptual and theoretical frameworks of current literature.

For example, it was when I arranged a ceasefire between the two warring factions in the Cape Town squatter settlement of Crossroads that I realised that we could not have peace without justice. The ceasefire was only *apparent* peace, because justice was not restored to the weaker party that was driven out of Crossroads. Justice is a condition for *real* peace.

During the Soweto revolt of 1976 I responded to the growing cycle of violence and polarisation between government authorities and the black communities by bringing the leaders together. While I set out as a neutral mediator, my role spontaneously and gradually shifted towards that of an advocate of the deprived. I found that I could not remain neutral on moral issues. I also responded positively to the particular needs of the black communities at that time.

In contrast to this shift towards greater identification with one group, I have tended towards a mediating and facilitating role in my recent contacts with the South African government and the liberation groups. Because of the state of polarisation and the stated unwillingness to negotiate, the parties were not interested in mediation or in mediators. But they were indeed interested in the facilitation of meaningful communication.

This chapter is largely concerned with what I term *facilitation* and not mediation. Needless to say, I am discussing *informal*, and not official, mediation or facilitation. I argue in this chapter that careful consideration of nine basic principles could contribute significantly to the success of any intermediary initiatives in South Africa. I have not included some of the most obvious principles, such as credibility of the intermediary, but have focussed on those that have taught me particular lessons. Quite obviously these lessons have applicability to many other situations of conflict.

FROM MEDIATION TO FACILITATION

Various processes and intermediary roles can be employed in the communication process between contending groups. I am arguing that the neutral, almost technical, services of the facilitator are often more acceptable than the services of the mediator who is morally committed to peacemaking. Where negotiation between conflicting parties is absent a neutral intermediary may be needed to mediate, mediation being "a voluntary process for settling disputes or resolving conflict in which an unbiassed third person assists the conflicting parties in negotiating a mutually beneficial settlement or truce" (Albert, 1986, p. 29). Mediation is closely related to conciliation, an informal process in which the third party tries to bring the parties to agreement by improving communications, lowering tensions, interpreting issues, providing technical assistance, exploring potential solutions and bringing about a negotiated settlement, either informally or in a subsequent step, through formal mediation. Conciliation is frequently used in volatile conflicts and in disputes where the parties are unable, unwilling or unprepared to come to the table to negotiate their differences (Meyer et al., 1986, p. 16). The mediator or conciliator thus "facilitates" exchange, suggests possible solutions and assists the parties in reaching a voluntary agreement.

However, I want to make a clear distinction between mediation and facilitation. Facilitation is restricted to the *first* of the tasks of mediation listed above: the facilitation of communication between conflicting parties. It does not suggest solutions and is not primarily concerned with reaching agreement or consensus. It is more concerned with technical than moral issues; the improvement of communications, rather than the promotion of solutions.

The mediator is usually motivated by a concern to reach a peaceful solution, consensus, conciliation or some such goal. He can claim neutrality regarding the stands taken by conflicting parties, but not regarding the outcome of the exercise. For the mediator, facilitation of communication is a means to an end. For the facilitator, facilitation of communication is an end in itself, in the same way that one can pursue knowledge for the sake of knowledge or develop atomic power for the sake of developing power. While the mediator is relatively more concerned with the use made of new insights gained from reliable communication, the facilitator is primarily concerned with the fact that the relevant parties gain accurate information, regardless of what use they make of it.

For these reasons a facilitator may, in situations of extreme polarisation and intense suspicion, be more acceptable to conflicting parties than a mediator.

I want to argue, therefore, that at this stage in South Africa we would consider facilitation as a first step before attempting mediation between the major contending parties. In my experiences with the South African estabishment and the African National Congress (ANC) in exile, I have always argued that I served as a facilitator assisting both parties in having meaningful communication and reliable information. I did not convey my experiences and insights urging the parties to put the knowledge to good use, to make peace, to forgive or to behave like good boys. It was up to them to decide how they would use these insights.

This approach probably accounted for the positive responses I have had from both sides. The facilitator is less likely than the mediator to be seen as a meddler or a busybody, a preacher or a moralist. The facilitator is there *not* as a peacemaker or conciliator. He also does not offer or attempt to bring the parties together. Obviously, should the parties be ready to take that step, the facilitator may be an appropriate person to assist.

This is exactly what has happened in my efforts to facilitate between conflicting parties in Natal. While one party urged me to arrange a meeting between them and to make an effort to make peace or reconcile them, the other party, which at that time felt they were strategically at a disadvantage, did not want any reconciliation, fearing that it would serve the purpose of merely maintaining the status quo, which, from their point of view, was unjust. They wanted the assurance that justice would be done before there was any peacemaking. Being the weaker or losing party, they were also suffering heavy losses when it came to physical conflicts and violence. While they did not favour any meeting for peacemaking, they were indeed willing to participate in any ad hoc effort to reduce physical violence. This wish gave rise to the idea of setting up a Joint Monitoring Committee and eventually a meeting was held in order to establish such a committee. While one party was unwilling to meet with the enemy for purposes of peacemaking, it was indeed willing to meet (almost by default) for a more specific strategic purpose. The intermediary presented himself and was accepted as somebody who was providing a *technical* rather than a *moral* service.

INFORMAL FACILITATION IN PREPARATION FOR OFFICIAL MEDIATION

Any involvement by governments or official bodies or any of their representatives as an intermediary tends to give some kind of official status to the communication process between contending parties. This is exactly what the parties want to avoid while they are not ready for mediation.

Such circumstances call for the quiet, informal services of "unofficial diplomats"—individuals without official status, power or vested interests. Unofficial or non-official mediators are people not employed by or responsible to national governments or inter-governmental organisations. While they have no political, economic or military clout (Martin, 1984, p. 974) they have "the freedom to be flexible, to disregard protocol, to suggest unconventional remedies or procedures, to widen or restrict the agenda or change the order of items, to propose partial solutions or package deals, to press the case for constructive initiatives or magnanimous gestures" (Bailey, 1985, p. 211). Private initiatives may contribute to the alleviation of problems in communication. "By providing auxiliary channels of communication, by serving as intermediaries between governments, by performing various third party functions, including negotiating and mediating in conflict situations, and by contributing to a climate in which policy-makers can usefully work, private citizens may augment and facilitate official diplomacy" (Berman and Johnson, 1977, p. 7). "The intent of some of the individuals who initiate private efforts is to prepare the way for intergovernmental action, and often they act with the blessing or at least the knowledge of officials of governments or international organizations. When it suits their purposes, governments may support and use private channels" (Berman and Johnson, 1977, p. 7).

CONFLICT ACCOMMODATION AND MANAGEMENT RATHER THAN RESOLUTION

"Conflict resolution" denotes the termination of a conflict through the elimination of the underlying bases or causes of that conflict. It is a far more complex and comprehensive process than mere conflict settlement, which is based on the notion of mutual compromise. Although the term is widely used in other countries, we do not favour the use of "conflict resolution" in the present South African context, because of its comprehensive and far-reaching implications. Indeed the majority of conflicts in the world are settled or accommodated rather than resolved. To use the term "resolution" loosely could therefore be interpreted as unrealistic, even irresponsible (Meyer et al., 1986, p. 9).

We use the term "conflict accommodation" as a generic term to include all methods, practices and techniques—formal and informal, traditional and "alternative", within and outside the courts—that are used to resolve or settle disputes. For some, the term "accommodation" refers to a form of compromise or giving in without taking a stand. However, we use the term to refer to the processes by which conflicting parties come to a settlement or *accommodate* one another's claims, aspirations or needs, *within the given structural context*. It does not necessarily imply fundamental structural change, although I believe that structural change is, indeed, a necessary condition for a lasting settlement in South Africa.

We tend to use the term "management" to refer to the processes by which conflict is settled or resolved through *major structural adjustments and change*. The need for management arises when the structural context does not permit the peaceful and lasting accommodation of the interests, needs and aspirations of all, notably of the weaker parties. In this sense, the term "management" is closely related to the concept of "empowerment" defined elsewhere.

There is the possibility that the term "management" could carry the negative connotation of manipulation, where the conflict-manager is seen as one who foments discord and sharpens divisions in order to bring about a settlement. However, "management" also carries with it positive associations—it implies that conflict is not *per se* something to be ignored or shunned, but can be positively and creatively handled. "Conflict management" can therefore be used to describe this positive approach (Meyer et al., 1986, pp. 8–9). In 1981 the Centre for Intergroup Studies, in cooperation with the Western Province Council of Churches, initiated our first Conflict *Management* Programme. The name of this programme reflected a deliberate decision not to use the term "resolution" which was widely used in the United States at that time.

FROM DETACHMENT TO CONCERN FOR HUMAN SUFFERING

Objectivity and detachment are essential conditions for facilitation and mediation which require no further explanation here. But such detachment can also be interpreted as lack of feeling, care and concern by suffering, deprived or oppressed parties, who believe they had been wronged or who feel threatened. This is especially true in the case of black South Africans, but it applies to many groups in particular situations, including the white South African minority group and the Nationalist government as a pariah state.

The use of the term "resolution" has given rise to the fear that inequalities, injustice and violations of human rights will be ignored or smoothed over by intermediaries who do not share their anguish and pain, but who undertake peacemaking for ulterior motives. Academics with grand plans that they want to try out, providing material for books, foreigners who build up reputations as successful mediators and gain international acclaim for their achievements, are suspect and often unacceptable. Expression of genuine concern is not always easily reconcilable with the very necessary quality of impartiality of the facilitator. Can concern with the "oppressed" be expressed without sacrificing this impartiality, and without estranging the "oppressor"? I believe it can be done, provided that concern for suffering is distinguished from support for any one party in the conflict. Such concern can be expressed without supporting the particular stands, goals, policies or methods of that party. Adam Curle (1986, p. 19) explains how expressions of shock and horror about atrocities committed may seem to one party to imply sympathy with the enemy. He suggests: "Perhaps the best approach is to express sorrow, but in a way that suggests no blame except to the practice of war which makes such tragedies, committed by either side, inevitable". This is often possible in situations of extreme violence where both parties are suffering from physical and human losses, as in the case of the violent confrontations between opposing parties in Natal. In most particular incidents one of the parties suffers greater losses than the other and the series of incidents offers sufficient opportunities for expression of concern by the intermediary towards both sides. But even in situations where the suffering is predominantly on the one side, as in the case of the oppression of blacks in South Africa, it is now widely accepted in government circles that past policies have been wrong and unjust and have caused suffering with which any person should sympathize.

Injury and death caused by political violence by various parties in South Africa give sufficient cause and occasion for public statements by concerned people such as church leaders. However, because of the state of polarisation, the occasions at which these statements are made, the media through which they are conveyed to the public and their content or tone almost invariably reflect the partisan political stands of such leaders. Conservative or pro-establishment church leaders show comparatively greater horror at the acts of protest of liberation movements and more concern and sympathy for their victims; while anti-government church leaders express comparatively much greater horror at the acts of the security forces and concern and sympathy for their victims. This leaning towards selective expressions of concern does not contribute towards the development of common ground, but towards further polarisation.

Examples of selective concern or horror are reflected in statements by different parties in relation to the increasing number of acts of political violence and counter-violence in South Africa. The cross-border attack of the South African Defence Force (SADF) on Maseru in December 1982, the bomb detonated by ANC supporters or agents in Pretoria on 20 May 1983 and the retaliatory attack by the SADF on Maputo three days later, left victims on both sides and elicited numerous public statements and denunciations. These events and the responses to them in both white and black circles, among conservatives and liberals, made me intensely aware of the spiral of polarisation that is driving South Africa into rigidly opposed camps of mutual hatred and commitment to revenge. This element of revenge was evident in the pubic statements of both the ANC and the South African government. On Monday 23 May, General Malan, the minister of defence, stated in Parliament that "the security forces of South Africa will revenge every drop of blood shed by the innocent—white, black or brown—with all the force at its disposal". This element pervades the whole of South African society. Blacks cheered when they heard of the Pretoria bomb, and so did whites when they heard of the revenge a few days later.

I could not help noticing in private conversation and in public statements by my colleagues and church leaders how the intensity of their responses reflected their political biases. These expressions of selective concern reinforced the relations of polarisation. In response to this situation I then formulated a statement of concern which I intended to serve as a contribution towards conciliation. In this statement I expressed:

1. my disapproval of violence on both sides;
2. my sympathy with the victims on both sides;

3. my belief in the elements of goodwill on both sides;
4. my intention to make financial contributions to the victims on both sides.

This statement, together with a small donation, were conveyed to the trustees of the State President's Fund in South Africa which was established to assist victims of terrorism, and to the Lesotho Christian Council, which assisted victims of the SADF attack on Maseru. The statement and the general sentiments expressed in it were also shared with black and white leaders of different and conflicting political views with whom I came in contact.

To my disappointment (but not to my surprise) this statement was deplored and attacked by colleagues and church leaders—some of whom accused me of supporting the terrorists and others of supporting apartheid (the government should take care of their own victims!).

Such expressions of concern can, however, open up channels of communication and promote the development of a middle ground, the narrowing of the gap between the conflicting parties and the lessening of the cycle of polarisation and violence. Such a development enhances the chances of contact, dialogue, negotiated settlement and conciliation. In contrast, expressions of selective horror and concern merely increase polarisation.

These concerns are shared by fellow Quakers with experience in international conciliation. Mike Yarrow explains that impartiality implies an aloofness or indifference, which does not adequately describe the Quaker approach:

A more appropriate though paradoxical description might be "balanced partiality"—that is, they listened sympathetically to each side, trying to put themselves in the other party's place. The evidence is clear that they were perceived as sympathetic listeners on both sides. [Yarrow, in Berman and Johnson, 1977, p. 99]

Adam Curle (1986, p. 19) argues that it is through this "concerned impartiality" that mediators are able to remain on good terms with both sides.

PEACE WITH JUSTICE

The two goals of *peace* and *justice* are normally accepted by all parties and by mediators. The unique relationship between these two goals is, however, not always fully appreciated. They are ideal states which can never be fully achieved; they are complementary, in the sense that one cannot be achieved without the other; and the roles of peacemaker (or conciliator) and prophet (or proponent of justice) stand in a relation of tension towards each other.

The peacemaker or conciliator must have credibility on both sides of a conflict. Building and maintaining good relations and credibility with all parties are not compatible with exposition of, and attacks on, injustice and public confrontation with the perceived perpetrators of injustice. The roles, tasks and styles of peacemakers and prophets are different and can cause severe tension within any one person, or between persons and groups.

This tension between peace and justice is manifested in various ways. The peacemaker who is trying to make or obtain peace at all costs is likely to underplay injustice and overlook its manifestations. By doing so, he may be able to arrange some kind of truce or apparent peace, leaving the relations of inequality and injustice unchanged. The weaker or deprived party will want an assurance that the intervener will not be obsessed with peacemaking only, but will also be concerned with the promotion of justice.

To what extent can the mediator express himself on issues of injustice without confronting or offending one party? It was pointed out earlier that it is possible to express *concern* about a problem, an injustice, an atrocity, without attributing blame. However, to do so in practice is indeed a fine art. Genuine concern is not something that can be taught in academic courses on peacemaking. In conflict situations where injustice is not a primary issue, or where mediators are seen as completely detached, these problems are less severe. In South Africa, however, injustice is seen as *the* primary issue by the deprived groups and by the international community. Furthermore, apartheid has become an international issue and no citizen of any other country is seen as quite detached or neutral on this major issue.

Justice in South Africa has become an obsession in the anti-apartheid movement, leading to the slogan: "There can be no peace until there is justice".

This atmosphere contributes to the discrediting of any conciliation or peacemaking. Given the complementary relation of the two goals of peace and justice, and the fact that justice is an ideal state that can never be fully achieved, the slogan that peacemaking should be shelved, or even opposed, until justice has been achieved obviously implies that peacemaking is not on the agenda.

In the same sense that peace and justice as goals are complementary, peacemaking and the promotion of justice as *means* towards these goals are also complementary. The one should not be conducted without the other. An obsession with the promotion of justice at all costs will undermine the foundations of peace and of a stable lasting future society. What kind of justice will it be without peace?

It has been argued that the styles and roles of peacemakers and prophets of justice are different. So do individuals differ in personality types, and organisations differ in goals and functions. It is thus obvious that each individual and organisation will lean more towards one than the other role. In my case, I have found that I tended to respond to the needs of the groups I dealt with and to specific situations. During the 1976 revolt I set off as a neutral mediator between government officials and black community leaders but spontaneously shifted towards a more partisan stand in support of the deprived groups. I attributed this shift to two factors: my responses to the needs of the black community at that time, and the fact that one cannot be neutral on moral issues (van der Merwe, 1983).

During the immense clampdown in the early 1980s I was a member of a delegation of the South African Institute of Race Relations to a regional head of police. The intention of the delegation was to bring reported atrocities and police torture to his attention in a friendly way. The meeting, however, developed into a confrontation and, with the permission of my colleagues, I withdrew from the delegation because I believed that my role as a go-between would be much more constructive and valuable than merely adding my voice to the protest movement. Subsequent developments gave support to that decision (see van der Merwe, 1986b). The art of peacemaking requires constant vigilance to maintain a balanced approach and sensitivity. There are no scientific recipes or easy answers.

BALANCING PRIVATE AND PUBLIC ROLES

Confidentiality and even secrecy are essential conditions for mediation and faciliation between public bodies. Such confidentiality poses no problems for most intermediaries. Academics, such as the members of the Centre for the Analysis of Conflict, have produced numerous publications based on their experiences in international mediation without revealing any details of the parties involved or their respective stands (Burton, 1969; Mitchell, 1981). In other cases, such information is given subsequent to the event in a way that causes no embarrassment to either party. There can be, however, good reasons for going public during the process of mediation. Third parties can help in resolving disputes constructively to the extent that they are known and prestigious. The mass media can help in this task by making them known to the parties but, even more important, by helping to promote public opinion in favour of third-party intervention and a negotiated settlement.

In my own case, I have experienced, and still do, a serious dilemma and ambivalence between my private role as facilitator and my public role as opinion maker. The latter is attached to my position as director of an institute that promotes educational and training programmes in conflict management on local, regional and national levels. The promotion of these programmes requires not only the provision of an infrastructure and organisational facilities, but also a public atmosphere favourably disposed towards negotiation and the constructive management of conflict. Over many years, this academic task has been closely matched with strong community and religious roles. I have represented the Religious Society of Friends (Quakers) of South and Southern Africa on several occasions and have been involved in various programmes and conferences of the South African Council of Churches. A Conflict Management Programme was launched in 1981 under the joint auspices of the Centre for Integrating Studies and the Western Province Council of Churches.

These activities give occasion to public statements by myself, either in my private capacity or on behalf of one or more religious or community groups. The mass media seldom distinguish clearly between the various capacities in or auspices under which public statements are made and often merge (and even confuse) the respective roles of academic, community leader or private individual.

This conflict is manifested in several aspects: (1) The public opinion maker is seen as somebody making a contribution to public thinking and political action. To the extent that he is successful and has an impact on developments, he may claim and deserve credit. Such credit may hamper progress if the facilitation should get any credit for progress or success instead of the contending parties. Preferably, the facilitator should stay out of the public eye. (2) In private communication between parties the results and impact of errors in judgement, wrong choice of words or wrong interpretations remain confined to the parties directly involved and can be rectified within that confined group. Public statements, however, have widespread impact and if these repercussions are negative, it is much harder to rectify mistakes. Furthermore, operating through mass media enables other groups with vested interest to colour or slant interpretations and statements.

In 1986 I was involved in the facilitation of communication between Inkatha and the United Democratic Front (UDF) in Natal. There was good progress and both parties accepted my interpretations of the situation. During the time I wrote an article on the current situation in South Africa at the request of the *Sunday Times* with reference to the visit of the Eminent Persons Group (EPG) (van der Merwe, 1986a). A week later Chief Mangosuthu Buthelezi, president of Inkatha, objected strongly to the fact that he had been "singled out" in the article as "the aggressive party" in South African politics. In a long letter to me he argued that I had become a propagandist of the UDF and had failed to remain neutral. It appeared that two things had gone wrong. The *Sunday Times* had either deliberately, or merely because of shortage of space, omitted one sentence in which special tribute was paid to Buthelezi as somebody willing to negotiate and compromise. The second mistake was my own poor choice of words. In the article I referred to "the growing antagonism of Buthelezi towards the UDF and ANC" instead of the "growing antagonism between Buthelezi and the UDF and ANC". My explanation and apologies were accepted and I was able to continue my role as "neutral" facilitator. But this "public" incident could have ruined the "private" task.

Another occasion where I had gone public also had various repercussions. In December 1984 I introduced Dr. Piet Muller, assistant editor of *Beeld*, the largest pro-government Afrikaans daily paper to members of the ANC executive committee in Lusaka. He wrote two articles (*Beeld*, 12 and 13 December) in which he described common ground between the National Party and the African National Congress, and in an editorial *Beeld* called on the Government to talk to the ANC. This was the first contact of its kind in 24 years and because of its positive, constructive interpretation of an organisation hitherto described only in antagonistic terms in pro-government papers, it received world-wide publicity. Since *Beeld* mentioned that this unique meeting was arranged by me, it led to much speculation among newspapermen and others about my auspices and motives. There was speculation that I was sent out as a feeler by the government to test the ANC on the matter of negotiation.

I decided it was necessary to make a public statement to explain my position. In it, I emphasized the independence of my position and mission and my positive approach and belief in the value of constructive steps. These statements received much publicity in South Africa and, together with the positive stand of *Beeld*, contributed towards the development of a more constructive approach, public acceptance of a negotiated settlement and also growing public acceptance of the ANC as a legitimate contending party within South Africa. During the following two years more than two dozen delegations of white and black South African businessmen, academics, church leaders and so forth met with the ANC in Lusaka. In a public opinion poll published by the Afrikaans Sunday paper *Rapport*, by the middle of 1986 almost 50 percent of whites favoured talks with the ANC (*Rapport*, 20 July 1986).

I believe that the Eminent Persons Group (EPG) of the Commonwealth maintained a healthy balance between their tasks of private mediation and public education. While many observers described their mission as a failure, I have no doubt that they made an invaluable contribution not only in formulating common ground between the parties, but especially by making third-party intervention and a negotiated settlement respectable in the public eye. What they achieved in public may far exceed the benefits of their private negotiations with the respective leaders.

INCREMENTAL STEPS WITH A RADICAL GOAL

Provision should be made for incremental steps within a radical, fundamental change programme. It is possible to reconcile gradual and radical change. The demands for radical change should not be contrary to a rational plan of action which, because of its provision for a logical sequence of events, is more likely to assure the achievement of a desired goal than one cataclysmic outburst.

The disagreement about the pace or rate of change is an important and genuine one. Quite naturally, whites who *do* realise that fundamental change, power-sharing and loss of privileges are inevitable will do whatever is within their power to postpone this transition and to propagate incremental change for that very reason. Those who want to hasten that transition will favour quick change. But this disagreement is on *means* and pace of change and not on eventual *goals*. While differences over means do constitute very severe causes of conflict, they are often more amenable to rational debate than differences over goals. Both parties presumably favour orderly change, and the formulation of a reasonable compromise in this particular case should not be impossible.

PRESSURE AND COOPERATION

It is important to recognise that pressure (violence) and cooperation (negotiation) are complementary outputs of the process of communication between conflicing parties in South Africa. Negotiation (the primary concern of the intermediary) should not be seen as a substitute for, or alternative to, pressures for change. Pressures are required to bring about change in South Africa. Negotiation should be seen as a complement to pressure in the communication process between conflicting parties. By improving the quality of communication and understanding, negotiation will ensure more rational and effective pressures and more orderly change. Meaningful and accurate information helps to put pressure in perspective. Third-party facilitation and mediation should be seen within this wider context.

South African newspapers have reported extensively on the ANC's intentions to step up the struggle in South Africa. One particular feature that aroused the horror of many South Africans was the ANC's reputed decision to focus on soft targets. These reports reinforced the popular opinion among whites that the ANC is merely a terrorist organisation and not interested in a negotiated settlement.

I want to make two observations to put the ANC's stand on this issue in perspective. First, many papers distorted Oliver Tambo's statements at a press conference. Contrary to the impression fostered by the South African authorities and their academic supporters the ANC has never employed a policy of indiscriminate terrorism. Tambo did not say they would now go for soft targets, but that "the distinction between 'soft' and 'hard' is going to disappear in an intensified confrontation, in an escalating conflict. The question of soft targets was quite out of place during World War II" (Tambo, 1985, p. 44). Oliver Tambo's stand was thus no different from that of any head of government who conducts modern warfare, whether he be Russian, American or South African. During the Second World War, 34 million innocent civilians—soft targets—were killed as against only 17 million military personnel. The two atom bombs dropped by the Americans destroyed primarily innocent civilians—soft targets.

Many people regard the intensification of the struggle as an indication that negotiation is ruled out. Quite the contrary may be true. It is normal for parties in conflict to do their very best to increase their bargaining power before negotiations commence. It is also normal for political leaders (both ANC and government) publicly to deny negotiations at such times.

At the same time that Tambo announced the intensification of the armed struggle, the National Executive Committee of the ANC in their Political Report referred to recent contacts between the ANC and South African businessmen, journalists, intellectuals and politicians. They did not condemn these contacts, but clearly stated that such negotiations should be handled with caution. "It is absolutely vital that our organisation and the democratic movement as a whole should be of one mind about this development to ensure that any contact that may be established does not have any negative effects on the development of our 'struggle'" (*African National Congress*, 1985, p. 36). Tom Lodge observed a "new note of conciliation" in the ANC since Nkomati. Even the dogmatic Communist leader Joe Slovo conceded that one day dialogue might well take place: "There were conditions under which all states or movements must be prepared to negotiate" (Lodge, 1985, p. 85). The ANC's serious commitment to negotiate was unequivocally confirmed in press statements by Oliver Tambo in January 1987.

While I do not want to play down the intensity and viciousness of the security clampdown in the mid-1980s, I firmly believe that this is not endemic in South African society, but a passing phase. To the extent that the moral base of apartheid has been eroded (Hund and van der Merwe, 1986, Chap. IV), white (including Afrikaner) leaders lack the moral commitment to such repressive measures as part of a long-term policy. For the moralists and pragmatists in the establishment, such measures can only be justified as control mechanisms during the process of reform.

PRESSURES AS CONDITIONAL AND CONSTRUCTIVE

Pressure on the government should be seen as part of the communication process and should be constructive and conditional, rather than punitive. Given this relationship between pressure and cooperation and the inevitability of pressure in power politics, a comment on the nature of sanctions against South Africa is in order.

Selective sanctions would be coupled with conditions that are not merely destructive but demand, and have a chance of obtaining, improved conditions in Southern Africa. These conditions should be specific, realistic and attainable and there should be a very clear commitment that the sanctions will be lifted when and if these conditions have been met.

This suggests a positive approach to the ruling parties in South Africa, a belief in their ability to meet these conditions (albeit under pressure and not willingly), and an open line of communications with the adversaries to enable the sender parties to review the situation, to discuss conditions and terms and, eventually, to agree on the lifting of the sanctions. Such an approach is not consistent with hate campaigns, mass hysteria and the belief that Afrikaners, Nationalists, business leaders or whites are all evil, or at least so evil that they cannot change, adapt or negotiate. If sanctions are to pave the way for negotiations, then serious rethinking seems to be called for in the emotional, international, public boycott campaign being waged.

CONCLUSION

This chapter has described several contrasting options open to the intermediary in the South African conflict. While it is readily admitted that such options could result in ambivalence (or even schizophrenia), the theme of this chapter is that, given the necessary sensitivity and initiative on the part of an intermediary, creative and constructive intervention is possible. While I have made a strong case for *facilitation* rather than *mediation* at times of extreme polarisation (such as we have in South Africa at present), I have demonstrated how, in my own case, facilitation has paved the way for mediation, and how I have responded to it.

The chapter reflects my current leanings towards the neutral role of facilitator or mediator. I have, however, great appreciation of the need for pressures on the establishment and argued that mediation and negotiation should be seen as *complementary* to pressure, not a substitute for it. However, I also argue, in the last section, that pressures, in order to complement negotiation, should be constructive and selective.

As a Quaker I am committed to non-violence. I have come to realise, however, that violence is endemic in mankind and in South Africa. Resort to violence is justified by virtually all religious and political leaders in all major conflicting groups in South Africa. I therefore do not talk about "peaceful" change in South Africa. But I do believe that the constructive approach described in this chapter does contribute towards a reduction of violence in the change process. My efforts are directed towards the promotion of justice and peace in South Africa. These two goals, are, however, unattainable ideals. Any new government in South Africa will fall short of these ideals. The struggle for justice, accompanied by violence, will continue, and so will the need for intermediaries.

11

Hypergames as an Aid to Mediation

Peter G. Bennett

THE TROUBLE WITH GAME THEORY

For an approach that showed such intellectual promise, the Theory of Games has proved surprisingly unhelpful. That, at least, seems to be something approaching a consensus view among those concerned with the practice of conflict management, negotiation, conflict resolution, and so on. By the same token, Game Theory is not generally welcomed with open arms by those who are already working in the field. At best, one hears the view that it may be helpful at the "conceptual" level (for example, by providing insight into what a threat "is"), while not being useful at a practical level, for guiding action in some particular situation. That is a comparatively charitable opinion. At worst, Game Theory may be seen as totally irrelevant (Blackett, 1962), or, indeed as positively harmful (Green, 1966; Martin, 1978). There are partial exceptions, to be sure, for there are fields in which the theory has been taken seriously. That of deterrence springs to mind. Even there, however, the theory's initial impact (particularly through Schelling's classic work) does not appear to have been maintained (Schelling, 1980).

As to why this should be so, there is no shortage of possible reasons. Clearly, the "game" terminology does not help, carrying as it does not only an air of trivialisation, but also an unhelpful "win–lose" connotation. That neither of these connotations is actually reflected in the content of the theory does not diminish their effectiveness in putting people off. It is thus no surprise that where approaches derived from Game Theory have had some success in getting applied "for real", they tend to enter under an assumed name (that of "options analysis"—of which more below—being probably the best known). A second problem has been a tendency for the theory to get taken over by those interested in developing the mathematics, more or less for its own sake. I am happy to be able to quote an unimpeachably authoritative source to back up this opinion; in the Preface to the 1980 edition of *The Strategy of Conflict*, Schelling remarks:

In putting these essays together to make the book, I hoped to estabish an interdisciplinary field that had been variously described as "theory of bargaining" or "theory of strategy". I wanted to show that some elementary theory . . . could be useful not only to formal theorists, but also to people concerned with practical problems, I hoped too, and I think now mistakenly, that the theory of games might be redirected toward application in these several fields. With notable exceptions like Howard Raiffa, Martin Shubik, and Nigel Howard, game theorists have tended to stay instead at the mathematical frontier. The field that I had hoped would become established has continued to develop, but not explosively, and without acquiring a name of its own.

Here, then, are two reasons for an apparent lack of practical impact and acceptability. Until recently I should have been tempted to add a third at this point: that the theory's association with both free-market economics and with rather hawkish versions of deterrence made it unpalatable with many on the left of the political spectrum—regardless of whether this association was justified.[1] In the last few years, however, Marxist theoreticians have "rediscovered" Game Theory (Lash and Urry, 1984), so perhaps this particular problem has disappeared.

None of the issues noted so far call into question the theoretical framework itself. In principle, they can be tackled while leaving the theory unchanged. Nothing in it prohibits one from developing an alternative terminology, or compels one to become preoccupied with mathematical ramifications. If there has grown up a tradition of looking for neat solutions to mathematically well-defined but highly artificial "problems", there also exists a strong stream of thought that may be termed structural game theory, developed inter alia by the writers mentioned above by Schelling. Mathematically, the models used here are comparatively rough-and-ready. Little emphasis is placed upon quantification (for example, preference orders are normally employed in place of the utility functions of the classical theory), or on finding unique "right answers" (the search is for outcomes "stable" in various senses; there may be several of these in a given case, or none).

Though there is much of value in "structural" game theory, however, it can be convincingly argued that even in this form the approach has some major inadequacies. Two seem to be of particular importance: lack of attention to process, and lack of attention to perceptions. By the first, I mean that a game-theoretic model presents a "snapshot" formulation of an issue; though moves and counter-moves are played out, the parameters of the problem itself remains static. For example, the parties' preferences do not change as the situation unfolds. By the second, I mean that the players are normally assumed to share a common view of the situation. While their interests may differ, their perceptions do not. Specifically, each is well informed of everyone's available strategies and preferences.

Both of these represent dimensions that are, by common consent, of crucial importance in real-life conflicts. If they are ignored, it is hardly surprising that people fail to take the resulting models seriously. As will become clear below, the argument here is not for "super models" that try to take into account everything at once. Such an approach would surely prove self-defeating. However, a way of looking at the world drawing solely on game theory seems conceptually unsatisfactory. In practical terms, the insights available will inevitably be very limited with so much assumed away from the beginning. One should have at least the option of constructing richer models. If this is accepted, there would seem to be two ways of moving forward, while still making use of game-theoretic concepts. The first would be to modify the structure and assumptions of the theory itself, while the second would be to combine game-type analysis with other approaches that are complementary, in the sense of providing insight into factors not dealt with by Game Theory alone.

The main theme of this chapter is an attempt, represented by hypergame analysis, to modify and expand Game Theory in order to rectify one of the problems suggested above, that is, the lack of attention given to perceptions. A second theme, only touched on here but potentially just as important, is the possibile combination of this approach with others that (among other things) help one to take proper account of the processes of decision-making and conflict resolution. The next section gives a brief introduction to the basic idea of a hypergame. The following three sections then give a resumé of subsequent developments, both at a theoretical level and in terms of practical methodology, while the final section outlines some implications for work in the specific field of mediation.

FROM GAMES TO SIMPLE HYPERGAMES

The fundamental concepts of Game Theory—players, strategies, outcomes, and utilities or preferences—will need no introduction here. Nor will the usual game-theoretic assumption that all the players see the same game; each is well-informed as to the parameters of the game (and furthermore, each has sufficient reasoning power to make use of all this information).

To get away from this assumption, the hypergame approach takes as its starting point the notion that the "players" may be quite literally "playing" different games. In its original and most basic form, a hypergame thus consists of a set of subjective games, each intended to reflect a given party's beliefs about the situation. Formally, such a model is defined in the same way as a game, except that the viewpoint of each player has to be considered. In other words, we must specify the strategies and preferences that each of them perceives—both for himself and for each of the other players.[2]

At this point a brief illustration may be helpful for any readers who have not come across hypergames before. This is deliberately chosen as a very simple example, which makes it artificial to a degree. Suppose our "players" are the rulers of two nations. Each desires to live in peace, but is suspicious of the other's intentions. Such a situation forms the basis for a well-known cautionary tale—the "Andersland–Jedesland" story (Richardson, 1939; Rapoport, 1960). A search for "security" prompts an arms race, in which each side sees itself as making defensive moves to counter the threat of the other's armaments. In its extreme form, the story ends with a "mad dash to the launching platforms" as each side tries to preempt the other's expected attack. A hypergame model of this "mutual suspicion" problem provides a rather interesting alternative to the usual game-theoretic models of arms races. Sticking, for the sake of argument, to the "arms race" part of the story, let us suppose that each side has a straight choice between two policies, arm or disarm (we are at liberty to keep things simple!). Further, we suppose that both see the choices in this way—there are no differences in perception as to the strategies available. Let us assume that player 1 places the four possible outcomes in the following order of preference:

Mutual disarmament (most preferred)

Arms lead for player 1

Arms race—both sides arm

Arms lead for player 2 (least preferred)

Unfortunately, this is not how 2 sees it. He believes that 1 would most prefer to get an arms lead for himself. In other words, in 1's preference order as perceived by 2, the first two outcomes in the list are reversed.

Finally, let us suppose that the same assumptions hold with the roles of the players reversed, both as regards 2's preferences and as regards his beliefs about player 1. The result is a hypergame as shown in Figure 11.1.

There are a number of ways of analysing this model, the appropriateness of which would, in a real example, depend on the conditions of play. Looking at the problem at a strictly individual level, consider the game seen by 1. He perceives 2 to have a dominant strategy; whatever 1 does it pays 2 to arm. So his natural reasoning will be to suppose that 2 will arm; he, 1, is then faced with a choice between an arms race and getting left

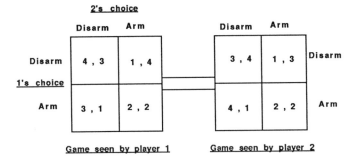

Figure 11.1. "Mutual suspicion" hypergame.

behind. The latter is his least preferred outcome, and to avoid it 1 "has" to arm. The logic of 2's game is, of course, analogous. In terms of the overall system, the result is an arms race that nobody wanted.

Alternatively, and a little more realistically, suppose the two sides engage in negotiations to stop the race. The problem then is to agree a joint move from "arms race" to mutual disarmament. Unfortunately, the logic of the situation is again unhelpful. If there were no misperceptions, the two sides need only to be able to co-ordinate their choices for such a move to be safe for each (see Figure 11.2a). Once agreement is reached, there is no incentive for either side to move from it. But in the hypergame, each believes that it would be in the other's interest to renege on any agreement, so obtaining—at least temporarily—an arms advantage. So unless there is some mechanism for enforcing a binding agreement—and

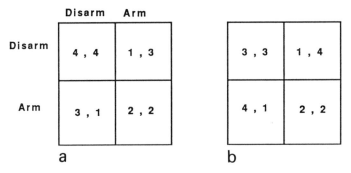

Figure 11.2. *A:* Game resulting if misperceptions are removed. *B:* Prisoners' Dilemma.

lack of one is arguably the most realistic feature of the model—neither side will "rationally" make a deal and stick to it.

The model described here may or may not be relevant to the current East–West arms race. We have argued elsewhere that it may have some relevance (Bennett and Dando, 1982, 1983),[3] but the discussion below on the analysis of real cases should make it clear that this is not advocated as "the" model of the problem. The point is that this approach can provide a reasonably systematic way of tracing out the consequences of a set of assumptions, including hypotheses about how any given interaction is perceived by the parties involved. Not all the features of the "mutual suspicion" model, for example, could have been captured in a single game. If each side were well-informed of the other's preferences, there would be no problem. The game that would result if each side really had the preferences assumed by the other, by contrast (see Figure 11.2b), turns out to be that of "Prisoners' Dilemma". Though an interesting model of arms races, this applies only to relatively aggressive players; no element of misunderstanding is involved. The hypergame case shows how an arms race could persist even if each side would genuinely like nothing better than mutual disarmament; the driving force is not a desire for superiority as such, but rather of fear of being left behind.

"Realistic" or not, this simple case should suffice to illustrate the basic structure of a hypergame. More generally, the games specified on each side would differ as regards perceived strategies too, rather than just preferences. (For example, cases of "strategic surprise" can be modelled by assigning one player strategies not appearing in the game seen by another.)

THEORETICAL DEVELOPMENTS

In some ways the hypergame concept has moved on beyond the simple "set of games" idea to become more general. Two such developments are worth describing briefly here.

The first has to do with "levels of perception". As can be readily seen, once perceptions are brought into the picture, something of a logical "Pandora's box" is opened. If one side's perception of the other is important, should we not also worry about the first side's perceptions of those perceptions? To return briefly to the "paranoia" hypergame, would it make a difference if 1 knew that 2 believed him to be more warlike than he really was? Similarly, of course, if there are more than two players, we might need to consider 3's beliefs about 1's beliefs about 2's beliefs about ... Some way of dealing with this potentially infinite hierarchy is needed. The hypergame concept has thus been expanded to allow all orders of belief to be considered, if necessary. More to the point, one can often show that it is not necessary to do so. The general theory of stability shows us which properties of the system will depend on what orders of belief; in many cases a "law of diminishing returns" applies. (This is one point at which the mathematical logic behind the approach, which is not something that we normally lay great stress on, is of some usefulness.)

The second line of development has been to take an increasingly radical view about the differences in perception that one may need to model. In their original form, hypergames allowed for differing beliefs about preferences, and allowed specific strategies to be seen by one party but not by another. It was implicitly assumed, however, that the different games were commensurable. That is, the strategies that were seen would be definable in similar terms; within the model there would be no problem in "translating" from one perceptual system to another. (In formal terms, the games' strategy spaces were assumed to intersect.) If the parties have radically differing frameworks, this approach will not suffice. On theoretical grounds, it seems justified to start from the possibility that the games seen on each side may have nothing in common at all. In other words, if one were to construct games reflecting as faithfully as possible the perceptions of any two parties in an interaction, these might, a priori, be totally different in terms of strategies and even perceived players (see Bennett, 1982, 1987; Bryant, 1984). Thus each "actor" might see a quite different "case list". For example, three decision-makers might have very different macro-level views of the world. One might see the international scene as a struggle between nation-states, another may see as relevant actors "economic classes", while for the third everything is seen in terms of conflict between religions. Even if all those involved are agreed who the relevant "players" are, the issues at stake—and hence the "game"—may be defined in different ways. For example, it has been quite plausibly suggested that the parties to the Vietnam conflict had quite different conceptions as to what the war was "about", successive U.S. administrations seeing the issue as that of containing communism, with the North Vietnamese seeing it as a war of national self-determination.

Nevertheless, the case is only "interesting" if the decisions taken on each side do actually have some significance for the others. That is, the "games" may be dissimilar, but they are "connected". In terms of the general hypergame model, such linkages are expressed by "strategy linkages" which, in effect, translate the way actions are interpreted from one game to another. Their logical form is thus "If A adopts some move m (part of a strategy in A's own game), then B interprets this as a manifestation of A* having taken move m* (where A*, m* appear in B's game)".

This digression into theory is, in itself, of little relevance here. The point, however, is to illustrate how far it is possible to get away from the assumption of a commonly perceived game. We are now dealing with actors who may construe the world in quite different ways. It is not claimed that this will always be the case. If it is found useful to model a problem in a more straightforward way, that is all to the good. (The "simple" hypergame is merely a special case of a more general concept, and the "ordinary" game a special case of that.) Nor, of course, need the situation be static. Thus, for example, successful mediation may lead the parties towards a common view of some issue. Nevertheless, it seems justifiable to start from the view that radically different perceptions of a problem may abound. Though intended in a different context, the diagram in Figure 11.3, adapted from Sharp and Dando (1978), is relevant here. This shows the types of models that any one participant in a conflict might have of the "other players", ranging upward from "totally ignored". Sharp and Dando make the point that it is always easy to move down the scale, from an initially complex view. Indeed there is much evidence for pressure on decision-makers to do just that, especially in conditions of crisis. What is not easy, however, is to move away from a simple model, unless at least the possibility of its inadequacy is acknowledged from the start. This observation leads us conveniently away from the realms of theory towards consideration of the practice of modelling, the subject of the next section.

DEVELOPING A DECISION-AIDING APPROACH

Let us now consider how models based on games, hypergames and related ideas can be used to provide something of practical use to decision-makers. This has been a major concern of recent work; it has also led increasingly to the linkage of hypergame analysis with other ways of

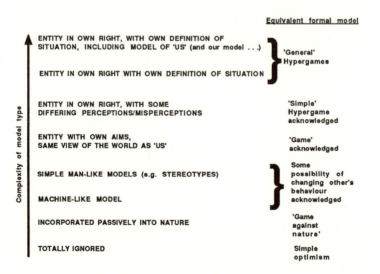

Figure 11.3. Categorisation of "models of other parties" in conflicts.

helping with complex decisions. The next section will outline some of the specific forms of model available, concentrating mainly on game-based analyses but touching briefly on some other approaches. First, however, there are some general comments on the modelling process to be made, concerning how one can tackle the analysis of complex, multi-layered conflicts and what might be gained by doing so.

The weakest form of "application" is the post hoc case study done with no involvement with the actors concerned. This sort of work has been much criticised, sometimes justifiably. Retrospective examples have been used to illustrate various concepts involved in hypergame analysis (Bennett and Dando, 1979; Geisen and Bennett, 1979), and in that role post hoc studies have a valid place. They can also provide a preliminary test of applicability; if one cannot make sense of history, then anything more ambitious seems hardly worth attempting! However, this sort of "application" is not to be confused with the real thing. One can move forward from the post hoc case study in two senses. One is temporal; analysis deals with current and future events rather than being confined to the past. The other concerns the degree of involvement with the relevant decision-makers: analysis done with, or for, at least some of the participants. The two dimensions are independent. The outside observer might produce a "stand-off" predictive analysis; in principle, one might even test models by, say, leaving predictions in sealed envelopes. Contrariwise, a restrospective study might be carried out with some of the actors involved, to improve understanding of what had happened and perhaps draw general lessons.

The development of "decision-aiding" methods has involved movement along both dimensions, with the analysis of live problems done with decision-makers. For present purposes, it will be convenient to cover some of the conflicts described elsewhere in this volume, and the illustrations used below will consequently be mainly of "stand-off" models, covering a mix of retrospective and current cases.

In approaching analysis, we start from a presumption that it is always important to ask certain general questions about actors in conflicts, centered around their options, aims and perceptions. For example:

What is their business and raison d'être, and what are their guiding values?

What are their relationships to us/each other? Are they competitors, obstacles, partners, suppliers, clients? How uncertain or changeable are these roles?

What outcomes might they prefer? Which would they most seek to avoid? Do they have a (de jure or de facto) veto over certain outcomes?

What are their current agendas, their linked decisions? How do these constrain their choices or the options they might consider? What are their time horizons for decisions? What internal games might be affecting them?

Whom do they see as actors of relevance? What possible strategies do they attribute to them? What aims or objectives are they perceived to have?

Such questions may, of course, be phrased in various terms, according to context. By asking them one attempts to build up a picture of the relevant "games" being played. In practice, however, one result will be to find questions that cannot be answered with any confidence (for example, by indentifying actors of probable relevance without being able to define their strategies). Modelling then proceeds as a structured learning process. The models help to identify what the crucial quesions are, and to suggest possible answers or procedures through which they can be sought— whether through intelligence gathering, making exploratory moves, or setting up special internal procedures to simulate other actors' perspectives (Radford, 1984). Analysis itself will tend to be done on a "what if . . ." basis; indeed, the analyst may well end up in a devil's advocate role, challenging assumptions previously held with confidence.

All this leads to a view of analysis far removed from that of following a recipe—"define all the players, all the available options and preferences seen by each side"—at the end of which one emerges triumphant with "the answer". This would be unhelpful even if technically possible; after all, models are supposed to simplify. Deliberate choices about what sorts of complexity to include have to be made as modelling proceeds. With these points in mind, we have suggested a methodology that is "mixed-scanning, iterative, and piecemeal" (Bennett and Huxham, 1982; Huxham and Bennett, 1983; Bennett and Cropper, 1987a).

We use the term "mixed-scanning" to describe an approach that moves between a broad overview of the perceived problem and more detailed analysis. Both the levels of aggregation of actors and options and the breadth of scope of models can be usefully varied. Thus, a conflict involving many parties can be simplified by narrowing the scope of the model—for example, by focussing in on a key interaction between two or three participants. Or the broad view can be maintained, and simplification maintained by losing detail—for example, by aggregating participants together and ignoring internal "games" for the time being. Similarly for strategies or options;[4] one aim of mixed-scanning is to maintain a creative tension between breadth and detail.

The "iterative" view of modelling acknowledges the futility of forcing analysis to proceed in a linear sequence. If learning is taking place, it is essential that all models should be open to later revision, and that opportunities to do so are built into the methodology.

Finally, the emphasis in hypergame theory on perceptions and misperceptions, and the associated uncertainty about the validity of models, suggests the importance of generating multiple alternative models. The "piecemeal" methodology takes this further, in suggesting the advantages not only of different models, but of different types of model, each used to capture different aspects of the problem. Different representations are used alongside each other without necessarily being brought together in some single "best" model. The hope is that complexity can be tackled using a mix of comparatively simple models. Some of the models available will now be illustrated.

TYPES OF MODEL

Two broad types of model are used within the hypergame approach, roughly corresponding to modes of work known as problem structuring and formal analysis. We use these headings here to discuss a somewhat wider range of game-based models. Several exist in each category, forming a repertoire from which to choose. As will be seen, it is also possible to use some models in either mode.

Problem Structuring

In problem structuring the aim is to represent the problem in broad terms, identifying relevant parties, how they interact, and over what issues. A structured picture (always open to later revision) is produced, serving as a reference point for more detailed work. This helps in organising large volumes of data, in selecting relevant information from more general background and in choosing areas for more detailed investigation. The picture will already be selective and dependent on the point of view from which the study is conducted, whether that of protagonist, mediator or outside researcher.

Two problem-structuring notations have been developed specifically as adjuncts to hypergame analysis. The first, *Preliminary Problem Structuring* (PPS), focusses attention on the actors involved in a situation and the pattern of interactions between them. As outlined in Figure 11.4a, the notation shows players (actors, participants) joined by lines representing interactions over specific issues. Because "players" can be defined in more or less aggregated terms, various levels of interaction will co-exist. The idea behind PPS is to display these as a starting point for further analysis, rather than choosing to consider just one level. This contrasts, in particular, to models that necessarily treat nations as unitary actors. To say that for some purpose it makes sense to speak of a "national policy" is not to deny that these policies may be the resultants of a multitude of internal political and bureaucratic games.[5] Nor is there generally one right way to draw up a PPS diagram; one could start with nations, then add internal structure, or start with individuals, then build outwards.

Where PPS focusses attention on actors and patterns of linkages, the *decision arena* notation primarily addresses the nature of the interactions. This model is formed as shown in Figure 11.4b. Arenas again correspond

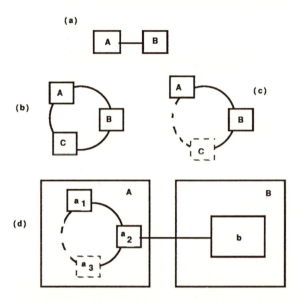

Figure 11.4a. PPS notation.

(a) Shows a straightforward dyadic interation between A and B.

(b) Shows a situation of all three parties interacting.

(c) Schematically indicates a "many-player game".

The idea of "games within games" is shown in (d). A and B again interact, but A's policies now depend on an internal game between a1, a2, a3, . . . Meanwhile A's interaction with B is conducted through a specific sub-system of B, b (who adds effective power for B's policy, though by definition is also party to an interaction with the rest of the B system).

to interactions over specified issues. Relevant information is structured as follows. On one side of each arena are shown starting conditions, to do with the parties' available options, their preferences, beliefs, particular strengths and weaknesses, and so on—what each side "takes into the arena". On the other are possible outcomes of the interaction. Factors affecting the starting conditions appear as input, the wider consequences of outcomes as output. These also provide links between arenas, or back into the same arena.

Figures 11.5 and 11.6 sketch applications of these models to some current aspects of the Falklands/Malvinas problem. They were developed in the course of a one-day workshop with a group of experts on the situation. This took place in April 1986 with the aim of exploring how the situation might develop following the elections then forthcoming in both Britain and Argentina.

Figure 11.5 is a PPS model built up to show the main parties to the situation, and the issues in which they are involved. A natural starting

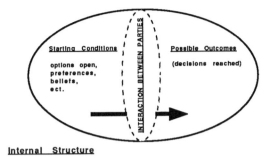

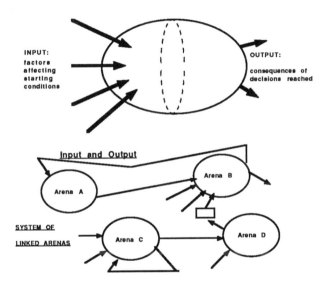

Figure 11.4b. "Arena" notation.

point is an interaction between the United Kingdom and the Argentine over "the future of the islands"—the central issue under study. A somewhat separate three-way "game", also involving the Falkland Islanders, concerns the mutual acceptability of any proposals. Some of the main internal interactions are also shown. British government policy is seen as a resultant of an interaction primarily between the Cabinet, the Foreign and Commonwealth Office, and the Ministry of Defence (issue: whether to maintain a "fortress Falklands" policy or attempt to compromise). Outside the government, the main actors of influence are the Opposition and the Falkland Islands Lobby. On the Argentinian side, the main actors are the Alfonsin administration, the Peronists and the

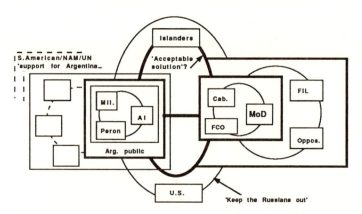

Figure 11.5. PPS diagram for Falklands/Malvinas situation (as of April 1987).

military (essentially in competition for power to govern), all operating in a "sea" of strong public opinion (at which point the Malvinas issue becomes entwined with that of human rights). Some linked external issues are also relevant. In particular Britain, the Argentine, the United States (and others) are involved in a game that might well be termed "keep the Russians out", while the Argentine is also acting in a series of games to do with maintaining support from other Latin American states, in the United Nations and within the Non-Aligned Movement. Clearly, these are not the only interactions that might be considered. The aim of the model was to represent those that seemed most important in affecting the parties' behaviour over the central issue. The consensus view of the group (experts acting, in this sense, as clients for the analysis) was that other interactions—e.g., between Britain and her EEC partners, or within the United Nations—were much less relevant in that specific sense.

As a very brief illustration of how an "arena" model operates, Figure 11.6 sketches some input into the central interaction, looking at the Argentinian position. Recalling that the study was conducted prior to the June 1987 election, it was argued that the key variable would be the re-election of a UK government headed by Mrs. Thatcher (as against any other outcome). It is argued that this would lead the Argentinians to discount the possibility of serious negotiations. Various inputs are also shown from internal Argentinian arenas, several (though not all) suggesting a growing preference for a campaign of military harassment, stopping short of an attempt to retake the Islands but imposing heavy costs on the British.

In focussing on slightly different aspects of decision situations, the PPS and arena models are complementary, as well as both being also compatible with other game-based representations. The Linked Decision Situations model of Radford and Corneil (Radford, 1980) provides another way of displaying multiple interactions. Perhaps more importantly, the Strategy and Tactics model of Geisen (1981) and Radford (1986) provides a further view of complex decision problems, by considering their development through time. In classical Game Theory, situations are defined once and for all at the start; comprehensive strategies then cover every eventuality up to the end of the game. This model, by contrast, considers a series of partly separable "rounds", each resulting in a tactical outcome, until the series culminates in a (more broadly defined) strategic outcome. As actions are evaluated both for their immediate and their longer-term consequences, the analysis helps to separate strategic from tactical goals, and to decide on priorities between them. The structure of "rounds" in a conflict is of interest in its own right. Opportunities for particular sorts of decision are often arranged in advance (e.g., through

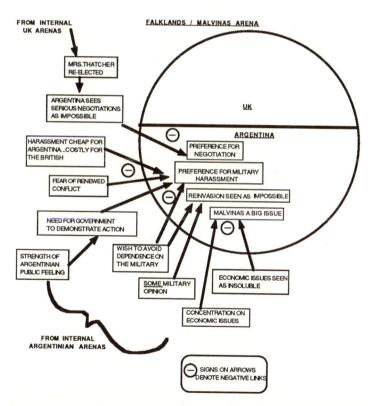

Figure 11.6. Fragment of "arena" model for Falklands/Malvinas situation.

committee cycles) as part of the formal and informal rules of the game. On occasion, these become part of the "game" itself—as when one party attempts to bypass "normal procedures". Yet again, events may be set in train that impose a structure beyond anyone's control.[6]

Models for Formal Analysis

Here, within necessarily simplified models, very specific hypotheses are set up to define perceived players, options and preferences. Analysis then seeks to set out the consequences of these. Again, various types of model exist; in particular, games and hypergames can be represented in matrix form, as trees or as option tableaux. The first has already been illustrated; we now briefly introduce the other two.

Option Tableaux   Developed as part of metagame analysis or "analysis of options" (Howard, 1981), this format can handle systems containing (relatively) many actors and strategies. Players ("participants") are listed and each is assigned a set of options. These represent possible courses of action, formulated as simple "yes-no" alternatives. More complicated strategies can be considered as conditional combinations of options. Outcomes (or "scenarios") are columns constructed by specifying "yes" or "no" for each option, often represented by writing 1 and 0, respectively. Usually some combinations are infeasible—logically or physically impossible, or impossible to implement for some other reason. These are separated out prior to further analysis. Analysis establishes the stability of different outcomes by finding any "improvements" for any participant, and then considering what "sanctions" other parties might have against that improvement. This can be done in a series of easy steps, taking each outcome and each participant at a time. To illustrate the notation, Figure 11.7 reproduces one of a series of tableaux used to analyse the conflict in Northern Ireland and presented to the Northern Ireland Constitutional Convention (Alexander, 1975). This example shows a tableau assumed to be seen by all; in a hypergame different perceived tableaux attach to each actor.

Game and Hypergame Trees   While tableaux are helpful in handling the complexity occasioned by combinations of possible options, trees are especially useful in representing sequences of decisions. The branches of the tree represent moves under the control of specified players. For hypergame analysis, different trees attach to each actor; if necessary these are linked to show how each player's moves are interpreted by the others. Figure 11.8 shows a very simple historical model of part of the Falklands conflict—taking the situation as seen by the Junta and the War Cabinet immediately prior to the outbreak of fighting. We first suppose that each side sees the same "tree" of possible moves, but has differing perceptions

SANCTIONS AGAINST BRITAIN AND ALLEGIANTS FROM IMPROVEMENTS FROM ASSEMBLY WITH LINKS WITH SOUTH

		Britain		Allegiants		Moderates		IRA		Dublin		Allegiants	
		P	NP	P	NP	P	NP	P	NP	P	NP	P	NP
BRITAIN	(1) Aid	10-	1 ---	1		1		1		1		-	1
	(2) Minority Participation	11-	1 ---	1		1		1		1		-	1
	(3) Law and Order	---	0 ---	0		0		0		0		-	0
	(4) United Ireland	001	0 ---	0		0		0		0		-	0
	(5) Integrated Parliament	00-	0 ---	0		0		0		0		-	0
	(6) Dominion	00-	0 ---	0		0		0		0		-	0
	(7) Links with South	11-	1 ---	1		1		1		1		-	1
	(8) Troops as and When	0--	1 ---	1		1		1		1		-	1
ALLEGIANTS	(9) Support Coup		0 1--	-	0	0		0		0		-	0
	(10) Support Violence		0 -1-	-	0	0		0		0		-	0
	(11) Support Violence		0 ---	-	0	0		0		0		-	0
	(12) Support Power Holders		1 --0	0	1	1		1		1		0	1
MODERATES	(13) Support Power Holders	1	---	1		1	0	1		1		-	1
	(14) Support Violence	0	--1	0		0	-	0		0		-	0
IRA	(15) Attack Britain	0	---	0		0		0	-	0		-	0
	(16) Attack Northern Ireland	0	---	0		0		0	-	0		-	0
DUBLIN	(17) Suppress IRA if	-	---	-		-		-		-	-	-	-
	(18) Intervention	0	---	0		0		0		0	-	0	

NOTES: BRITAIN has preferred outcomes of (i) United Ireland, or (ii) and Assembly with no link with South and with minority participation, and either no financial aid, or financial aid but no troops

ALLEGIANTS have sanctions against BRITAIN moving: ALLEGIANT violence or coup, regardless of all else, or any form of ALLEGIANT non-support together with MODERATE violence.

There are no sanctions to prevent Allegiants from moving to non-support positions: the Allegiants have a guaranteed improvement by non-support.

MODERATES, IRA, and DUBLIN have no unilateral improvements.

P - Preferred   NP - Non Preferred

Figure 11.7. Analysis of options tableaux (after Alexander, 1975).

of each other's preferences. These are shown on the end-points of the tree, with higher numbers again denoting more highly preferred outcomes.

The game as seen by the Junta can be analysed as follows, by reasoning "backward" from the end-points. If the British attack, Argentina prefers to fight. Given this, the British would do better ("2" rather than "1") by confining themselves to "bluff and protest". Therefore the Junta can get its most preferred outcome ("4" rather than "2") by staying put. However the "Cabinet game" differs in several respects. Firstly, the British misperceive Argentinian preferences, believing that they would be more likely to

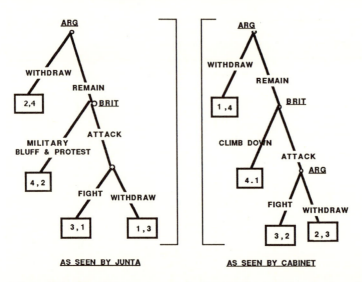

Figure 11.8a. Simple hypergame tree (preferences for Argentina shown on left in each case).

withdraw if the British fight (perhaps in a limited way). This actually has no effect on the expected course of events. More importantly, the War Cabinet prefers "fight" to "bluff and protest" (which they see as "climb down"). Analysis of this game suggests fighting as the only possible outcome; so does the hypergame as a whole.

Though surprising to the Junta, the outcome is not the result of misperception; rather this is an interesting model of an overdetermined conflict. True, the Junta believes that the British will not fight (and one of the problems is that any preparations to do so will be indistinguishable from "bluff" by definition).[7] But even if this misperception were removed, the Junta would still prefer the consequences of "remain" to those of withdrawing,[8] and the fight is still predicted.

Starting from this simple model, one can expand the games on each side to make them more realistic. For example, it seems that at some stages the Argentinians saw the United States as a full participant with the power (and perhaps the inclination) to stop the British fighting by applying extreme economic and political pressure—as with the Suez crisis. This suggests expanding their side of the model to a three-player tree, perhaps as in Figure 11.8b.

All the above forms of model can also be used in a problem-structuring role, typically by drawing up a partly defined model. If decisions are to be taken on several related issues, it can be worthwhile using an Analysis of

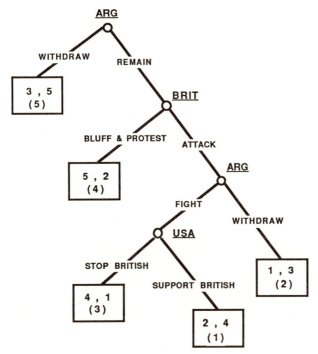

Predicted Outcome: ARG remains, BRIT chooses "bluff"
in preference to fighting ARG with US "doing a Suez"

Figure 11.8b. Expansion of ARG game to include United States (with "optimistic" perceptions of preferences; those for the United States show beneath others).

Options tableau just to help examine what the feasible outcomes are, without necessarily going on to do stability analysis. Similarly, a partly defined tree can be used to show how a sequence of choices is liable to unfold. An example, produced for the current Falklands/Malvinas situation as part of the study mentioned above, is shown in Figure 11.9.

LINKS WITH OTHER APPROACHES

Whatever its other merits or demerits, a methodology that is "piecemeal, mixed-scanning and iterative" at least avoids the illusion that one type of model can represent all that there is to say about a complex problem. The way is very much open to combining hypergame analysis with other approaches, and collaborative work is currently in progress in this area. Links with two such approaches are currently of particular interest: Cognitive Mapping, and Strategic Choice. These both form part

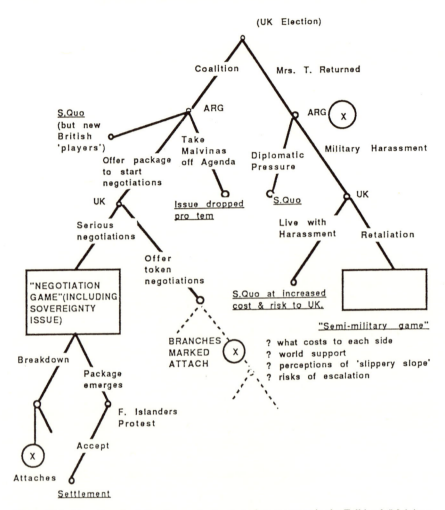

Figure 11.9. Use of partly defined game to structure future moves in the Falklands/Malvinas conflict.
Further examination of (especially) the "semi-military harassment game" and other sub-games may then allow one to assign perceived preferences. Some key uncertainties are noted.

of a range of approaches within what is sometimes known as "soft OR"—that part of operational research concentrating on problems that may not be amenable to quantification, and where subjective factors predominate.

The former will be familiar to many present readers through the work of Axelrod and others, in which mapping provides a sophisticated form of content analysis for documentary data. Our own main interest is in a rather different set of methods, developed by Eden et al. (1983), and with an intellectual background provided by personal construct theory in which maps are primarily used to structure verbal data about decision problems. Here mapping is used "on line" as a medium through which, firstly, the views of each individual within a decision-making group can be expressed and, secondly, the group can work towards an agreed definition to their problem. To facilitate these processes, highly interactive computer programs have been developed that allow maps to be rapidly built up, examined, modified, merged together and so on. The Strategic Choice methodology (Friend and Jessop, 1977; Friend and Hickling, 1987) has its roots in studies of decision processes in local government, though the ideas have been applied to a wide variety of settings. Again, the emphasis is on helping small groups to manage decisions. In this case, the methods concentrate specifically on handling different kinds of uncertainty (including uncertainties about the group's own values), and the interconnections made between decisions to be made in different areas.

These methods differ from game/hypergame analysis in at least two ways. First, they take a different conceptual slice through problems (through looking at uncertainty rather than conflict, for example); second, they pay close attention to the process of decision, rather than just modelling the structure of situations. This is something not well covered by game-based approaches alone—one of the inadequacies with which this chapter started. Recent work has investigated how these different methods can be used in combination, either by using different methods in sequence, or by designing models that can bridge the different approaches (for example, the arena model outlined above provides such a bridge between mapping and hypergame analysis). Though much further work remains to be done in this area, successful combined applications already exist (Huxham and Bennett, 1985; Matthews and Bennett, 1986; Bennett and Cropper, 1987b).

IMPLICATIONS FOR MEDIATION

So far we have written of "decision-aiding" without having considered the question of whose decisions we might be trying to help. The methods discussed above have largely been developed in an Operational Research (OR) context. This, it might be argued, implies a perspective quite different from that of a mediator. The normal OR assumption is that analysis is carried out for the benefit of some "client" (in a financial sense or otherwise). In a conflict setting the natural tendency might be to visualise the client as one or other of the warring parties. After all, the historical origins of OR are with work done to improve the fighting performance of one side in war! So perhaps any transfer of ideas to the problem of disinterested mediation would appear to be inapt.

There is certainly a need to tread carefully here. Nevertheless, the two sorts of situation are not as far divorced as they might seem to be at first sight. From the OR point of view, it is increasingly recognised that, whatever the official definition, the "client" is hardly ever a monolithic being. Even if only a small group of decision-makers is involved in the study, each can be expected to have an idiosyncratic view of what the problem is about. Futhermore, each will generally have particular axes to grind, whether for individual reasons or from the need to protect the interests of some group in an inter-organisational "game". To use the terminology of the previous section, there will typically be at least two levels of interaction going on. The analyst's official task may be to help the client group act effectively in some interaction with external parties. In trying to do this, however, he may well find himself acting as a sort of de facto mediator in an internal conflict, in which the group arrives (hopefully) at a (more or less) agreed definition of the problem and decides on a policy to adopt. In the present context, perhaps the most relevant feature of the "soft OR" approaches discussed above is the extent to which they have developed ways to facilitate the process of—to use Eden's phrase—"negotiating the problem". There do seem to be genuine parallels here with "real" mediation, and particularly with respect to the problem-solving approach to mediation (Burton, 1969; de Reuck, 1974, 1983; Groom and Webb, 1987; Light, 1984).

Having made this analogy, I should not want to press it too far. The analyst as described above seldom remains in a "neutral" position. Quite legitimately, he will form his own ideas about the problem—as he is supposed to do—and will thus tend to inject his own views, in effect becoming an interested participant. More important is the nature of the client group. The OR analyst's group may be a loose coalition of different interests, but they are normally "all on the same side" in some vague sense. Whatever the internal differences, the acknowledgement of external problems faced by the group provides at least a starting point for cohesion. It remains to be seen how the methods outlined here might cope with cases where a large part of the task would be to reach just such a starting point. Quite apart from that, special skills are obviously needed to handle any group whose members have very high levels of mutual hostility.

Leaving these caveats aside, it might still be felt worthwhile to try using hypergame analysis (probably in alliance with other methods) in the context of mediation. If so, there seem to be two possible ways of going about this. The first would be to use hypergames as a vehicle for mediation. That is, models would be built "on-line", with the participation of the interested parties, who would eventually share a common model, and the conclusions that might come from analysing it. The second approach would be to use such analysis as a form of decision-aiding for mediators. In other words, the mediator himself (or herself) would be the immediate client, rather than the group as a whole. Analysis would be done out of the mediation sessions. One aim would be to help the mediator trace through the ramifications of the problem by analysing the consequences of positions being taken, the effects of possible differences in beliefs, and so on. Even if specific proposals were not analysed in full detail, broad models of the problem might form a useful conceptual backdrop for the mediator to work with.

At first sight, the second of these two approaches appears the easier option. Experience suggests that hypergame modelling is much easier to carry out when there is some backroom time available to the analyst. As against this there is the potential problem of anything being done out of session appearing mysterious, and therefore suspicious, to the parties involved in the mediation attempt. In a sense, this is also an argument for the analyst working for the mediator, who can then use his own discretion as to what analysis, if any, is introduced explicitly into the sessions. The separation of roles may be useful for there is no particular reason why a skilled analyst should also have the rare inter-personal skills necessary to manage a group with very high levels of hostility and distrust.

However, I would not want to dismiss the possibility of using the forms of analysis described here as "on line", particularly in the context of problem-solving workshops. Practitioners of mediation approaches have noted the usefulness of the judicious interjection of "theoretical ideas; the parties then find that they can use these to analyse their situation. There are also comparatively gentle ways of leading up to live analysis. Initially, models can be used in a backward-looking sense to help the parties explore alternative explanations as to how the current situation has arisen, or even to examine some other problem which (as the parties discover for themselves) has at least some parallels with their own. From there, it is a less unthinkable idea to try the same models to look forward at how the conflict may develop. Hypergame analysis—at least under a more attractive name—appears well suited to these tasks, and may thus provide one useful way of helping participants to re-conceptualise their problems.

So far, of course, these remarks are highly speculative. I have outlined some possible modes of work that seem to fit in with existing expertise on mediation. The only way of finding out which are practicable, and helpful, is to try them. Arrangements are now in train for some preliminary trials to be carried out in "demonstration" workshops; time will tell to what extent these forms of analysis are a useful addition to the mediator's armoury.

NOTES

1. In fact, Game Theory can be seen as undermining some of the tenets of free-market economics. For example, the "Prisoners' Dilemma" paradox shows that the "invisible hand" of individual rationality does not necessarily lead to a good overall outcome.

2. See Bennett (1977). It should be stressed that the basic idea of paying attention to differing perceptions—at least, of preferences—was not new. This had been mentioned as an area warranting future research in Von Neumann and Morganstern's original treatise (1944). Mathematical developments continued, in particular through the work of Harsanyi on games with incomplete information. On the whole, though, these theroretical advances seem to have had little impact on those concerned with the application of game models—at least outside the field of economics. The work of Brams (1977) and his colleagues on the effect of deception in games is also relevant here.

3. In a striking parallel development, the same model has been independently proposed (under the apposite name of the "Perceptual Dilemma") by Plous (1985/1987) who has also assembled evidence to support it.

4. Many analyses used to illustrate games and hypergames not only use very high-level actors (e.g., nations), but also consider strategies in broad terms only —e.g., the arms race modelled as a 2 × 2 game. While obviously "unrealistic" if taken in isolation, such models serve as a useful backdrop against which to examine more specific choices.

5. Or, to quote Laurence J. Peter, "neither sound nor unsound proposals can be carried out efficiently, because the machinery of government is a vast series of interlocking hierarchies, riddled through with incompetence" (in Peter and Hull, 1969, p. 63).

6. In the Falklands Crisis, for example, it was clear that important decisions would have to be made when the British Task Force reached the Islands. Once it had set out, the decision about what to do with it could not be delayed forever—despite some flexibility occasioned by slow steaming. To use Haig's phrase, the fleet "moved down the South Atlantic like a weight on a clock".

7. This belief is stressed in most accounts of the conflict, particularly by Haig: "Even after all that I had said to the contrary, I feared that Galtieri and his colleagues were unable to believe that the British would fight. In one final attempt to persuade them, I sent Dick Walters to see Galtieri alone and tell him in crystal-clear terms, in the Spanish language, that if there was no negotiated settlement, the British would fight and win—and that the United States would support Britain. Galtieri listened and replied 'Why are you telling me this? The British won't fight'" (Haig, 1986, p. 280).

8. To make the point again, national "preferences" and available strategies express the resultant of internal forces. Though true also of Britain, this point appears to have been particularly crucial in shaping Argentine actions: "British ministers described Argentina as a dictatorship. . . . It was no such thing. It was an oligarchy; weak, unstable, and extraordinarily brutal. . . . The institutions of legitimacy were the service councils . . . Argentina's parliaments, her ruling elite in conclave. It was before these bodies that the Junta members had to defend any compromises they might offer Haig. . . . Any hierarchical responsibility now collapsed as each junta member guarded his rear. At consultative meetings, hands would shoot up, hard-liners would form factions, moderates would be heckled into silence . . ." (Hastings and Jenkins, 1983). In this context, it is significant that where Haig (especially) seems to have seen a mixture of anarchy and bad faith, others insist that perfectly well-defined procedures were being followed. See, especially, Kinney (Chapter 5, this volume).

12

Paradigms, Movements, and Shifts: Indicators of a Social Invention

Dennis J. D. Sandole

In his seminal work, Thomas Kuhn (1970) has provided the world with a metaphysic and a theory which, though compatible with bits and pieces of psychology and anthropology, were at odds with a prevailing philosophical tradition that has dominated perceptions, thinking, and behavior for some three hundred years; the view associated with Descartes that the world is a stable given, an objective reality; that in spite of apparent cultural and other differences, we should all be able to perceive that world in pretty much the same way, and if some of us do not, then there is something "wrong" (Kuhn, 1970, Chap. 10; Sandole, 1984, 1986, 1987).

Kuhn's notions of "paradigm," "normal science," "anomalies," "crises," and "scientific revolutions" comprise an eloquent argument against the Cartesian thesis; indeed, they constitute, in true dialectic fashion, an antithesis to the prevailing view. Kuhn's message is not only that we can and do live in different perceptual worlds (Sandole, 1984, 1987), but that we tend to look only for confirmations of our expectations (Snyder and Gangstead, 1981); to resist, unconsciously as well as consciously, cognitively as well as emotionally, recognition of anomalies (Sandole, 1984); and, in violation of Karl Popper's (1959) falsification model, that we often "go to our graves" with assumptions which, at least for others, are no longer (if they ever were) valid. Nevertheless, change is possible. "Scientific revolutions," involving "paradigm shifts," do occur from time to time, though, as implied, not without considerable difficulty.

ALTERNATIVE APPROACHES TO CONFLICT AND CONFLICT MANAGEMENT

One metaphysical/theoretical system that influences thinking, perceptions, and behavior is associated with the political philosphy of *political realism*, often called "power politics." Political realism is associated with Morton Deutsch's (1973, 1987) notion of competitive processes of conflict interaction characterized by distrust and suspicion, expansion of the issues involved and of one's emotional investment in them, little or no productive communication, disinformation and espionage, hostility, a predominantly zero-sum (win/lose) view of the world, and a reliance on adversarial, coercive, power-based processes of conflict resolution. In terms of recorded history, competitive processes have been around at least since Thucydides observed them in action during the Peloponnesian War, for example, when the Athenians subjugated the inhabitants of Melos in 416 BC (1951, pp. 330–337).

Few human phenomena exist for long without being responded to, accompanied by, and sometimes replaced by their opposites. This is certainly true of political realism and the competitive processes of conflict resolution. The corresponding opposites are political idealism and the cooperative processes. The cooperative processes are characterized by a spirit of commonality, trust, reduction in the number of issues involved in conflict and of one's emotional involvement in them, productive communication, a fundamentally non–zero-sum, positive-sum (win/win) view of the world, and a reliance on nonadversarial, noncoercive, collaborative problem-solving techniques. Idealism and its variations have also been around a long time, at least since the sixth century BC, the time of Confucius and his emphasis on justice.

As I have pointed out elsewhere (Sandole, 1986, p.120), the relationship between competitive and cooperative processes

is not just one of an either/or dichotomy, for a gradient or continuum can be seen to exist between them. For instance, with competitive on one side and cooperative on the other, we can have actual or threatened use of deadly force, litigation/adjudication, arbitration, conciliation, traditional mediation, facilitated problem solving, and integrative/collaborative negotiation.

As is perhaps implied by the continuum metaphor, and as has been pointed out by Billig (1976), Folger and Poole (1984), and others, competitive and cooperative processes are not necessarily mutually exclusive. Elements of both may appear in the same conflict situation, indeed, may even appear in the same person, over time. Hence, "trust" may be a factor in an otherwise adversarial relationship. According to a former CIA intelligence officer (Matthias, 1987, p. 240):

There is a widespread view in this country, frequently expressed by responsible officials of the government, that the Soviet Union is an evil empire, that it cannot trust, that it is determined to destroy us by military force if necessary. However that may be, we have no alternative to relying upon their rationality and indeed their good will.

Aside from the fact that they have not blown us up yet, they have demonstrated, I think, a rather considerable capacity for being trustworthy and rational. The historical record shows, although there is always some debate about this, that whenever we have had a clear, unequivocal agreement with the Soviets, they have kept it.

Contrariwise, even in an overall cooperative relationship, we may have to put forward our cases firmly, which may be suggestive of subtle threats. To be firm in this sense, however, also means to be flexible and conciliatory (Pruitt, 1987). Nevertheless, although the real world rarely falls into, but instead, *between*, our neat conceptual categories, we can still speak of overall competitive and cooperative orientations and processes.

REALISM AND THE COMPETITIVE ORIENTATION: PERSISTENCE THROUGH TIME AND SPACE

Though it would surely be impossible to develop realist/idealist, competitive/cooperative comparisons for all interactions and events that have occurred throughout human history, we can say that political realism, with its attendant competitive orientation, is very compelling, very "attractive" especially to one who has experienced, directly or otherwise, some brutal assault to person, property, or values. We can also say that, at least at the international level, political realism has been, and is, the dominant paradigm (Banks, 1984a; Rothstein, 1972; Taylor, 1978; Sandole, 1984; Vasquez, 1983).

The international level, which logically and empirically affects all others, can be viewed as homo sapiens' most extensive approximation to a Hobbesian state of nature, a Social-Darwinistic struggle, as evidenced by the horizontal and vertical proliferation of nuclear weapons, plus the movement into earth orbit of weapons of mass destruction. This recognition would itself constitute proof for realists that they are right in their assumption, for example, that we have no choice but to prepare to defend ourselves against the inevitable. For others, however, this is just one more example of realism as a self-perpetuating, self-maintaining violent conflict system (Sandole, 1984, 1986, 1987). Either way, realism prevails, and the tendency to employ the competitive approaches to conflict management is extended and reinforced.

CRACKS IN THE REALIST ARMOUR:
ANOMALIES AND RESPONSES TO THEM

Kuhn tells us that as paradigms mature, the tendency for them to confront instances they cannot explain increases but, perhaps paradoxically, so does the resistance to detecting anomalies. When anomalies are detected, the paradigms involved may fail to account for them; after prolonged failure to do so, "crisis" may ensue, one response to which may be a search for alternatives. A significant anomaly with regard to realism is that, to a point, realism and the competitive processes may lead to perceived functional outcomes but, beyond that point, may be counterproductive and self-defeating. This seems to be what actors at all levels have been experiencing. Beyond some critical threshold, the use of competitive processes may appear to "settle" but not necessarily to "resolve" conflict (Burton, 1986) and attempts to impose solutions may lead to protracted conflict (Azar and Burton, 1986). Quite simply, at the international level, the more we endeavor to "deter" nuclear war by employing competitive means, the more likely it may be that nuclear war will occur. Hence, reflecting the classic "security dilemma" (Herz, 1962), the more that we are to pursue security, the more insecure we become. What could be more anomalous?

As already indicated, it is not only at the international level that anomalies are being detected and responses to them fashioned. Accompanying and following the American war in Vietnam, plus the civil rights struggles, Watergate, CIA exposures, and other events in the United States during the 1960s and 1970s, a number of developments have been emerging as cooperative alternatives to competitive processes: among others, in family and divorce mediation, neighborhood dispute resolution, environmental mediation, and hostage negotiations. These have all been associated with "alternative dispute resolution" (ADR), which is a response to "a significant dissatisfaction with the legal system's adversarial approach to resolving disputes" (Ray, 1982, p. 117). ADR always has a legal component: if differences are not managed and resolved to the satisfaction of all concerned, then there may be recourse to competitive means which, whether legal or non-legal, may involve the legal system. This is not the case at the international level where, international law and the International Court of Justice notwithstanding, there is no legal system in the generally more meaningful sense that there is at the national level. Hence, Rapoport's (1974, p. 175) distinction between "endogenous" and "exogenous" conflicts: situations where there are "mechanisms ... for controlling or resolving conflict" versus those where there may be no super-system to exercise control or resolve conflict."

Though the international level lacks the controlling or resolving "super-system" associated with the national level, this has not prevented—indeed, has stimulated—the development of alternatives to coercive, competitive processes at that level. This has taken the form, in part, of the development of information-disseminating, training, research, and funding organizations, such as the Canadian Institute for International Peace and Security (Pearson, 1986), the United States Institute of Peace (Laue, 1985; Smith, 1985), plus many others worldwide (UNESCO, 1981; Geldenhuys, 1985; *AFB-INFO* 1/87, 1987). It has also taken the form of efforts by John Burton (1969), Herbert Kelman (1972; Kelman and Cohen, 1979), Leonard Doob (1970, 1973, 1976), and others to bring together representatives of warring factions; and it has taken the form of the UN-affiliated University for Peace in Costa Rica (*University for Peace*, 1981).

Taken together, these few developments at the international level may not seem to amount to much. Paralleling these, however, has been the establishment of the Center for the Study of Foreign Affairs, Foreign Service Institute, U.S. Department of State, one of whose objectives is to bridge the gap between foreign service practitioners and theorists/ researchers in conflict management. To this end, the Center has organized a number of conferences and seminars involving practitioners and theorists/researchers (e.g., Bendahmane and McDonald, 1984, 1986; McDonald and Bendahmane, 1987). Just as the theorist/researcher can be influenced by the practitioner, so the practitioner can be influenced by the theorist/researcher. For example, negotiation techniques pioneered by Roger Fisher of Harvard Law School's Program on Negotiation "were instrumental in fashioning the Camp David Accords between Egypt and Israel in 1978" (Marquand, 1986a, p. B3).

These developments at the international level should be seen as part of cooperative trends in general, trends which, in the United States, include the development of the Harvard Law School's Program on Negotiation (Fisher and Ury, 1981; Raiffa, 1982; Ury, 1985), the American Bar Association's Standing Committee on Dispute Resolution (Ray, 1982, 1987), the Federal Mediation and Conciliation Service (FMCS) (Buckingham, 1982; Davis with Dugan, 1982; Davis, 1987), the Community Relations Service (CRS) of the U.S. Department of Justice (Pompa, 1985, 1987; Salem, 1982), the Consortium on Peace Research, Education and Development (COPRED) (Alger and Boulding, 1981), the Society of Professionals in Dispute Resolution (SPIDR), the American Arbitration Association (AAA) (Coulson, 1982), the National Institute for Dispute Resolution (NIDR) (NIDR *Progress Report*, 1985–1986), and the National Conference on Peacemaking and Conflict Resolution (NCPCR) (Herrman and Weeks, 1984; Herrman with Covi, 1986). Similar developments have been taking place in Australia (Schwartzkoff and Morgan, 1982), Canada (Sandler, 1986; Shrybman, 1986), Great Britain (Parker, 1983; Marshall, 1984; Marshall and Walpole, 1985), the People's Republic of China (Clayre, 1984, Chap. 4), South Africa (Centre for Intergroup Studies, 1986; Wahrhaftig, 1985, 1986), and elsewhere.

With some exceptions—for example the AAA in 1926, the FMCS in 1947, and the CRS in 1964 (also see Laue, 1987; Wehr, 1986)—most of these developments occurred during the 1970s and 1980s: COPRED, 1970, SPIDR, 1973; ABA Standing Committee on Dispute Resolution, 1976 (the committee has undergone various name changes since then: see Ray 1987); University for Peace (chartered by the UN General Assembly), 1980; NIDR, 1982; Center for the Study of Foreign Affairs, U.S. Department of State, 1982; Canadian Institute for International Peace and Security, 1983; Harvard Law School's Program on Negotiation, 1983; and the U.S. Institute for Peace, 1984. During this same period, the number of ADR challenges to the formal legal system in the United States went from "three centers in 1971 to more than 180 in 1982" (Ray, 1982, p. 117), and as Olson (1986, p. 1; also McBride, 1987) indicates:

There is, we are told, a dispute resolution "explosion." Statistics bear that out. When the [Standing] Committee [on Dispute Resolution] was established in 1976, there were only a handful of mediation programs. Today, as our recent survey has shown . . . more than 350 mediation programs are in operation. In 1976, there were perhaps 2,500 community mediators. Today, there are more than 20,000. While today more than 20 states have specific dispute resolution statutes, 10 years ago not a single one did. In 1976, no bar association had a committee on dispute resolution. Today, more than 120 do (*Bar Association Directory on Dispute Resolution*, 1986). And although in 1976 no law school offered a course in dispute resolution, today more than half do so.

These trends have been accompanied by other developments, such as an emphasis in the literature on the constructive management (including resolution) as well as the analysis of conflict (e.g., Bacow and Wheeler, 1984; Banks, 1984b; Bercovitch, 1984; Burton, 1987a, 1987b; Deutsch, M., 1973, 1987; Folberg and Taylor, 1984; Folger and Poole, 1984; Goldberg et al., 1985; Himes, 1980; Kriesburg, 1982; Mitchell, 1981a, 1981b; Moore, 1986; Pruitt and Rubin, 1986; Sandole and Staroste-Sandole, 1987; Saposnek, 1983). Journals have been launched as well, the vast majority during the 1970s and 1980s: *Bulletin of Peace Proposals; Conflict Management and Peace Sciences; Current Research on Peace and Violence; International Journal on World Peace; Journal of Collective Negotiations in the Public Sector; Journal of Conflict Resolution; Journal of Peace Research; Mediation Quarterly; Missouri Journal of Dispute Resolution; Ohio State Journal on Dispute Resolution; Peace and Change; Peace Research Reviews;* plus others which feature articles and sometimes devote entire issues to aspects of conflict management (e.g., *American Behavioral Scientist; Conciliation Courts Review; Family Law Quarterly; International Studies Quarterly; Journal of Social Issues; Political Psychology*).

Another development has been the growing number of newsletters: for example, *AFB-INFO* (Arbeitsstelle Friedensforschung Bonn), *Canadian Environmental Mediation Newsletter* (York University, Ontario), *Conflict*

Resolution Notes (Conflict Resolution Center, Pittsburgh), *Dispute Resolution* (ABA Standing Committee on Dispute Resolution, Washington, D.C.), *Dispute Resolution Forum* (NIDR, Washington, D.C.); *International Peace Studies Newsletter* (Centre for Peace Studies, University of Akron, Ohio); *International Peace Research Newsletter* (International Peace Research Association/IPRA); *Mediation* (Forum for Initiatives on Reparation and Mediation, London, England); *Negotiation* (Harvard Law School Program on Negotiation); *Peace Chronicle* (COPRED); *PEACE in Action* (Foundation for P.E.A.C.E., Arlington, Virginia); *Peace Research Centre Newsletter* (Australian National University, Canberra); *Prospectus* (Community Boards, San Francisco); *Resolve* (The Conservation Foundation, Washington, D.C.); *SPIDR Notes* (Washington, D.C.); *The Mediator* (Development Association of British Columbia, Canada); *The New York Mediator* (Unified Court System of the State of New York); plus others (see spring and summer 1985 issues of the ABA Standing Committee's *Dispute Resolution* for further listings).

There has also been a growing number of local, national, and international conferences addressing issues in conflict and conflict management. In 1986, the United Nations International Year of Peace, there were many (see 1986 issue of COPRED's *Peace Chronicle*), including the First International Conference on Conflict Resolution and Peace Studies, Suva, Fiji (Maas and Stewart, 1986); Pre-Conference Seminar on Managing Conflicts in a Multicultural Context, Amsterdam, The Netherlands (Kakonen, 1986; van der Wulp, 1986); General Conference of the International Peace Research Association (IPRA), Sussex, England (Alger and Stohl, 1988); Twelfth Annual Congress of SIETAR, Amsterdam (van der Wulp, 1986); Third National Conference on Peacemaking and Conflict Resolution (NCPCR), Denver (Herrman, 1987); and the Fourteenth International Conference of the Society of Professionals in Dispute Resolution (SPIDR), Chicago (Cutrona, 1987).

Part of the cooperative trend in the United States has been a meteoric rise in the number of people and organizations providing training and teaching in conflict management. According to Baur (1983, p. 82):

In recent years there has been a phenomenal growth of interest in ways of coping with social conflict and applying intervention techniques in areas of human activity where they were previously little used. This trend has expanded the need for personnel who are skilled in the general principles of conflict management applicable to any situation of tension between and among individuals and groups. A number of organizations, agencies, foundations, and institutions of higher education have responded to this need. They have been providing services, giving instruction, developing teaching materials, and subsidizing innovative projects.

Many of the organizations, foundations, and agencies providing short-term workshops are listed in NIDR's *Dispute Resolution Resource Directory* (1984) and in the ABA Standing Committee's *Dispute*

Resolution Program Directory (1986–1987). Undergraduate and post-graduate programs have been discussed by Baur (1983), Crohn (1985), Gerschenfeld (1985), Hall (1986), Katz (1986), Kemp (1983), Koopman (1985), Lewicki (1986), Malone (1985), Sandole (1985), Volpe (1985), Wedge and Sandole (1982), and others. Some 100 of these, mostly in the United States, are listed in COPRED's *Directory of Peace Studies Programs* (1986). "During the 1970s conflict resolution studies proliferated in scores of universities and colleges around the nation" (Wehr, 1986, p. 4); "The number of colleges granting degrees in peace-related studies has vaulted from 5 to more than 100 during the last decade" (Marquand, 1986b, p. B1); "peace studies ... has been adopted by more than 160 American universities" (Elias, 1986, p. B8). According to the first national survey of dispute resolution teaching in higher education in the United States, there are "838 courses taught by 636 instructors in 294 institutions across 43 states" (Wehr, 1986, pp. 3–4); hence, Drake's (1986) observation that "Nowhere has the dispute resolution field experienced as much ferment and growth as in higher education." Again, there are comparable developments elsewhere in the world: for example, the Irish Peace Institute and Irish School of Ecumenics in Ireland; Kyung-Hee University in South Korea; La Trobe University in Australia; the Polemological Institute of the State University of Groningen and the University of Utrecht in The Netherlands; Universities of Bradford, Kent and Lancaster in England; University of Haifa in Israel; University of Ulster in Northern Ireland; University of Waterloo in Canada; Uppsala and Lund Universities in Sweden; plus others. One especially positive note here is that the Irish Peace Institute, which is in the Republic of Ireland, and the University of Ulster, which is in Northern Ireland, are collaborating in offering an MA in Peace Studies.

In the United States, "The increased attention given to peace education in colleges ... is being paralleled, to a degree, in elementary and secondary schools" (Marquand, 1986c). And although some 74 private foundations have provided funds for peace studies programs—"from 1982 to 1984 their grants increased by over 200 percent, to $52 million"—most of this money has gone to support research rather than education: "Grants grow, but most schools pay for peace studies themselves" (Rowe, 1986).

PARADIGM SHIFT, SOCIAL MOVEMENT OR DOES IT REALLY MATTER?

John Burton and I (Burton and Sandole, 1986, p. 336) have argued elsewhere that "A shift is in progress in the United States and elsewhere from the *settlement* of conflict by authoritative controls to conflict *resolution* by the parties themselves, and has been made possible by a fundamental paradigm shift in thought." As has been suggested above, this "shifting" has been occurring at many, if not all levels of human experience, from the interpersonal to the international, and is a general reaction to the failure of simple-minded realism and the competitive processes to bring about positive, enduring outcomes. This is not to suggest, however, that competitive processes no longer have any useful role, or that they are about to become totally eclipsed by cooperative processes, but that a "second track" is coming more and more to complement the "first track" associated with political realism (Burton, 1984, Chap. 17; McDonald and Bendahmane, 1987). For example, rather than send in SWAT (special weapons and tactics) teams to terminate, with "extreme prejudice," hostage-taking sieges, police departments are using, as a first resort, hostage-negotiators to end such situations without bloodshed (Hassel, 1987). Rather than sue for divorce via their respective attorneys, separating couples are seeking the services of divorce mediators (Gaughan, 1987; Koopman, 1987). If such "second track" approaches do not succeed, then the conflicting parties may be forced to fall back on the "first track." What we have been addressing here, therefore, is not about the old ways being replaced by the new, but about increasing our options.

How extensive is this "shifting," and what can we expect in the future? Returning to the notion of a gradient between competitive and cooperative processes, the developments that we have looked at thus far, plus the emergence of a new "realism" in East–West relations, suggest that the cooperative trends will continue at all levels worldwide. The nuclear superpowers may be, in fact, conflict role models for others: if they can handle their disputes via the "second track," then perhaps the tendency for others to do the same will be established or reinforced. Moreover, cooperative processes, like competitive ones, can be self-maintaining (Deutsch, 1987). Life has never been the same for the Israelis and the Egyptians since President Sadat personally went to the Knesset. Overall, this "shifting" may constitute a social movement in the making.

Social movements are organized efforts to bring about or to resist social change. McCarthy and Zald (1977) indicate that social movement *writ large* is comprised of the following (Hess et al., 1982, p. 548):

Social movement (writ small): the set of opinions and beliefs in a population that are in favor of bringing about social change.

Countermovement: the set of opinions and beliefs that are opposed to the objectives of the social movement.

Social movement organizations: structures designed to realize the objectives of the social movement or counter-movement.

Social movement industries: the collaboration of various organizations in the pursuit of a single issue.

These various components also comprise the "natural history" or "life course" of a social movement. For example, according to a review of relevant literature conducted by Hess et al. (1982, pp. 552–55), there are at least four major phases from the inception to the dissolution of a social movement: (1) a preliminary period of personal discontent and vague unrest in the society; (2) the crystallization of concern and the construction of information networks; (3) formation of organizations to embody movement beliefs; and (4) either the institutionalization of the movement's goals or its decline through attrition of membership.

Our discussion above indicates that there is considerable discontent with realist philosophy and the adversarial processes; there are beliefs and opinions favoring changes at all levels of human society, from reliance on competitive to progressive use of cooperative processes; there are information networks (e.g., the journals, newsletters, and conferences) and clearly there are "social movement organizations" to embody and institutionalize the beliefs of the movement (e.g., AAA, CRS, FMCS, NIDR, SPIDR, the U.S. Institute of Peace; all the programs listed in the various directories, etc.). I would also argue that there are "social movement industries" comprised of organizations pursuing the same specific goals and around which there is some type of consensus. Others, such as Larry Ray, argue that "The search for alternative methods to the formal legal system for resolving . . . disputes . . . has burgeoned into a 'movement'" (1982, p. 117, also 1987). I am, of course, talking about "exogenous" as well as about "endogenous" conflict management processes and, although I agree with Alder that disagreement exists on many fronts, including among members of the same program (Sandole, 1985), I think there is sufficient consensus on other aspects to label what we are observing as—or at least, as part of—a growing social movement.

But does "labelling" really matter? I think not. What does is that, as Adler's own analysis and our discussion re-indicate, something is clearly happening in the way people are handling their disputes. Although "ADR is still a new phenomenon in which the perceived need for ADR services and the supply of able and willing ADR providers seems to have outstripped actual demand for services" (Adler, 1987, p. 69)—or, as Roger Fisher (1983) has put it, "we are a field for which there is a great need but little demand"—it nevertheless seems to be the case that nothing less than a "revolution" is taking place in the conflict management dimension of human experience. As Burton and I (1987, p. 98) have argued:

The "paradigm shift" that we are addressing is not merely some Kuhnean phenomenon occurring within the context of one or more disciplines where academic theory and practice might be affected. It is a more general phenomenon taking hold in various professions and in society-at-large.

CONCLUSION

We have been discussing approaches to conflict management, plus developments that are suggestive of a "shifting" from competitive to cooperative processes. Conflict management is part of conflict and peace studies (CAPS), or, depending upon one's preference, peace and conflict studies (PACS), which also includes conflict analysis, peace research, peace education, and peace action. The bits and pieces comprising CAPS/PACS have been around for some time. What is new is that relatively recent development of the overall field into a "metadiscipline," various professions, probably a social movement—certainly a composite "social invention" (Deutsch et al., 1971)—spurred on by the growing realization that the "time-proven" competitive processes may be leading more and more to counterproductive, self-defeating outcomes. And if, as Adler has argued, ADR lacks shared goals, then surely CAPS/PACS must lack coherence. According to Wehr (1986, p. 4): "The building blocks for integrating conflict resolution studies—the courses, research projects, training programs, networks, and literature—exist. It remains to interconnect them."

It is an open question, however, "whether proliferating courses and research efforts will result in cumulative and integrative development of the field" (ibid., p. 13), or whether the future of the field will be dominated by Platonic elitism or Aristotelian pluralism. I agree with Burton (1987b) that the "right framework" in conflict management should be comprised of appropriate theoretical, methodological, and applied components. Whether this will translate, once the "shifting" has run its course, into one paradigm with one or multiple interpretations, or into multiple paradigms, is not clear. I also agree with Wehr (1986, p. 13) that "some hybrid" of the Platonic and Aristotelian models"—what he calls the competitive/hierarchical and collaborative/network models—is the one most likely to develop. He goes on to say: "Without combining the strengths of the two, it will be difficult to achieve the necessary multidisciplinary collaboration of those engaged in teaching of theory and practice."

Whatever the mix between the Platonic and Aristotelian models; between theory, research, practice, and education; between track one and track two, the "shifting" should continue to generate new approaches until we are fairly certain about what works and where. And since, as Kuhn and others have shown, "certainty" may be a relatively short-lived phenomenon, we in the field should continue to monitor our assumptions, theories, methodologies, and application lest the parameters governing our "Standard Operating Procedures" change without our knowing—a fate that seem to have befallen the "realist" advocates of the competitive processes.

Bibliography

AACC (1966). *Report on the AACC Goodwill Mission to the Sudan*. Nairobi, Kenya (Geneva: WCC Archives).

Adcock, F. A., and D. J. Mosley (1975). *Diplomacy in Ancient Greece*. London: Thames and Hudson.

Adler, P. S. (1987). "Is ADR a Social Movement?" *Negotiation Journal* 3(1) (January): 59–71.

AFB–INFO 1/87 (1987). *Mitteilungen der Arbeitsstelle Friedensforschung Bonn*. Newsletter of the Information Unit Peace Research Bonn, Federal Republic of Germany.

African National Congress (1985). "Political Report of the National Securities Committee to the National Consultative Conference. June 1985." In *Documents of the Second International Consultative Conference of the African National Congress*, Zambia, 16–23 June 1985 (Lusaka: African National Congress).

Albert, Jean (1986). *Negotiation Skills: A Handbook*. Rondebosch: Centre for Intergroup Studies.

Albino, Oliver (1970). *The Sudan: A Southern Viewpoint*. London: Oxford University Press.

Alcock, A. E. (1970). *The History of the South Tyrol Conflict*. London: Michael Joseph.

Alexander, J. (1975). "An Operational Analysis of Conflict in Northern Ireland: An American Perspective." *Northern Ireland Constitutional Convention*, Belfast (October).

Alger, C. F., and E. Boulding (1981). "From Vietnam to El Salvador: Eleven Years of COPRED." *Peace and Change* 7(3) (Spring): 35–43; also in *International Peace Research Newsletter* 19(2) (May): 14–22.

Alger, C. F., and M. Stohl (Eds.) (1988). *Proceedings of the Eleventh General Conference*, International Peace Research Association.

Ashmore, H. S., and W. C. Baggs (1968). *Mission to Hanoi.* New York: Berkeley Publishing.

Azar, Edward, E., and John W. Burton (Eds.) (1986). *International Conflict Resolution: Theory and Practice.* Brighton: Wheatsheaf; Boulder: Lynne Rienner.

Bacow, L., and M. Wheeler (1984). *Environmental Dispute Resolution.* New York: Plenum.

Bailey, Sydney D. (1982). *How Wars End: The UN and the Terminations of Armed Conflict* 1946–1964. Oxford: Oxford University Press.

Bailey, Sydney D. (1985). "Non-Official Mediation in Disputes: Reflections on Quaker Experience." *International Affairs* 61(2) (Spring): 205–22.

Banks, Michael H. (Ed.) (1984a). *Conflict in World Society: A New Perspective on International Relations.* Brighton: Wheatsheaf; New York: St. Martins's.

Banks, Michael H. (1984b). "The Evolution of International Relations Theory." In Michael H. Banks (Ed.), *Conflict in World Society: A New Perspective on International Relations.* Brighton: Wheatsheaf; New York: St. Martin's.

Bar Association Directory on Dispute Resolution, 1986 (1986). Washington D.C.: American Bar Association (ABA) Standing Committee on Dispute Resolution.

Barber, J. (1983). *The Uneasy Relationship: Britain and South Africa.* London: Heinemann (for The Royal Institute of International Studies).

Barber, J., et al. (1982). "The West and South Africa." *Chatham House Papers*, 14. London: Royal Institute of International Studies.

Barros, J. (1968). *The Aland Island Question.* New Haven: Yale University Press.

Baur, E. J. (1983). "College Curricula in Conflict Regulation: The Emergence of a Discipline." *Peace and Change* 9(1) (Spring): 81–92.

Bedjaoui, Mohammed (1979). *Towards a New International Economic Order.* Paris: UNESCO.

Bendahmane, Diane B., and John W. McDonald (Eds.) (1984). *International Negotiation: Art and Science.* Washington D.C.: Center for the Study of Foreign Affairs, Foreign Service Institute, U.S. Department of State.

Bendahmane, Diane B., and John W. McDonald (1986). *Perspectives on Negotiation: 4 Case Studies.* Washington, D.C.: Center for the Study of Foreign Affairs, Foreign Service Institute, U.S. Department of State.

Bennett, P. G. (1977). "Toward a Theory of Hypergames." *Omega* 5: 749–51.

Bennett, P. G. (1982). "Hypergames: Developing a Model of Conflict," *Futures* 12: 589–607.

Bennett, P. G. (1987). "Beyond Game Theory—Where?" In P. G. Bennett (Ed.), *Analysing Conflict and Its Resolution: Some Mathematical Contributions.* Oxford: Oxford University Press.

Bennett, P. G., and S. A. Cropper (1987a). "Helping People Choose: Conflict and Other Perspectives." In V. Belton and R. O'Keefe, *Recent Developments in O.R.* Oxford: Pergamon Press/O.R. Society, pp. 13–25.

Bennett, P. G., and S. A. Cropper (1987b). "Maps, Games, and Things in Between." *European Journal of Operational Research* 32: 33–46.

Bennett, P. G., and M. R. Dando (1979). "Complex Strategic Analysis; a Hypergame Study of the Fall of France." *Journal of the Operational Research Society* 30: 23–32.

Bennett, P. G., and M. R. Dando (1982). "The Arms Race as a Hypergame: A Study of Routes towards a Safer World." *Futures* 14: 293–306.

Bennett, P. G., and M. R. Dando (1983). "The Arms Race: Is It Just a Mistake?" *New Scientist* (17 February): 432–35.

Bennett, P. G., and C. S. Huxham (1982). "Hypergames and What They Do: A 'Soft O.R.' Approach." *Journal of the Operational Research Society* 33: 41–50.

Bercovitch, Jacob (1984). *Social Conflicts and Third Parties: Strategies of Conflict Resolution*. Boulder, Col.: Westview Press.

Berman, Maureen R., and Joseph E. Johnson (Eds.) (1977). *Unofficial Diplomats*. New York: Columbia University Press.

Beshir, Mohammed O. (1968). *The Southern Sudan: Background to Conflict*. New York: Praeger.

Bilig, M. (1976). *Social Psychology and Intergroup Relations*. London/New York: Academic Press.

Blackett, P. M. S. (1962). "A Critique of Some Contemporary Defence Thinking." In *Studies of War*. Edinburgh: Oliver and Boyd.

Blake, R. R., H. A. Shepherd, and J. S. Mouton (1964). *Managing Inter-Group Conflict in Industry*. Houston: Gulf Publishing Co.

Brams, S. (1977). "Deception in 2 × 2 Games." *Journal of Peace Science* 2: 171–203.

Brookmire, D. A., and F. Sistrunk. (1980). "The Effects of Perceived Ability and Impartiality of Mediators and Time Pressure on Negotiations." *Journal of Conflict Resolution* 24: 311–28.

Bryant, J. W. (1984). "Modelling Alternative Realities in Conflict and Negotiation." *Journal of the Operational Research Society* 35: 985–94.

Buckingham, Jr., G. W. (1982). "Variables Affecting Mediation Outcomes." *Peace and Change* 8(2/3) (Summer): 55–64.

Bull, Hedley (1979). *The Anarchical Society*. New York: Columbia University Press.

Burton, John W. (1969). *Conflict and Communication: The Use of Controlled Communication in International Relations*. London: MacMillan; New York: Free Press.

Burton, John W. (1984). *Global Conflict: The Domestic Sources of International Crisis*. Brighton: Wheatsheaf; College Park: University of Maryland, Centre for International Development.

Burton, John W. (1986). "The Theory of Conflict Resolution." *Current Research on Peace and Violence* 9(3): 125–30.

Burton, John W. (1987a). *Resolving Deep-Rooted Conflict: A Handbook*. Lanham, Maryland/London: University Press of America.

Burton, John W. (1987b). "International Conflict and Problem Solving." In D. J. D. Sandole and I. Staroste-Sandole (Eds.), *Conflict Management and Problem Solving: Interpersonal to International Applications*. London: Francis Pinter; New York: New York University Press.

Burton, John W., and D. J. D. Sandole (1986). "Generic Theory: The Basis of Conflict Resolution." *Negotiation Journal* 2(4) (October): 333–44.

Burton, John W., and D. J. D. Sandole (1987). "Expanding the Debate on Generic Theory of Conflict Resolution: A Response to a Critique." *Negotiation Journal* 3(1) (January): 97–99.

Campbell, J. C. (Ed.) (1976). *Successful Negotiation: Trieste 1954*. Princeton, N.J.: Princeton University Press.

Cantril, Hadley (1965). *The Pattern of Human Concern*. New Brunswick: Rutgers University Press.

Cawthra, G. (1986). *Brutal Force: The Apartheid War Machine*. London: International Defence and Aid Fund.

Centre for Intergroup Studies (1986). *Nineteenth Annual Report*. Rondebosch, South Africa: University of Cape Town.

Clark, Ian (1980). *Reform and Resistance in the International Order*. Cambridge: Cambridge University Press.

Clayre, A. (1984). *The Heart of the Dragon*. Boston: Houghton Mifflin.

Coker, C. (1982). "The United States and South Africa: Can Constructive Engagement Succeed?" *Millenium* 11(3): 223–41.

Cooper, A. D. (1982). *U.S. Economic Power and Economic Influence in Namibia*. Boulder, CO: Westview Press.

Cot, Jean Pierre (1972). *International Conciliation*. London: Stevens.

Coulson, R. (1982). "The Functions of Arbitration." *Peace and Change* 8(2/3) (Summer): 65–72.

Crocker, C. A. (1980). "South Africa: Strategy for Change." *Foreign Affairs* (Winter).

Crohn, M. (1985). "Dispute Resolution and Higher Education." *Negotiation Journal* 1(4) (October): 301–5.

Cronje, Suzanne (1972). *The World and Nigeria*. London: Sidgwick and Jackson.

Curle, Adam (1971). *Making Peace*. London: Tavistock Publications.

Curle, Adam (1986). *In the Middle: Non-Official Mediation in Violent Situations*. New York: St. Martin's Press.

Cutrona, C. (Ed.) (1987). *Dispute Resolution: An Open Forum*. Proceedings of the Fourteenth International Conference. Society of Professionals in Dispute Resolution (SPIDR). Washington, D.C.: SPIDR.

Davis, H. (1987). "Managing Labour Relations: A More Complete Approach." In D. J. D. Sandole and I. Staroste-Sandole (Eds.), *Conflict Management and Problem Solving: Interpersonal to International Applications*. London: Francis Pinter; New York: New York University Press.

Davis, H., with M. A. Dugan (1982). "Training the Mediator." *Peace and Change* 8(2/3) (Summer): 81–90.

de Reuck, A. V. S. (1974). "Controlled Communication: Rationale and Dynamics." *The Human Context* 6(1): 64–80.

de Reuck, A. V. S. (1983). "A Theory of Conflict Resolution by Problem Solving." *Man, Environment, Space and Time* 3(1): 27–36.

Deutsch, K. W., J. Platt, and D. Senghass (1971). "Conditions Favouring Major Advances in Social Science." *Science* 171(3970) (5 February): 450–59.

Deutsch, M. (1973). *The Resolution of Conflict: Constructive and Destructive Processes*. New Haven/London: Yale University Press.

Deutsch, M. (1987). "A Theoretical Perspective on Conflict and Conflict Resolution." In D. J. D. Sandole and I. Staroste-Sandole (Eds.), *Conflict Management and Problem Solving: Interpersonal to International Applications*. London: Francis Pinter; New York: New York University Press.

Directory of Peace Studies Programs (1986). Urbana: Consortium on Peace Research, Education, and Development (COPRED). University of Illinois at Urbana-Champaign (August).

Dispute Resolution Program Directory, 1986–1987 (1986). Washington D.C.: ABA Standing Committee on Dispute Resolution.

Dispute Resolution Resource Directory (1984). Washington D.C.: National Institute for Dispute Resolution (NIDR) (January).

Documents Diplomatiques Suisses (1981). Volume 6, 1914–1918. Berne: Benteli Vorlag.

Doob, L. W. (Ed.) (1970). *Resolving Conflict in Africa: The Fermeda Workshop*. New Haven/London: Yale University Press.

Doob, L. W. (1973). "The Belfast Workshop: An Application of Group Techniques to a Destructive Conflict." *Journal of Conflict Resolution* 17(3): 489–512.

Doob, L. W. (1976). "A Cyprus Workshop: Intervention Methodology During a Continuing Crisis." *Journal of Social Psychology* 98: 143–44.

Douglas, A. (1972). *Industrial Peacemaking*. New York: Columbia University Press.

Drake, W. R. (1986). Introduction to "Dispute Resolution in Higher Education." *Dispute Resolution Forum*. Washington D.C.: National Institute for Dispute Resolution (NIDR) (April), p. 2.

Druckman, Daniel (Ed.) (1977). *Negotiations: Social Psychological Perspectives*. Beverley Hills: Sage Publications.

Dugard, J. (1973). *The South-West Africa/Namibia Dispute*. Berkeley, California: University of California Press.

Eckstein, Harry (1980). "Theoretical Approaches to Explaining Collective Political Violence." In T. R.Gurr (Ed.), *Handbook of Political Conflict: Theory and Research*. New York: The Free Press, pp. 135–66.

Eden, C., S. Jones, and D. Sims (1983). *Messing About in Problems*. Oxford: Pergamon Press.

Elias, R. (1986). "Grading the Peace Teachers: The Critics Are Unfair or Uninformed." *Christian Science Monitor* (31 January), p. B8.

Fisher, Roger (1983). "Is Dispute Settlement a Professional Speciality?" Plenary Luncheon Address, *First National Conference on Peacemaking and Conflict Resolution* (NCPCR), University of Georgia (4 March).

Fisher, Roger, and William Ury (1981). *Getting to "Yes": Negotiating Agreement Without Giving In*. Boston: Houghton Mifflin; London: Hutchinson.

Fisher, Ronald J. (1983). "Third Party Consultation as a Method of Intergroup Conflict Resolution: A Review of Studies." *Journal of Conflict Resolution* 27(2) (June): 301–34.

Folberg, J., and A. Taylor (1984). *Mediation: A Comprehensive Guide to Resolving Conflicts without Litigation*. San Francisco/London: Jossey-Bass.

Folger, J. P., and M. S. Poole (1984). *Working Through Conflict: A Communication Perspective*. Glenview: Scott, Foresman.

Friend, J. K., and A. Hickling (1987). *Planning Under Pressure*. Oxford: Pergamon Press.

Friend, J. K., and N. Jessop (1977). *Local Government and Strategic Choice*, 2nd ed. Oxford: Pergamon Press.

Gaughan, L. D. (1987). "Divorce and Family Mediation." In D. J. D. Sandole and
    I. Staroste-Sandole (Eds.), *Conflict Management and Problem Solving:
    Interpersonal to International Applications*. London: Francis Pinter; New
    York: New York University Press, 1987.
Geldenhuys, D. (1984). *The Diplomacy of Isolation*. New York: St. Martin's Press.
Geldenhuys, O. (1985). *Directory: Foreign Negotiation and Mediation Organisa-
    tions*. Rondebosch: University of Cape Town, Centre for Intergroup
    Studies.
Gerschenfeld, W. J. (1985). "Teaching Dispute Resolution." In C. Cutrona (Ed.),
    The Elements of Good Practice in Dispute Resolution. Proceedings of the
    Twelfth International Conference of SPIDR. Washington, D.C.: SPIDR.
Giesen, M. O. (1981). *Toward an Applied Theory of Complex Decision Making*.
    D.Phil. Thesis, University of Sussex.
Giesen, M. O., and P. G. Bennett (1979). "Aristotle's Fallacy: A Hypergame in
    the Oil Shipping Business." *Omega* 7: 309–20.
Goldberg, S. B., E. D. Green, and F. E. A. Sander (Eds.) (1985). *Dispute
    Resolution*. Boston: Little Brown.
Green, P. (1966). *Deadly Logic*. Ohio: Ohio State University Press.
Green, R. H., et al. (1981). *Namibia: The Last Colony*. London: Longman.
Groom, A. J. R. G., and K. Webb (1987). "Injustice, Empowerment, and
    Facilitation in Conflict." *International Interactions* 13(3): 263–80.
Gulliver, P. A. (1979). *Disputes and Negotiations*. New York: Academic Press.
Haig, A. (1986). *Caveat: Realism, Reagan, and Foreign Policy*. London:
    Weidenfeld and Nicholson.
Haig, A. *Time*, 9 April 1984.
Hall, L. (1986). "Preliminary Thought on Graduate Programs in Dispute
    Resolution." *Negotiation Journal* 2(2) (April): 207–11.
Halliday, F. (1984). *The Making of the Second Cold War*. London: Verso.
Haq, Barbara (1972). "Statements on Activities of Liberation (MCF) on the
    Question of Resolving the Problem of Southern Sudan." Unpublished ms.
Hassel, C. V. (1987). "Terrorism and Hostage Negotiation." In D. J. D. Sandole
    and I. Staroste-Sandole (Eds.), *Conflict Management and Problem Solving:
    Interpersonal to International Applications*. London: Francis Pinter; New
    York: New York University Press.
Hastings, M., and S. Jenkins (1983). *The Battle for the Falklands*. London: Joseph.
Herrman, M. S. (1987). *Final Report of the National Conference on Peacemaking
    and Conflict Resolution*, 5–8 June 1986. Athens, GA: The University of
    Georgia, Carl Vinson Institute for Government.
Herrman, M. S., with K. K. Covi (1986). *Final Report of the National Conference
    on Peacemaking and Conflict Resolution*, 18–23 September 1984. Athens,
    GA: The University of Georgia, Carl Vinson Institute for Government.
Herrman, M. S., and Weeks, Jr., E. S. (1984). *Final Report of the National
    Conference on Peacemaking and Conflict Resolution*, 4–6 March 1983.
    Athens, GA: The University of Georgia, Georgia Centre for Continuing
    Education.
Herz, J. H. (1962). *International Politics in The Atomic Age*. New York: Columbia
    University Press.
Hess, B. B., E. W. Markson, and P. J. Stein (1982). *Sociology*. New York:
    MacMillan; London: Collier MacMillan.

Himes, J. S. (1980). *Conflict and Conflict Management.* Athens, GA: The University of Georgia Press.

Hinsley, F. H. (1963). *Power and the Pursuit of Peace.* Cambridge: Cambridge University Press.

Hoivik, T. (1971). "Social Inequality: The Main Issues." *Journal of Peace Research* 8: 119–42.

Howard, Michael (1983). *The Causes of War.* London: Unwin Paperbacks.

Howard, N. (1981). *Paradoxes of Rationality.* Cambridge, MA: M.I.T. Press.

Howell, J. (1978). "The Horn of Africa: Lessons from the Sudan Conflict." *International Affairs* 54(3) (July): 421–36.

Hund, John, and Hendrik W. van der Merwe (1986). *Legal Ideology and Politics in South Africa: A Social Science Approach.* Rondebosch: Centre for Intergroup Studies.

Huxham, C. S., and P. G. Bennett (1983). "Hypergames and Design Decisions." *Design Studies* 4: 227–32.

Huxham, C. S., and P. G. Bennett (1985). "Floating Ideas: An Experiment in Enhancing Hypergames with Maps." *Omega* 13: 331–48.

Ikle, F. E. (1964). *How Nations Negotiate.* New York: Praeger.

Jackson, Elmore (1952). *Meeting of Minds.* New York: McGraw-Hill.

Kakonen, J. (Ed.) (1986). *Current Research on Peace and Violence.* Special Issue on Conflict and Conflict Resolution, 9(3).

Katz, N. H. (1986). "Report on Graduate and Undergraduate Programs in Conflict Resolution." *Peace and Change* 11(2): 81–94.

Kelman, H. C. (1972). "The Problem-Solving Workshop in Dispute Resolution." In R. L. Merritt (Ed.), *Communication in International Politics.* Urbana: University of Illinois Press.

Kelman, H. C., and S. P. Cohen (1976). "The Problem-Solving Workshop: A Social-Psychological Contribution to the Resolution of International Conflicts." *Journal of Peace Research* 13(2): 79–90.

Kelman, H. C., and S. P. Cohen (1979). "Reduction of International Conflict: An Interactional Approach." In W. G. Austin and S. Worchel (Eds.), *The Social Psychology of Intergroup Relations.* Monterey: Brooks/Cole.

Kemp, A. (1983). "A Paradigm for Peace Studies Programs?" *Peace and Change* 9(1) (Spring): 73–80.

Keohane, Robert O., and Joseph S. Nye (1977). *Power and Interdependence.* Boston, MA: Little Brown and Company.

Kohler, G., and N. Alcock (1976). "An Empirical Study of Structural Violence." *Journal of Peace Research* 13: 343–56.

Koopman, E. J. (1985). "The Role of Higher Education in Family Dispute Resolution: Current Developments and Future Challenges." In C. Cutrona (Ed.), *Elements of Good Practice in Dispute Resolution*, Proceedings of the Twelfth International Conference of SPIDR. Washington D.C.: SPIDR.

Koopman, E. J. (1987). "Family Mediation: A Developmental Perspective on the Field." In D. J. D. Sandole and I. Staroste-Sandole (Eds.), *Conflict Management and Problem Solving: Interpersonal to International Applications.* London: Francis Pinter; New York: New York University Press.

Korpi, W. (1974). "Conflict, Power, and Relative Deprivation." *American Political Science Review* 68: 1659–678.

Kreisburg, Louis (1982). *Social Conflicts*, 2d ed. Englewood Cliffs, NJ: Prentice-Hall.

Kressel, K. (1972). *Labor Mediation. An Exploratory Survey*. New York: Association of Labor Mediation Agencies.

Kuhn, T. S. (1970). *The Structure of Scientific Revolutions*, 2d ed. Chicago/ London: University of Chicago Press.

Lakatos, I. (1970). "Falsification and the Methodology of Scientific Research Programmes." In I. Lakatos and A. Musgrave (Eds.), *Criticism and the Growth of Knowledge*. London: Cambridge University Press, pp. 91–196.

Lash, S., and J. Urry (1984). "The Marxism of Collective Action: A Critical Analysis." *Sociology* 18: 33–50.

Laue, J. H. (1985). "The U.S. Institute of Peace: A Federal Commitment to Dispute Resolution." *Negotiation Journal* 1(2) (April): 181–92.

Laue, J. H. (1987). "The Emergence and Institutionalisation of Third Party Roles in Conflict." In D. J. D. Sandole and I. Staroste-Sandole (Eds.), *Conflict Management and Problem Solving: Interpersonal to International Applications*. London: Francis Pinter; New York: New York University Press.

Legum, C. (1972). "Fighting Ends in Sudan after 17 years of War." *The Times*, London (February).

Legum, C. (1979). *The Western Crisis Over Southern Africa*. New York/London: Africana Publishing.

Levi, H. M., and A. Benjamin (1977). "Focus and Flexibility in a Model Conflict Resolution." *Journal of Conflict Resolution* 21(3): 405–25.

LeVine, E. P. (1972). "Mediation in International Politics: A Universe and Some Observations." *Peace Research Society (International) Papers* 8(18): 23–43.

Lewicki, R. J. (1986). "Challenges of Teaching Negotiation." *Negotiation Journal* 2(1) (January): 15–27.

Light, M. (1984). "Problem-Solving Workshops: The Role of Scholarship in Conflict Resolution." In M. Banks (Ed.), *Conflict in World Society: A New Perspective on International Relations*. Brighton: Wheatsheaf, pp. 146–60.

Lodge, Tom (1985). "The Second Consultative Conference of the African National Congress." *South Africa International* 16(2) (October): 80–97.

Maas, J. P., and R. A. C. Stewart (Eds.) (1986). *Towards a World of Peace: People Create Alternatives*. Proceedings of the First International Conference on Conflict Resolution and Peace Studies, Suva, Fiji: University of the South Pacific.

McBride, N. C. (1987). "Many Americans Are Taking Disputes to Mediators, Not Courts: 350 Programs Across U.S. Help Solve Conflicts Quickly, Cheaply." *The Christian Science Monitor*, 2 March, p. 7.

McCarthy, J. D., and M. N. Zald (1977). "Resource Mobilisation and Social Movements: A Partial Theory." *American Journal of Sociology* 82(6) (May): 1212–41.

McDonald, Jr., J. W., and D. B. Bendahmane (Eds.) (1987). *Conflict Resolution: Two Track Diplomacy*. Washington, D.C.: Centre for the Study of Foreign Affairs, Foreign Service Institute, U.S. Department of State.

Mair, Lucy (1964). *Primitive Government*. London: Penguin Books.

Malone, J. A. (1985). "Dispute Resolution: An Emerging Discipline in Higher

Education." In C. Cutrona (Ed.), *Elements of Good Practice in Dispute Resolution*. Proceedings of the Twelfth International Conference of SPIDR. Washington, D.C.: SPIDR.

Marquand, R. (1986a). "Honing the Fine Art of Give and Take: The Real World is the Laboratory for Prof. Fisher and His Students." *The Christian Science Monitor*, 31 January, pp. B3 & B12.

Marquand, R. (1986b). "Teaching for Peace." *The Christian Science Monitor*, 31 January, pp. B1–B3 & B12.

Marquand, R. (1986c). "More Courses on Nuclear Issues—Information and Advocacy." *The Christian Science Monitor*, 31 January, p. B6.

Marshall, T. (1984). "Reparation, Conciliation, and Mediation." *Research and Planning Unit Paper No. 27*, London: Home Office.

Marshall, T., and M. Walpole (1985). "Bringing People Together: Mediation and Reparation Projects in Great Britain." *Research and Planning Unit Paper No. 33*, London: Home Office.

Martin, B. (1978). "The Selective Uses of Game Theory." *Social Studies of Science* 8: 85–110.

Martin, Walter (1984). "Quaker Diplomacy as Peace Witness." *The Friend*, 3 August, pp. 973–75.

Matthews, L. R., and P. G. Bennett (1986). "The Art of Course Planning: Soft O.R. in Action." *Journal of the Operational Research Society* 37: 579–90.

Matthias,W. (1987). "Surviving in the Post-Detente World." In D. J. D. Sandole and I. Staroste-Sandole, *Conflict Management and Problem Solving: Interpersonal to International Applications*. London: Francis Pinter; New York: New York University Press, 1987.

Mattingley, Garrett (1955). *Renaissance Diplomacy*. Boston: Houghton Mifflin.

Meyer, Gabi, Hendrik W. van der Merwe, and Wanita Kawa (1986). *Conflict Accommodation: Towards Conceptual Clarification*. Rondebosch: Centre for Intergroup Studies.

Mitchell, C. R. (1981a). *Peacemaking and the Consultant's Role*. New York: Nichols Publishing Company; Farnborough: Gower.

Michell, C. R. (1981b). *The Structure of International Conflict*. London: Macmillan; New York: St. Martin's.

Moore, C. W. (1986). *The Mediation Process: Practical Strategies for Resolving Conflict*. San Francisco/London: Jossey-Bass.

Morgenthau, Hans J. (1948). *Politics Among Nations*, 1st ed. New York: Alfred A. Knopf.

NIDR Progress Report 1985–1986 (1987). Washington, D.C.: National Institute for Dispute Resolution (NIDR).

O'Ballance, Edgar (1977). *The Secret War in the Sudan 1955–1972*. London: Faber and Faber.

Oberschall, A. R. (1969). "Rising Expectations and Political Turmoil." *Journal of Development Studies* 6: 6–23.

Olson, R. L. (1986). "Reflections of the Chair: Growth in the Dispute Resolution Field: Letting a Thousand Flowers Bloom." *Dispute Resolution*. Washington D.C.: ABA Standing Committee on Dispute Resolution, Summer, pp. 1–2.

Parker, P. (1983). "The Role of the Advisory, Conciliation, and Arbitration

Service (ACAS) in British Labour Relations." *Occasional Paper No. 83-3*. Washington, D.C.: Society of Professionals in Dispute Resolution (SPIDR), September.

Pearson, G. (1986). "The Canadian Institute for International Peace and Security." *PEACE in Action*. Arlington, VA: Foundation for P.E.A.C.E., August/September/October, pp. 23-25.

Peter, L. J., and R. Hull (1969). *The Peter Principle*. London: Pan Books.

Pickvance, T. J. (1975). *Peace with Equity: The Northern Ireland Problem*. Birmingham: Pickvance.

Plous, S. (1985/1987). "Perceptual Illusions and Military Realities." *Journal of Conflict Resolution* 29: 263–389; 31: 5–33.

Pompa, G. G. (1985). "'Public Agencies' Roles and Capabilities—Community Relations Service and State and Local Agencies." In C. Cutrona (Ed.), *Elements of Good Practice in Dispute Resolution*. Proceedings of the Twelfth International Conference of SPIDR. Washington, D.C.: SPIDR.

Pompa, G. G. (1987). "The Community Relations Service." In D. J. D. Sandole and I. Staroste-Sandole (Eds.), *Conflict Management and Problem Solving: Interpersonal to International Applications*. London: Francis Pinter; New York: New York University Press.

Popper, K. R. (1959). *The Logic of Scientific Discovery*. New York: Harper & Row; London: Hutchinson.

Probst, Raymond (1960). "Die Schweiz und die internationale Scheidsgerichtsbarkeit." *Annuaire suisse de droit internationale* 17: 99–146.

Pruitt, Dean G. (1981). *Negotiation Behaviour*. New York: Academic Press.

Pruitt, Dean G. (1987). "Creative Approaches to Negotiation." In D. J. D. Sandole and I. Staroste-Sandole (Eds.), *Conflict Management and Problem Solving: Interpersonal to International Applications*. London: Francis Pinter; New York: New York University Press.

Pruitt, Dean G., and J. Rubin (1986). *Social Conflict: Escalation, Stalemate, and Settlement*. New York: Random House.

Quandt, William B. (1986). *Camp David: Peacemaking and Politics*. Washington, D.C.: Brookings.

Radford, K. J. (1980). *Strategic Planning: An Analytic Approach*. Reston, VA: Reston Publishing.

Radford, K. J. (1984). "Simulating Involvement in Complex Situations." *Omega* 12: 125–31.

Radford, K. J. (1986). *Strategic and Tactical Decisions*. Toronto: Holt McTavish.

Raiffa, Howard (1982). *The Art and Science of Negotiation*. Cambridge: Harvard/Belknap Press.

Rapoport, A. (1960). *Fights, Games and Debates*. Ann Arbor: University of Michigan Press.

Rapoport, A. (1974). *Conflict in a Man-Made Environment*. Harmondsworth/New York: Penguin.

Ray, L. (1982). "The Alternative Dispute Resolution Movement." *Peace and Change* 8(2/3) (Summer): 117–28.

Ray, L. (1987). "Trends Towards Alternative Dispute Resolution." In D. J. D. Sandole and I. Staroste-Sandole (Eds.), *Conflict Management and Problem*

Solving: Interpersonal to International Applications. London: Francis Pinter; New York: New York University Press.

Richardson, L. F. (1939). "Generalised Foreign Policy." *British Journal of Psychology Monographs Supplements*, 23. Cambridge: Cambridge University Press, pp. 1–91.

Rocha, G. M. (1984). *In Search of Namibian Independence.* Boulder, CO: Westview Press.

Roffe, Pedro (1980). "UNCTAD: Code of Conduct for the Transfer of Technology—Progress and Issues under Negotiation." *Journal of World Trade Law* 14(2) (March–April): 160–72.

Rosenau, J. N. (Ed.) (1964). *International Aspects of Civil Strife.* Princeton, NJ: Princeton University Press.

Rothstein, R. L. (1972). "On the Costs of Realism." *Political Science Quarterly* 87(3): 347–62.

Rowe, J. (1986). "Grants Grow, But Most Schools Pay for Peace Studies Themselves." *The Christian Science Monitor*, 31st January, p. B7.

Rubin, J. Z. (Ed.) (1981). *Dynamics of Third Party Mediation.* New York: Praeger.

Salem, R. A. (1982). "Community Dispute Resolution Through Outside Intervention." *Peace and Change* 8(2/3) (Summer): 91–104.

Sandler, B. (1986). "Environmental Conflict Resolution in Canada." *Resolve*, Washington, D.C.: The Conservation Foundation, No. 18, pp. 1, 4–8: see also pp. 9–16.

Sandole, D. J. D. (1984). "The Subjectivity of Theories and Actions in World Society." In M. Banks (Ed.), *Conflict in World Society: A New Perspective on International Relations.* Brighton: Wheatsheaf, 1984.

Sandole, D. J. D. (1985). "Training and Teaching in a Field Whose Time Has Come: A Postgraduate Program in Conflict Management." In C. Cutrona (Ed.), *Elements of Good Practice in Dispute Resolution.* Proceedings of the Twelfth International Conference of SPIDR. Washington D.C.: SPIDR.

Sandole, D. J. D. (1986). "Traditional Approaches to Conflict Management: Short-Term Gains vs. Long-Term Costs." *Current Research on Peace and Violence* 9(3): 119–24.

Sandole, D. J. D. (1987). "Conflict Management: Elements of Generic Theory and Process." In Sandole D. J. D., and I. Staroste-Sandole (Eds.), *Conflict Management and Problem Solving: Interpersonal to International Applications.* London: Francis Pinter; New York: New York University Press.

Sandole, D. J. D., and I. Staroste-Sandole (Eds.) (1987). *Conflict Management and Problem Solving: Interpersonal to International Applications.* London: Francis Pinter; New York: New York University Press.

Saposnek, D. T. (1983). *Mediating Child Custody Disputes: A Systematic Guide for Family Therapists, Court Counsellors, Attorneys, and Judges.* San Francisco/London: Jossey-Bass.

Schelling, T. C. (1980). *The Strategy of Conflict.* Cambridge, Mass.: Harvard University Press.

Schmid, Herman (1968). "Peace Research and Politics." *Journal of Peace Research* 5(3): 217–32.

Schwartzkoff, J., and J. Morgan (1982). *Community Justice Centres: A Report on the New South Wales Pilot Project*. Sydney: Law Foundation of New South Wales.

Scott, D. (1981). *Ambassador in Black and White*. London: Weidenfeld and Nicolson.

Seigfried, Andre (n.d.). *Switzerland: A Democratic Way of Life*. New York: Duell, Sloan and Pearce.

Serfontein, J. H. P. (1976). *Namibia*. Randburg: Focus Suid.

Sharp, R. G., and M. R. Dando (1978). *Decision Resource Management*. Brighton, Sussex: O.R. Group, University of Sussex.

Shrybman, S. (1986). "Environmental Mediation: A Boon to Canadian Environmentalists?" *Resolve*. Washington D.C.: The Conservation Foundation, No. 18, pp. 2–3.

Smith, Arnold (1981). *Stitches in Time: The Commonwealth in World Politics*. London: Andre Deutsch.

Smith, C. D. (Ed.) (1985). *The Hundred Percent Challenge: Building a National Institute of Peace*. Cabin John, Maryland: Seven Locks Press.

Snyder, M., and S. Gangstead (1981). "Hypothesis-Testing Processes." In J. H. Harvey, W. Ickes, and R. F. Kidd (Eds.), *New Directions in Attribution Research*, Vol. 3. Hillsdale, NJ: Lawrence Erlbaum Associates.

Spero, Joan Edelman (1981). *The Politics of International Economic Relations*, 2d ed. New York: St. Martin's Press.

Spicer, M. (1980). "Namibia, Elusive Independence." *The World Today* 36 (October): 406–14.

Stenelo, Lars. G. (1972). *Mediation in International Negotiations*. Sweden: Studentlitteratur.

Stremlau, John J. (1977). *The International Politics of the Nigerian Civil War 1967–70*. Princeton, NJ: Princeton University Press.

SWAPO (1976). *Political Programme*. Lusaka: SWAPO.

Tambo, Oliver (1985). "Press Conference, Lusaka, June 25, 1985." In *Documents of the Second International Consultative Conference of the African National Congress*, Zambia, 16–23 June 1985. Lusaka: African National Congress.

Taylor, T. (1978). "Power Politics." In T. Taylor (Ed.), *Approaches and Theory in International Relations*. London/New York: Longman.

Thucydides (1951). *The Peloponnesian War*, Crawley translation. New York: The Modern Library (Random House).

Totemeyer, G., and J. Seiler (1980). "South-West Africa/Namibia: A Study of Polarisation and Confrontation." In J. Seiler (Ed.), *South Africa Since the Portugese Coup*. Boulder, CO: Westview Press.

Touval, S. (1975). "Biased Intermediaries: Theoretical and Historical Consideration." *Jerusalem Journal of International Relations* 1(1) (Autumn): 51–87.

Touval, S. (1982). *The Peace Brokers: Mediators in the Arab-Israeli Conflict, 1948–79*. Princeton, N. J.: Princeton University Press.

Touval, S., and I. W. Zartman (Eds.) (1985). *International Mediation: Theory and Practice*. Boulder, CO: Westview Press.

UNESCO (1981). *World Directory of Peace Research Institutes*, 4th ed. Reports and Papers in the Social Sciences No. 49. Paris: UNESCO.

University for Peace: Basic Documents (1981). San Jose, Costa Rica: Presidential Commission of the University for Peace.

Ury, W. (1985). *Beyond the Hotline: How Crisis Control Can Prevent Nuclear War.* Boston: Houghton Mifflin.

Vance, C. (1983). *Hard Choices.* New York: Simon and Schuster.

van der Merwe, Hendrik W. (1983). "Mediation and Empowerment." In A. Paul Hare (Ed.). *The Struggle for Democracy in South Africa.* Cape Town: Centre for Intergroup Studies.

van der Merwe, Hendrik W. (1986a). "Like It or Not, We May Need Third Party Help." *Sunday Times*, 1 June.

van der Merwe, Hendrik W. (1986b). "Peace Marshalling: A Case Study of Social Control." Paper presented at the *Seventeenth Annual Congress of the Association for Sociology in Southern Africa*, Durban, 30 June–4 July.

van der Wulp, P. (ed.) (1986). *Coming to Terms with Conflict: Third Party Intervention and Aspects of Culture.* Amsterdam: Royal Tropical Institute.

Vasquez, J. A. (1983). *The Power of Power Politics: A Critique.* London: Francis Pinter; New Brunswick: Rutgers University Press.

Volpe, M. R. (1985). "Teaching Alternative Methods of Dispute Resolution: Some Observations." In C. Cutrona (Ed.), *Elements of Good Practice in Dispute Resolution..* Proceedings of the Twelfth International Conference of SPIDR. Washington D.C.: SPIDR.

Von Neumann, J., and O. Morgenstern (1944). *Theory of Games and Economic Behaviour.* Princeton: Princeton University Press.

Wahrhaftig, P. (1985). "Conflict Resolution in South Africa." *Conflict Resolution Notes*, 2(2) (January): 21–22. Pittsburgh: Conflict Resolution Centre.

Wahrhaftig, P. (1986). "Preparing for a Post-Apartheid Society: Impressions on Meeting with South African Mediators, June 1986." *Conflict Resolution Notes*, 4(2) (September): 17–18. Pittsburgh: Conflict Resolution Centre.

Wai, Dunstan (1981). *The Arab-African Conflict in the Sudan.* New York: African Publishing Company.

Walbank, F. W. (1940). *Phillip V of Macedon.* Cambridge: Cambridge University Press.

Wall, J. A. (1981). "Mediation: An Analysis, Review and Proposed Research." *Journal of Conflict Resolution* March 25(1): 157–80.

Walton, Richard E. (1969). *Interpersonal Peacemaking.* Reading, Mass: Addison Wesley.

Webb, K. (1986). "Movimento Sociali: Fenomeni contingenti o inerenti?" In A. Melucci (Ed.), *Movimenti Sociali e Sistema Politico.* Milano: Fondazione Feltrinelli, pp. 35–58.

Wedge, B. and D. J. D. Sandole (1982). "Conflict Management: A New Venture into Professionalisation." *Peace and Change* 8(2/3) (Summer): 129–38.

Wehr, Paul (1979). *Conflict Regulation.* Boulder, CO: Westview Press.

Wehr, Paul (1986). "Conflict Resolution Studies: What Do We Know?" *Dispute Resolution Forum.* Washington DC: National Institute for Dispute Resolution (NIDR), April, pp. 3–4, 12–13.

Winham, Gilbert R. (1977). "Negotiation as a Management Process." *World Politics* 30(1) (October): 87–114.

Yarrow, C. H. (1978). *Quaker Experiences in International Conciliation.* New Haven, CT: Yale University Press.

Young, A. (1980). "The United States and Africa." *Foreign Affairs* 59(3): 648–66.

Young, O. R. (1967). *The Intermediaries: Third Parties in International Crisis.* Princeton, NJ: Princeton University Press.

Zartman, I. W. (1977). "Negotiation as a Joint Decision Making Process." *Journal of Conflict Resolution* 21(4): 619–38.

Zartman, I. W. (1985). *Ripe for Resolution.* London: Oxford University Press.

Zartman, I. W., and Maureen Berman (1982). *The Practical Negotiator.* New Haven: Yale University Press.

Name Index

Subject Index

About the Contributors

HEZEKIAH ASSEFA is a consultant on conflict resolution and an assistant professor in the graduate program of LaRoche College, Pittsburgh, specialising in management and international affairs. He has recently published a book on the ending of the Sudanese Civil War (*Mediation in Civil War*, Westview Press) and is the co-author of a forthcoming book entitled *Extremist Groups and Conflict Resolution: The MOVE Crisis in Philadelphia*.

PETER G. BENNETT received his B.Sc. (1st class hons) in physics from Southampton University, then an M.Sc. and D. Phil. in Philosophy of Science at the University of Sussex. He joined the Operational Research Group at Sussex University in 1976, moving to the Management Science Department, University of Strathclyde, in 1988. His research has involved the construction of models for analysing conflict based upon the notion of a "hypergame," and his main current interest is in combining conflict analysis with other aspects of complex decisions (e.g. the existence of multiple uncertainties). Dr. Bennett is the author of over forty papers on these and related subjects and is the editor of *Analysing Conflict and Its Resolution* (Oxford University Press, 1987). He is a member of the Conflict Research Society and the Centre for the Analysis of Conflict.

VIVIENNE JABRI received her doctorate from the City University, London, where her research concerns the activities of multi-party intermediaries, such as the Western Contact Group. Her first degree was in physiology at Kings College, London and she was subsequently awarded an M.A. in International Relations from the University of Kent. She is a member of the Conflict Research Society and the Centre for the Analysis of Conflict.

DOUGLAS KINNEY is a professional foreign service officer with the U.S. Department of State. He completed a book-length study of the diplomacy of the 1982 Falklands/Malvinas crisis while studying under the auspices of the Center for Conflict Resolution, George Mason University, Virginia. The resultant book is shortly to be published by Praeger. At present, Mr. Kinney is First Secretary in the Political Section of the U.S. Embassy in Caracas, Venezuela.

C. R. MITCHELL was Professor of International Relations at the City University, London, before accepting a chair at George Mason University, Virginia. He has written extensively about the theory and practice of mediation, including *The Structure of International Conflict* (Macmillan 1981) and *Peacemaking and the Consultant's Role* (Gower Press 1981). At present, he is working on a book-length study of concessions and conciliatory gestures. He is a member of the Conflict Research Society and the Centre for the Analysis of Conflict.

T. J. PICKVANCE is a science graduate of Reading and Oxford universities who acquired an early interest in national minority problems through school teaching in Wales (1933–37). After teaching at Christs Hospital in Sussex through the war years, he held a Fellowship at Woodbrooke, the Quaker College in Birmingham. From 1949 onward he was engaged in extra-mural work for Birmingham University and during this time developed ideas about active peacemaking. He was a member of the Quaker Study Mission in Italy and Austria (1966–75) in connection with the German-speaking minority in Italian Tyroi and in 1973 retired early to study the Northern Ireland problem.

DENNIS J. D. SANDOLE received his Ph.D. from Strathclyde University, Glasgow, and is presently Associate Professor of Government and Politics and Faculty Associate of the Center for Conflict Resolution, George Mason University. He has taught at University College, London, Garnett College, and the City University and on the University of Southern California Graduate Programs in International Relations in both England and Germany. He is a member of both the Conflict Research Society and the Centre for the Analysis of Conflict, while his research interests include international relations theory and methodology, conflict analysis and management, attitude change and paradigm shifts.

JOHN B. STEPHENS received his first degree from Earlham College, Indiana, and he then came to London to study at the City University, receiving his M. Phil. degree in 1984. After working on the staff of a U.S. Congressman in Washington, he moved to St. Louis where he is currently a legislative representative for the Home Builders Association of Greater St. Louis, Missouri.

HENDRIK W. VAN DER MERWE is Director of the Centre for Inter-group Studies at the University of Capetown and a graduate of the universities of Stellenbosch and California. He is the joint author and editor of a number of books, including *White South African Elites* and *Legal Ideology and Politics in South Africa*. He is past president of the Association for Sociology in Southern Africa and represented South Africa on the Council of the International Sociological Association. He founded the South African Association for Conflict Management, has mediated between major conflicting groups in South Africa, and, in 1984, initiated dialogue between South Africans and the African National Congress in exile. He is a member of the Religious Society of Friends (Quakers), and this relationship is reflected in his chapter in this book.

K. WEBB lectures in international relations at the University of Kent. His first degree was in philosophy and politics from the University of Keele and his second in politics from the University of Strathclyde. He has taught at the University of Iceland, the University of Strathclyde, and the Open University, and for six years was a research fellow at the City University, London. His research and teaching interests are in the epistemology and methodology of social science and in political conflict, particularly with respect to communal and international violence and their management. He is secretary of the Conflict Research Society and a member of the Centre for the Analysis of Conflict.

ANDREW WILLIAMS was born in Birmingham, England in 1951 and received his first degree from the University of Keele and then a doctorate from the University of Geneva. While in Switzerland he worked at the Graduate Institute of International Studies and the Centre for Applied Studies in International Negotiations, in the latter case working on issues related to the United Nations. He is presently a lecturer in International Relations at the University of Kent, where his interests include the history of East–West relations, revolutionary foreign policy, and international organisations. He is a member of the Centre for the Analysis of Conflict.